Merry Christmas!
much love from Justin + Anastasia - 2016

NEW ZEALAND

THE SOUTHERN REALM

JASON LAW

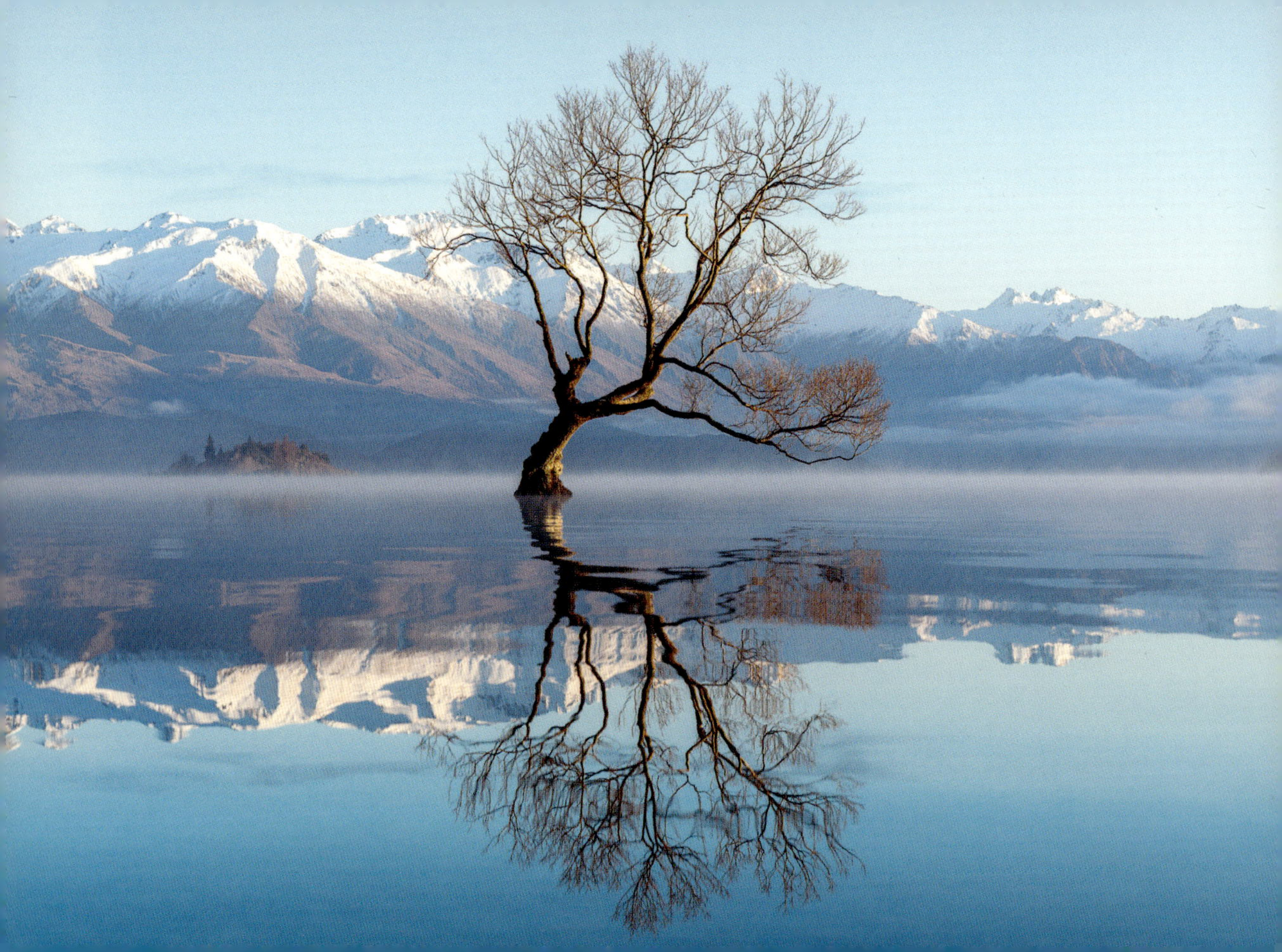

NEW ZEALAND
THE SOUTHERN REALM

JASON LAW

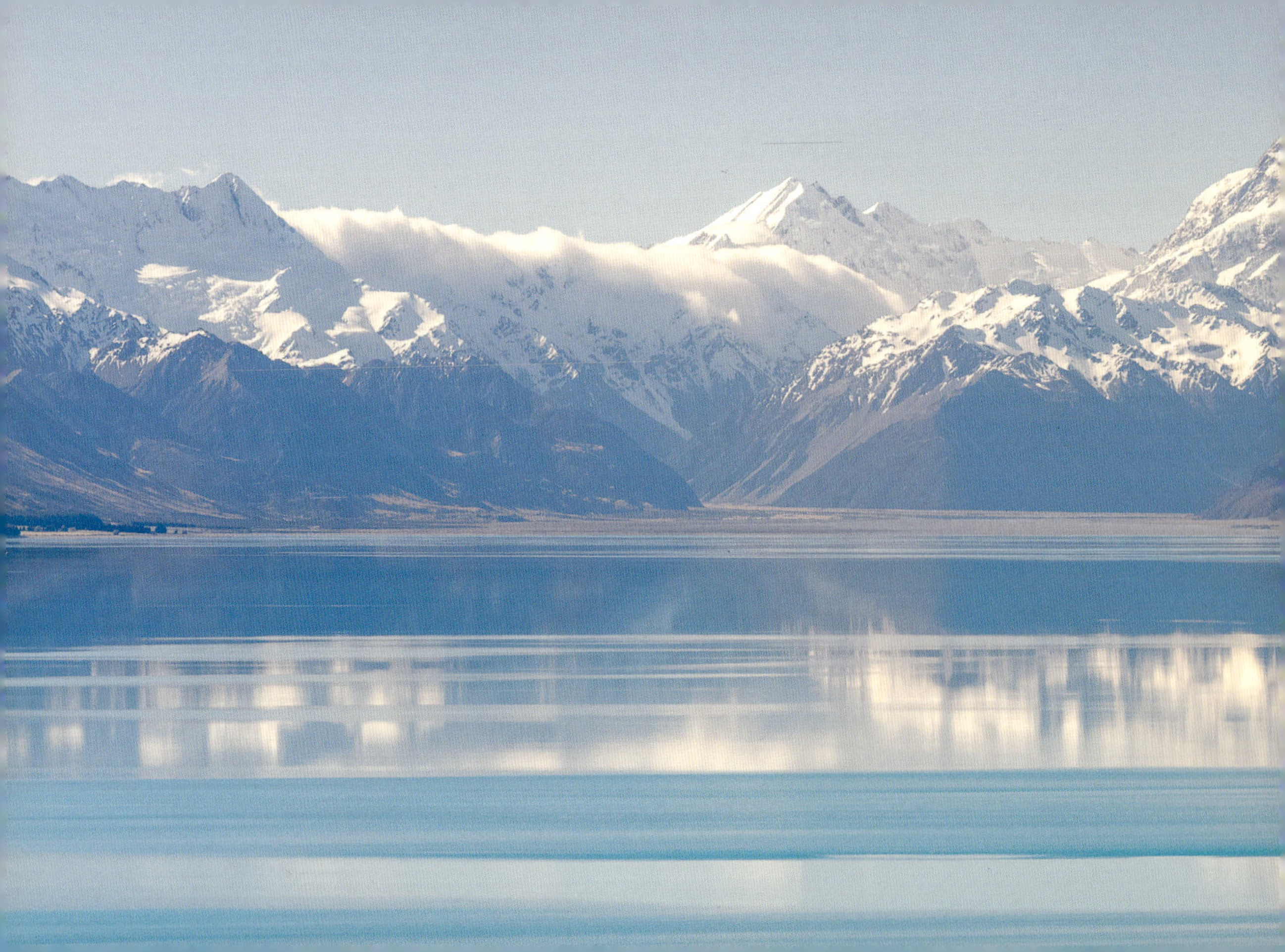

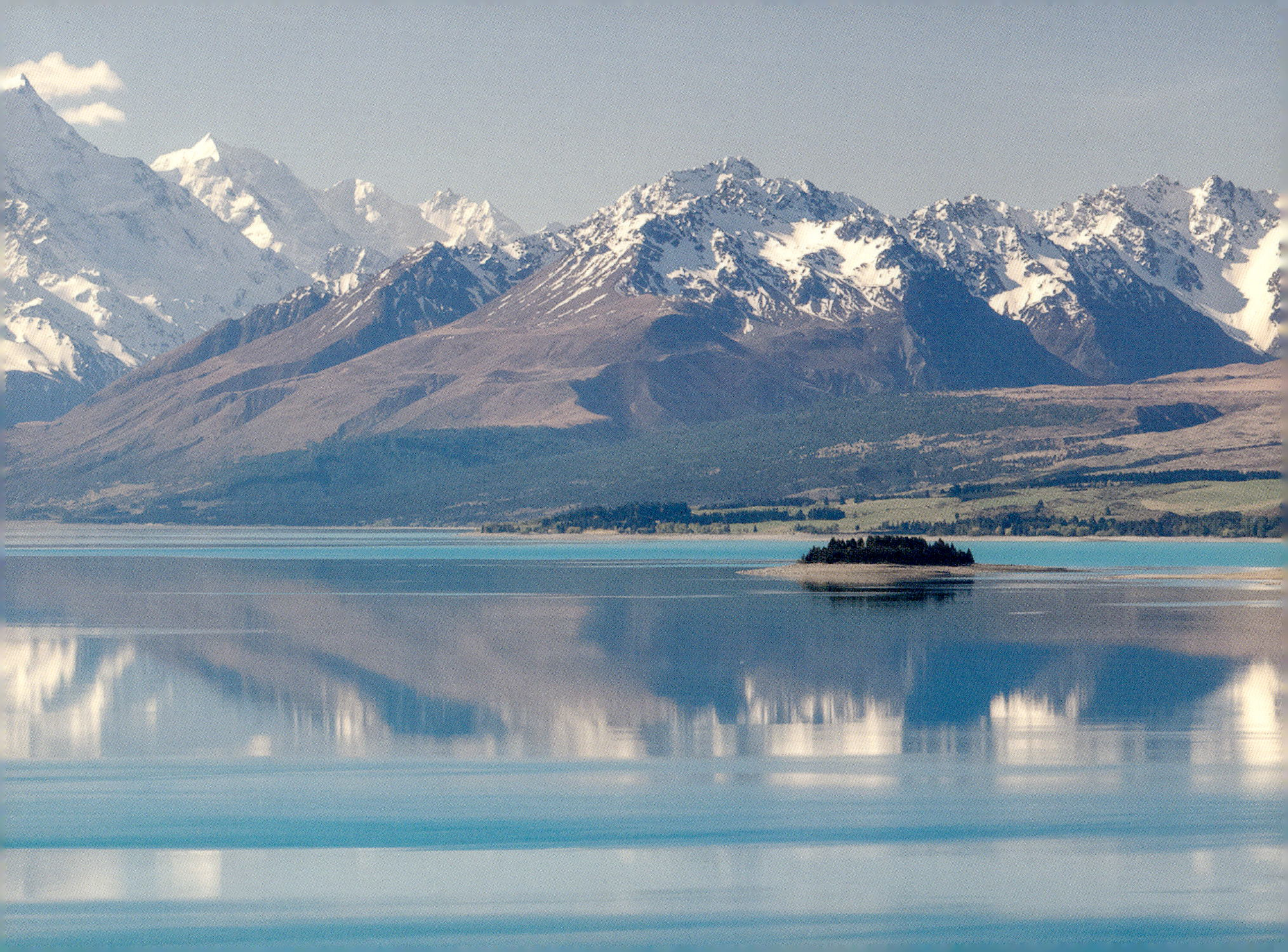

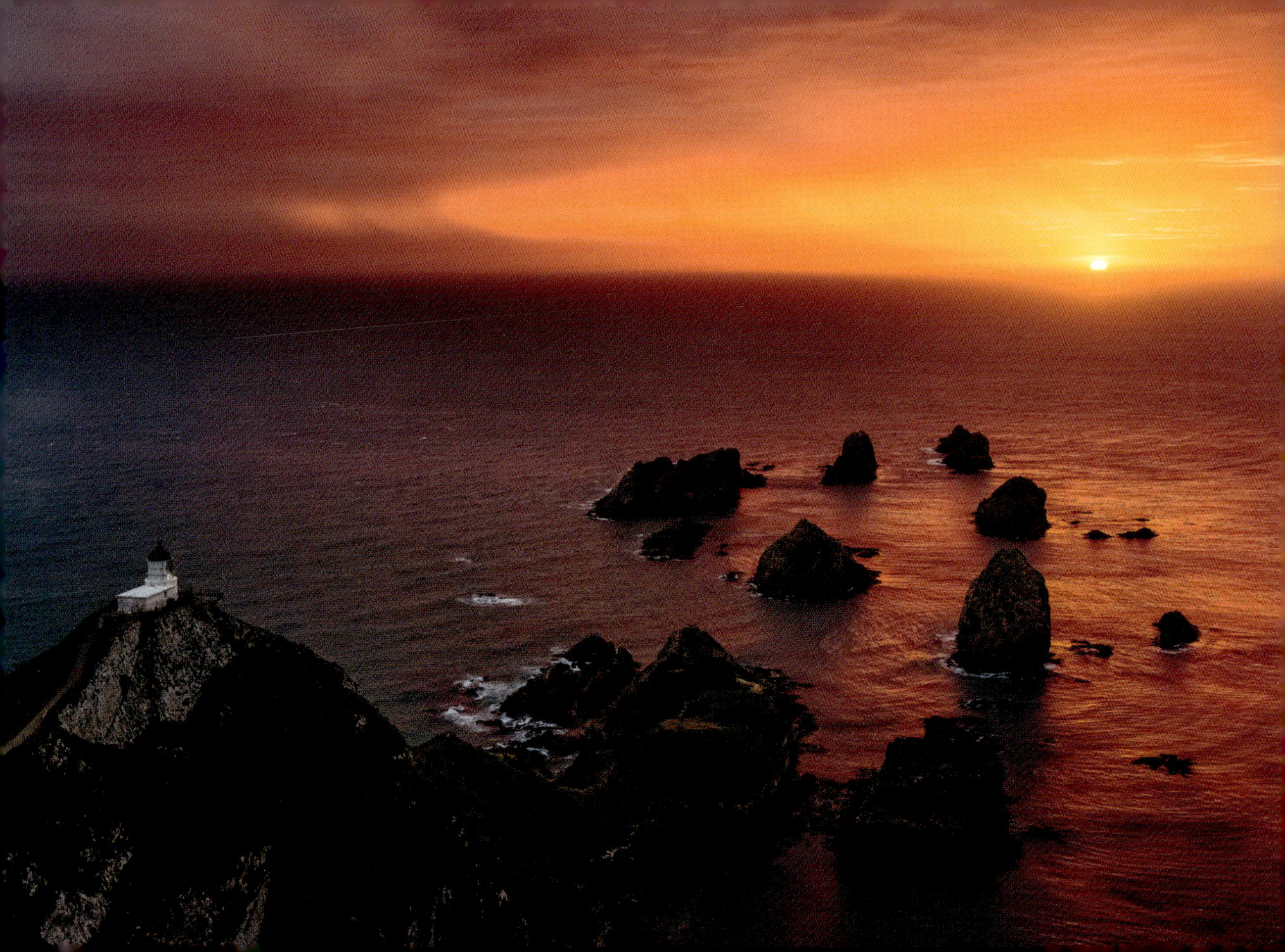

CONTENTS

page 2: Lone Tree reflections, Roys Bay, Lake Wanaka, Central Otago.
pages 4-5: Mt Cook reflections in Lake Pukaki, Mackenzie Basin.
page 6: Sunrise over Nugget Point, Catlins Coast.

INTRODUCTION

My true passion in life is the love of the outdoors: mountains, wildlife, oceans, rivers and lakes. That feeling of being surrounded by nature, the freedom of true peace and quiet and those moments of natural serenity calm my inner being. Photography makes me appreciate the world I live in. With my camera in hand I have seen sunsets I never thought possible; I have watched soaring birds for hours on end in the early golden sun; I have been mesmerised by the movement of crashing waves upon the foreshore and I have seen the most amazing and diverse landscapes through new eyes. I view the world afresh thanks to photography, and hopefully through my images I can share with you what I see and cherish about my beautiful country.

The world I see through my camera makes sense to me. Simple moments without the clutter of life's noise, without fear, doubt or worry. They are slices of time: the present, captured for all to see. They are glimpses of my journey through this life that I hope will someday mean something, expressions of inner ideas. They are My moments, My memories, My life.

I escaped into a world of photography five years ago, and it now consumes me. I love the adventures it takes me on, the moments of natural beauty I witness, my awakened awareness of the environment around me and the patience it has taught me. My eyes are constantly searching for beauty; little sun kissed scenes within the landscapes that captivate me.

I am very blessed to find my passion in life. Many let life pass them by without finding something that gives them focus and a purpose. This land, it calms my soul, fills my lungs with fresh life; it is a place that provides freedom to explore, to learn and grow amongst nature. We must protect this for future generations in all forms. It has been a blessing to me and I hope future generations will be able to experience this firsthand.

I have dedicated my life to documenting the natural wonders of this place: the light, the shape of the land and their interactions. The rugged wild coastline, the lush native bush, the rolling green grassland and the beautiful tranquil mountain clad lakes have all personalities that speak to me when I am still in their presence.

This is my first book, a documentation of the first five years of my photographic journey, one that has been full of many ups and downs; but I am dedicated to this land and this path. This place and I are inseparable and I only hope that through my imagery you can take with you, wherever in the world you may live, a part of New Zealand to cherish. Strive to look for the wonder of nature wherever you call home, and give time to find solitude in your everyday life. May this book be a reminder of that for you.

I am excited about the future, thankful for my past and trying to live in the present as best I can by doing what I love. The road is long and my journey with my camera has just begun. Thank you for being a part of it.

Jason Law

Queenstown, May 2016

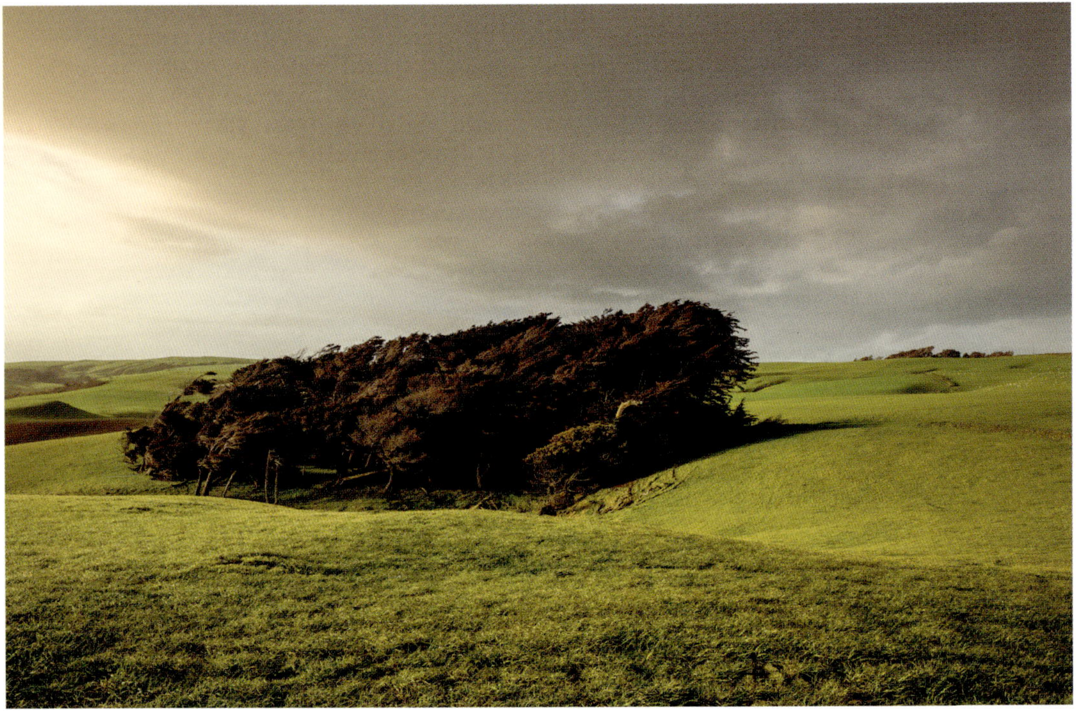

Late afternoon light over farmland at Slope Point, Southland.

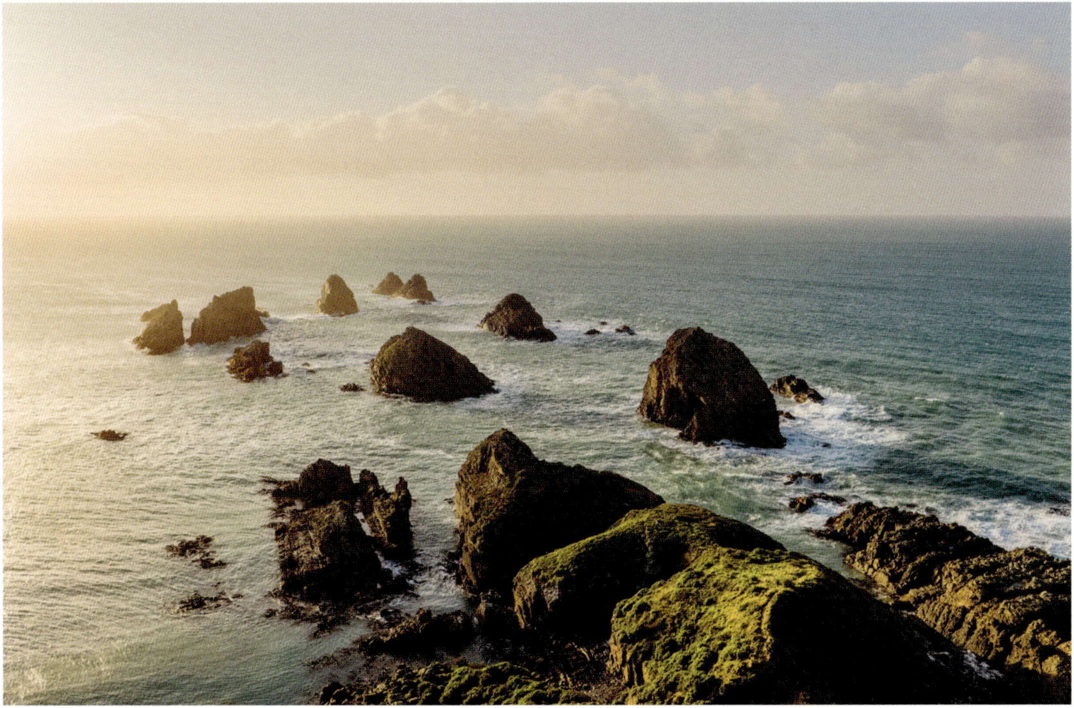

Rocky islets (The Nuggets) at first light, Nugget Point, Catlins Coast.

"The Catlins are Calling"

Sheep grazing near Owaka, The Catlins, South Otago.

Tucked away in the southeastern corner of the South Island lies a relatively forgotten area of New Zealand, known as The Catlins. This remote district is full of rolling grasslands, beautiful waterfalls, rugged coastlines and wildlife galore. A sparsely populated place where the locals enjoy a true community lifestyle, without the conveniences of city living.

In the summertime this remote part of New Zealand is a great coastal getaway for New Zealanders and tourists, however it is in the off season - winter and spring, when the roads are empty, the local shops are predominately closed and the land comes alive with adventures aplenty. The seemingly endless gravel roads that twist around beautiful undulating hills, wind twisted coastal trees, penguins that waddle through ancient fossilised forests to the Pacific ocean, all on display, with endless solitude if you seek it.

Take a walk along the Catlins River Trail in lush bush, escape to Nugget Point to watch the sunrise, spend time watching the water flow over one of the numerous waterfalls in the district or stroll along the untouched beach at Tautuku Bay. The entertainment is free in The Catlins if you are willing to spend time in nature's presence.

The Catlins are calling, and it is time to explore.

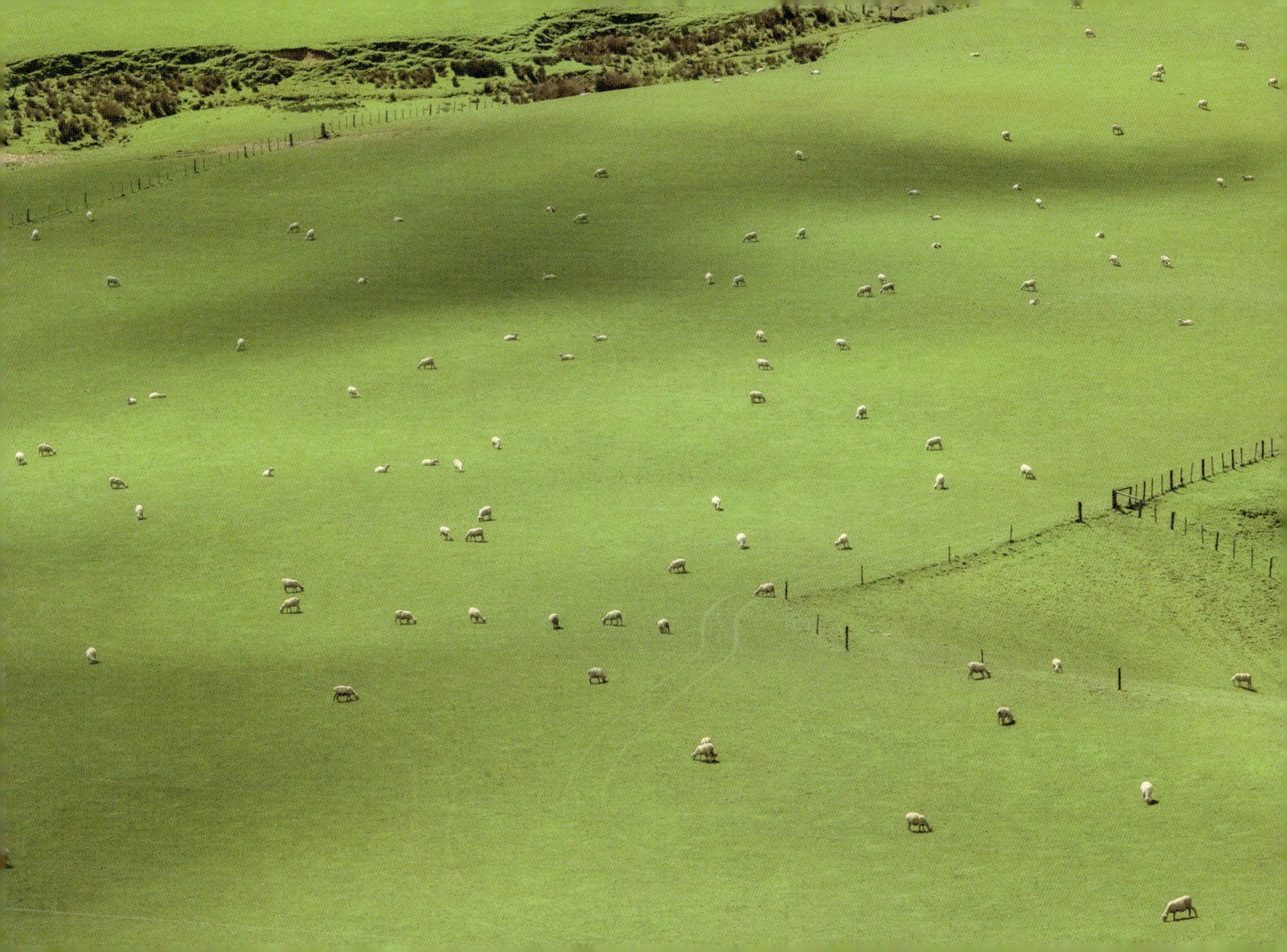

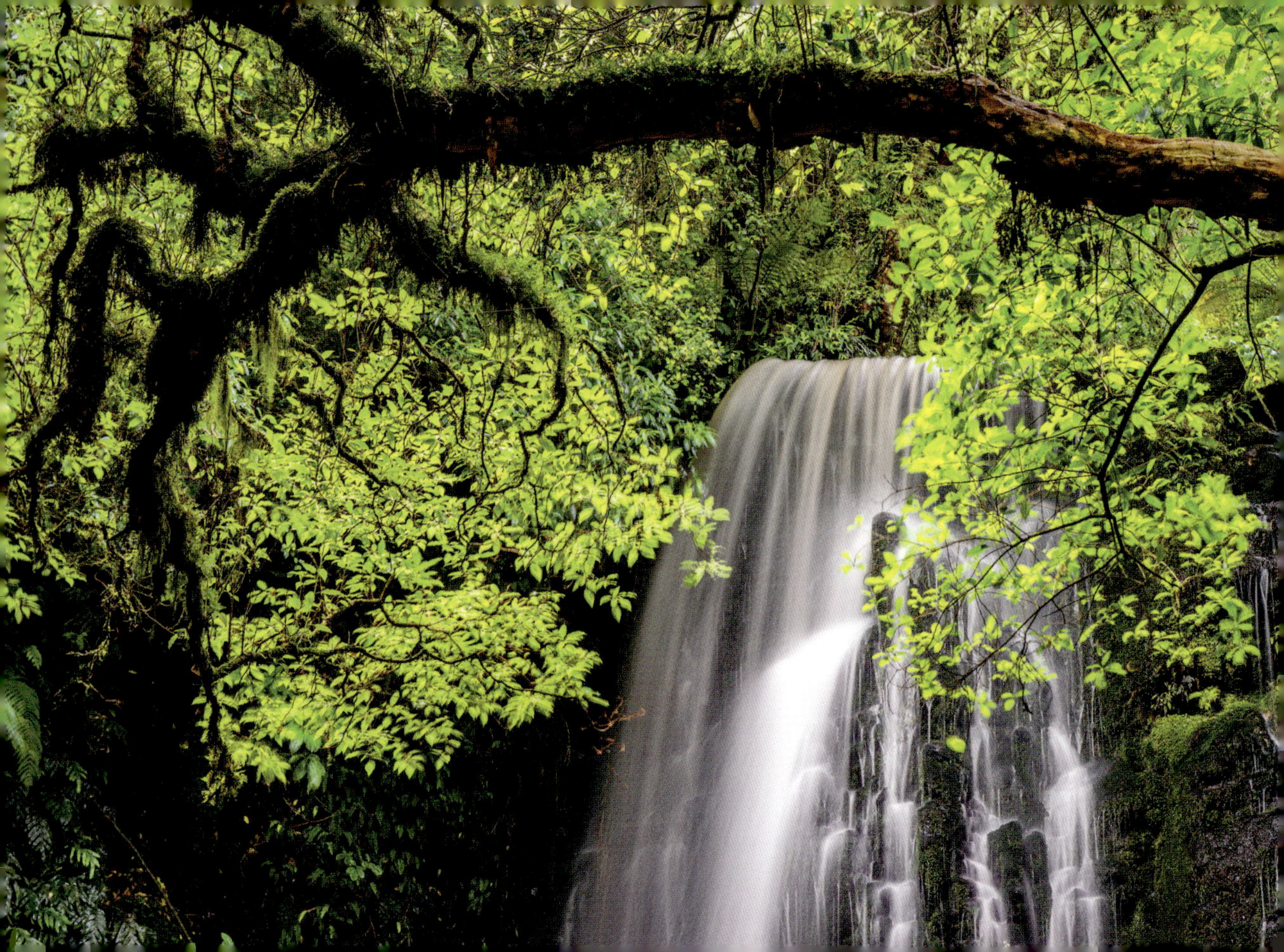

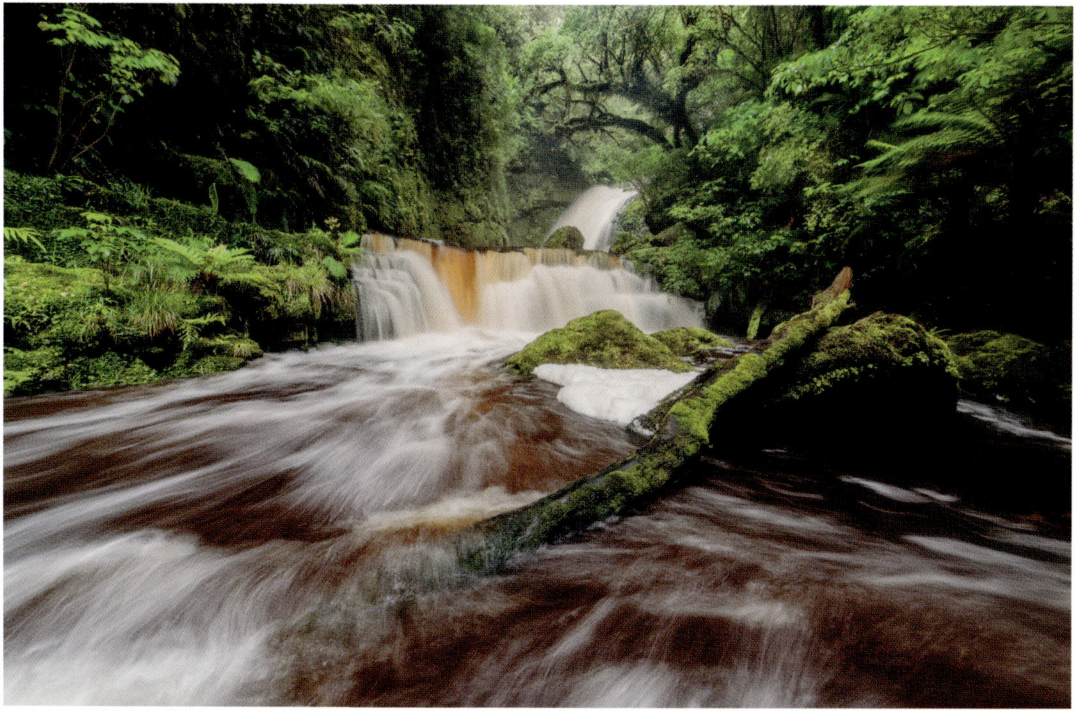

Lower McLeans Falls after a torrential downpour, The Catlins.
opposite: Light in the leaves, Matai Falls, The Catlins.

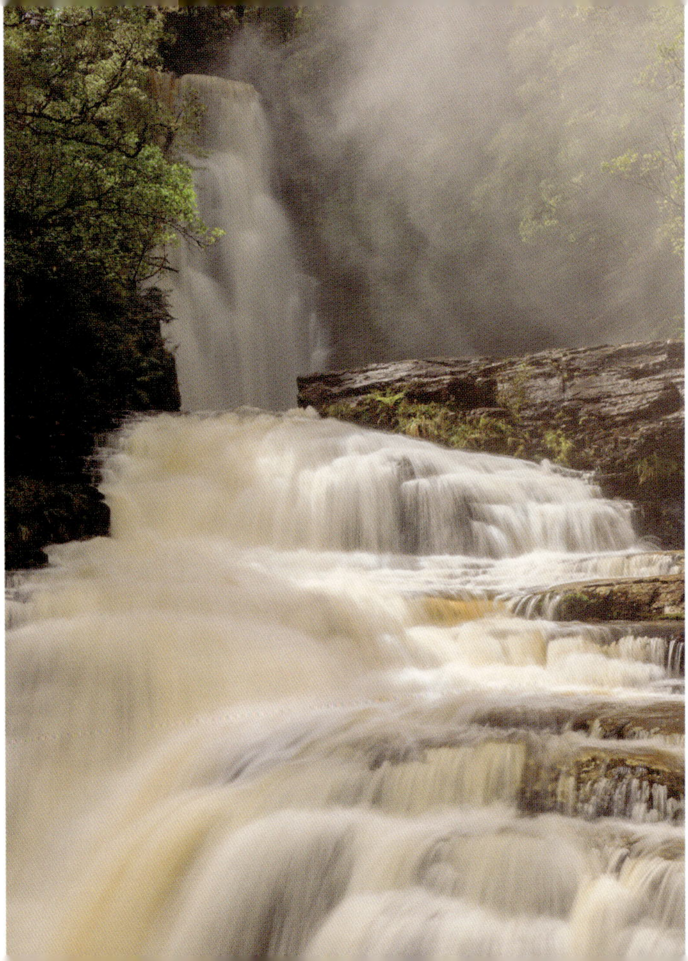

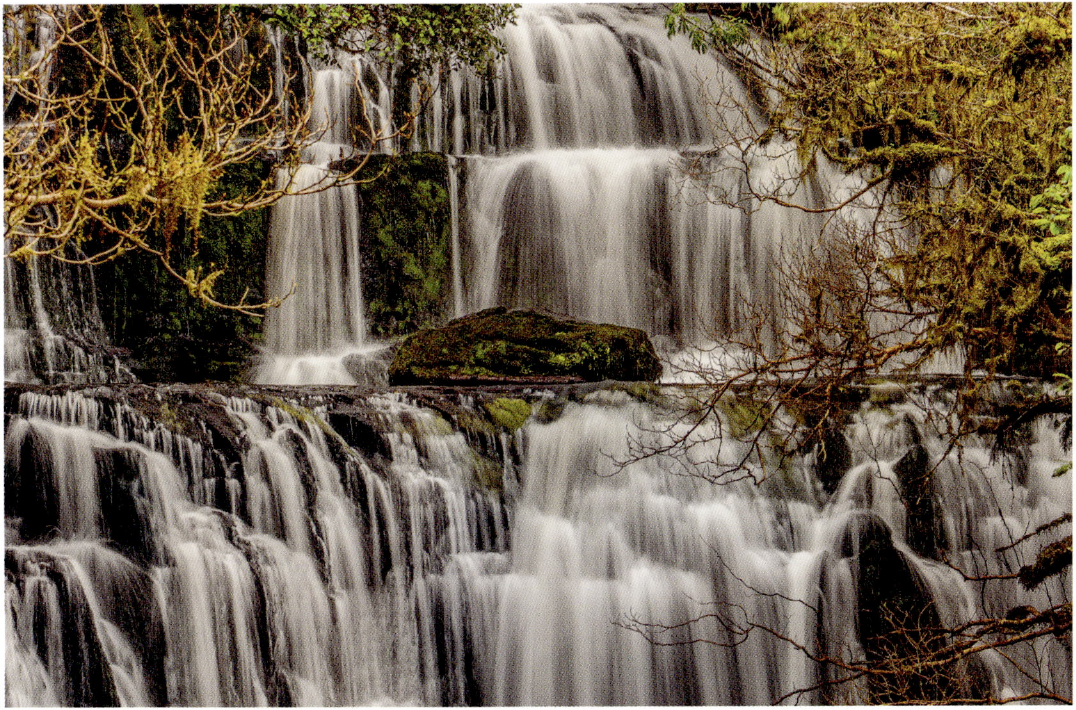

Branches surround Purakaunui Falls, The Catlins.
opposite: After a break in the rain the sun came out, McLeans Falls, The Catlins.

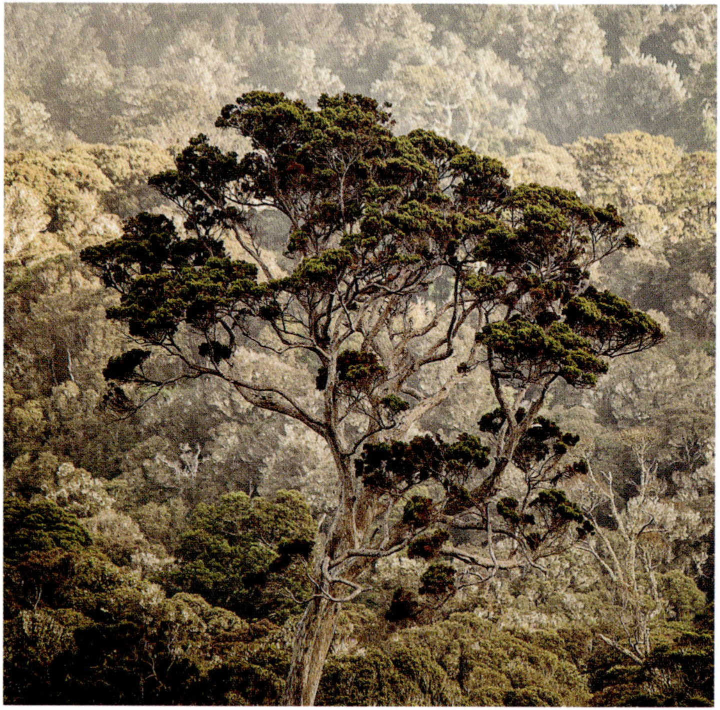

Above the canopy, The Catlins.

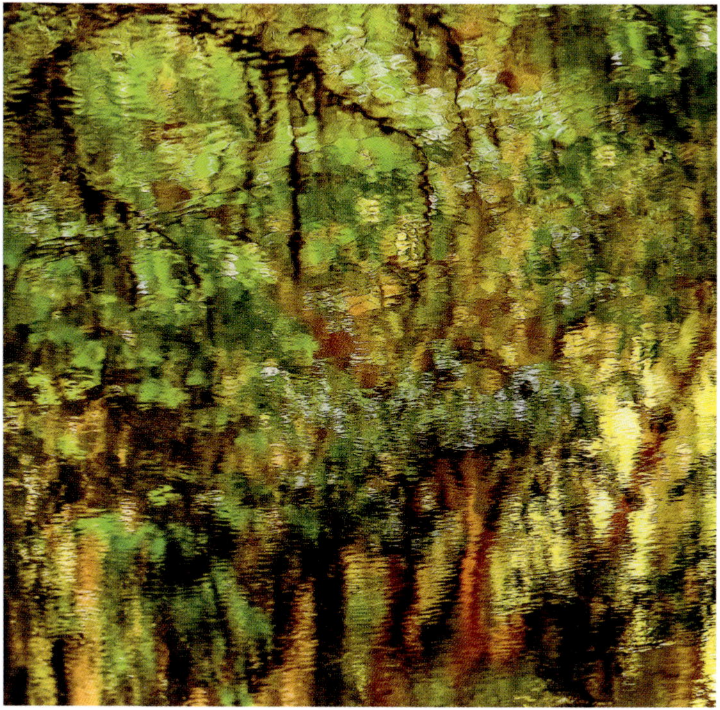

River reflections, Purakaunui, The Catlins.

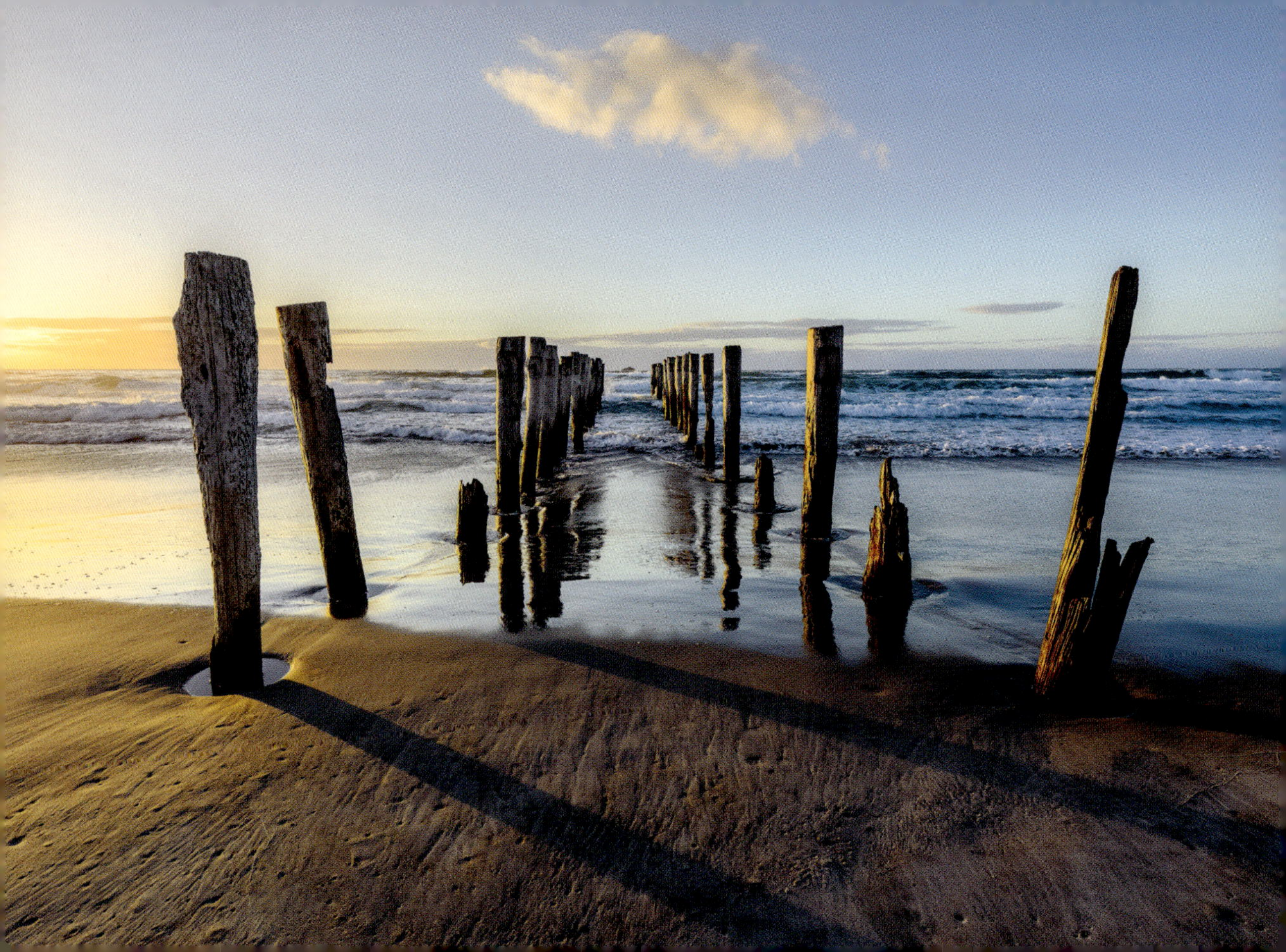

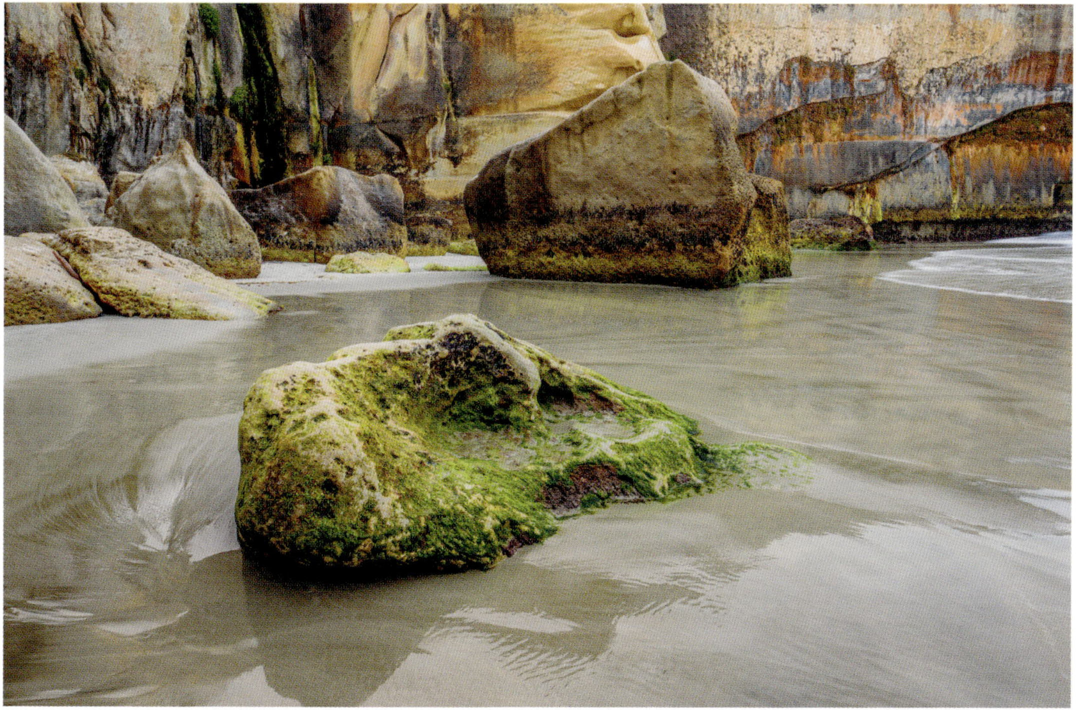

The incoming tide at Tunnel Beach, Dunedin, Otago Coast.
opposite: The popular breakwater, St Clair Beach, Dunedin.

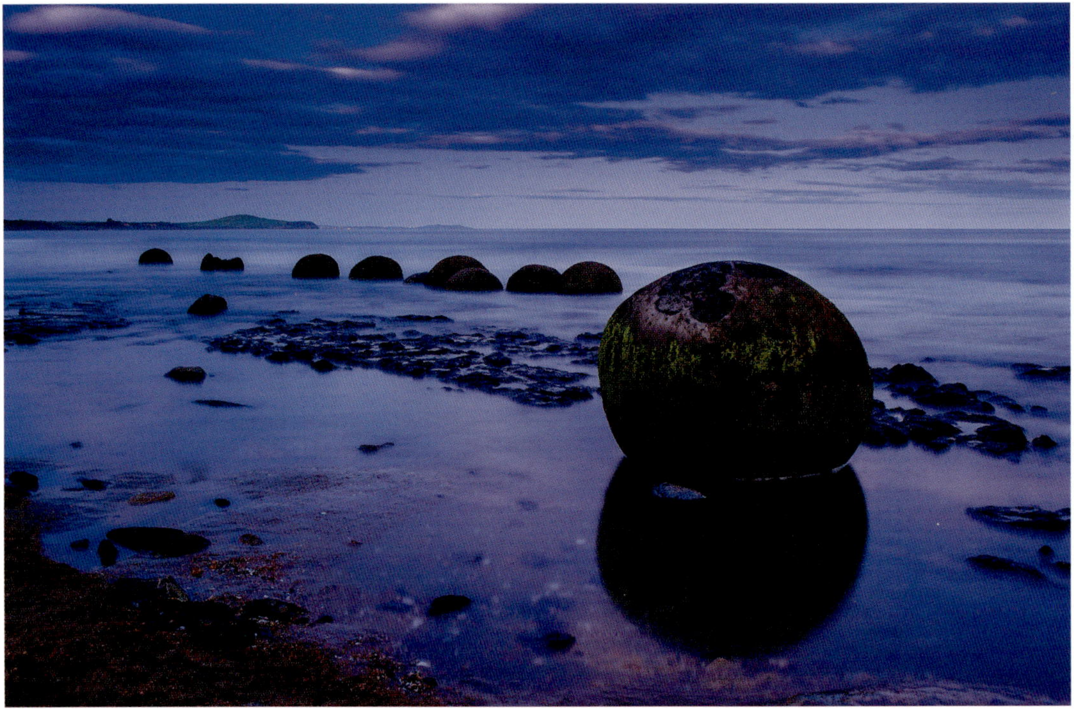

The line up at dusk, Moeraki Boulders, Koekohe Beach, Otago Coast.
opposite: 'The One' a single Moeraki Boulder buried deep in the sand.

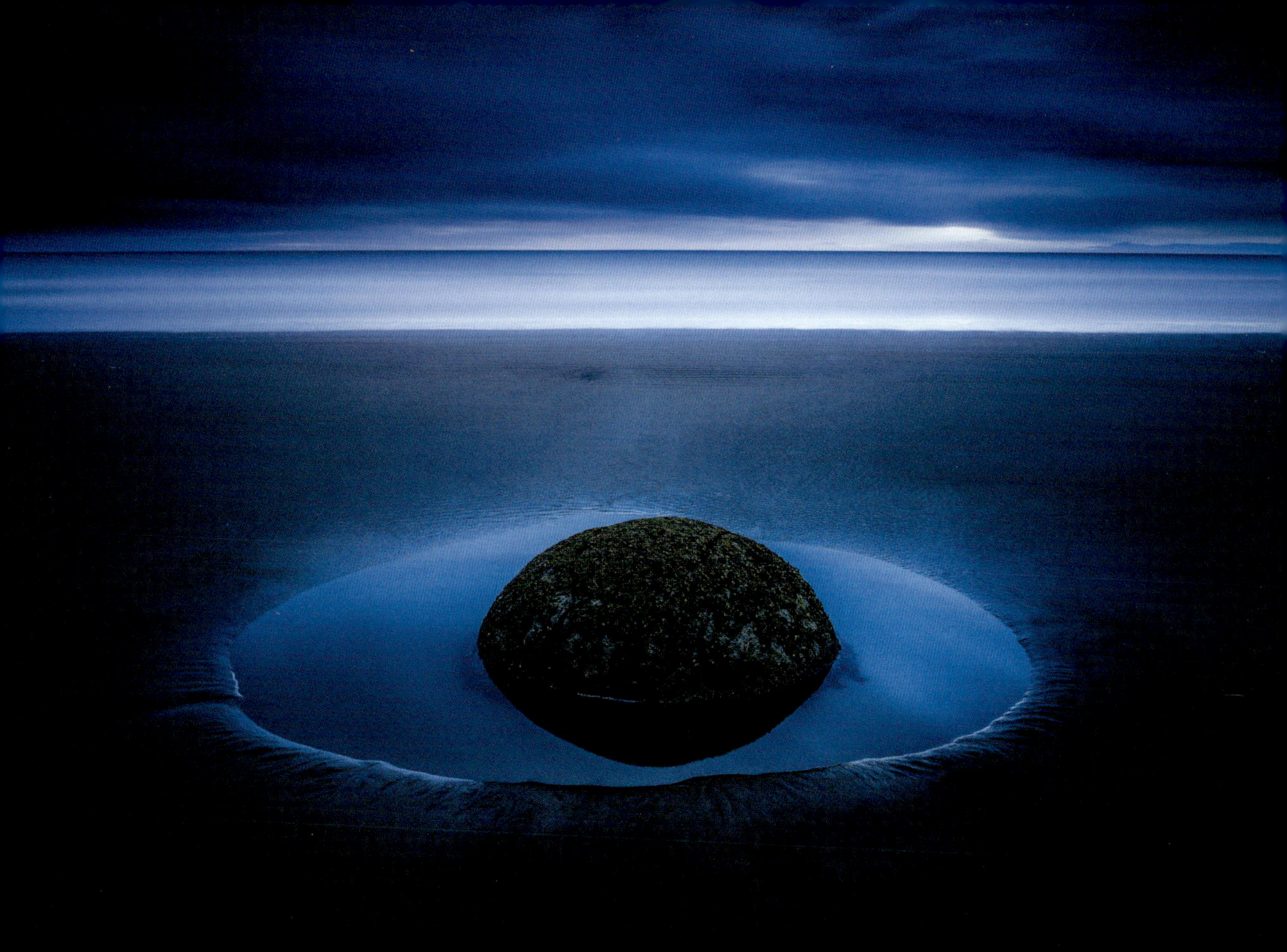

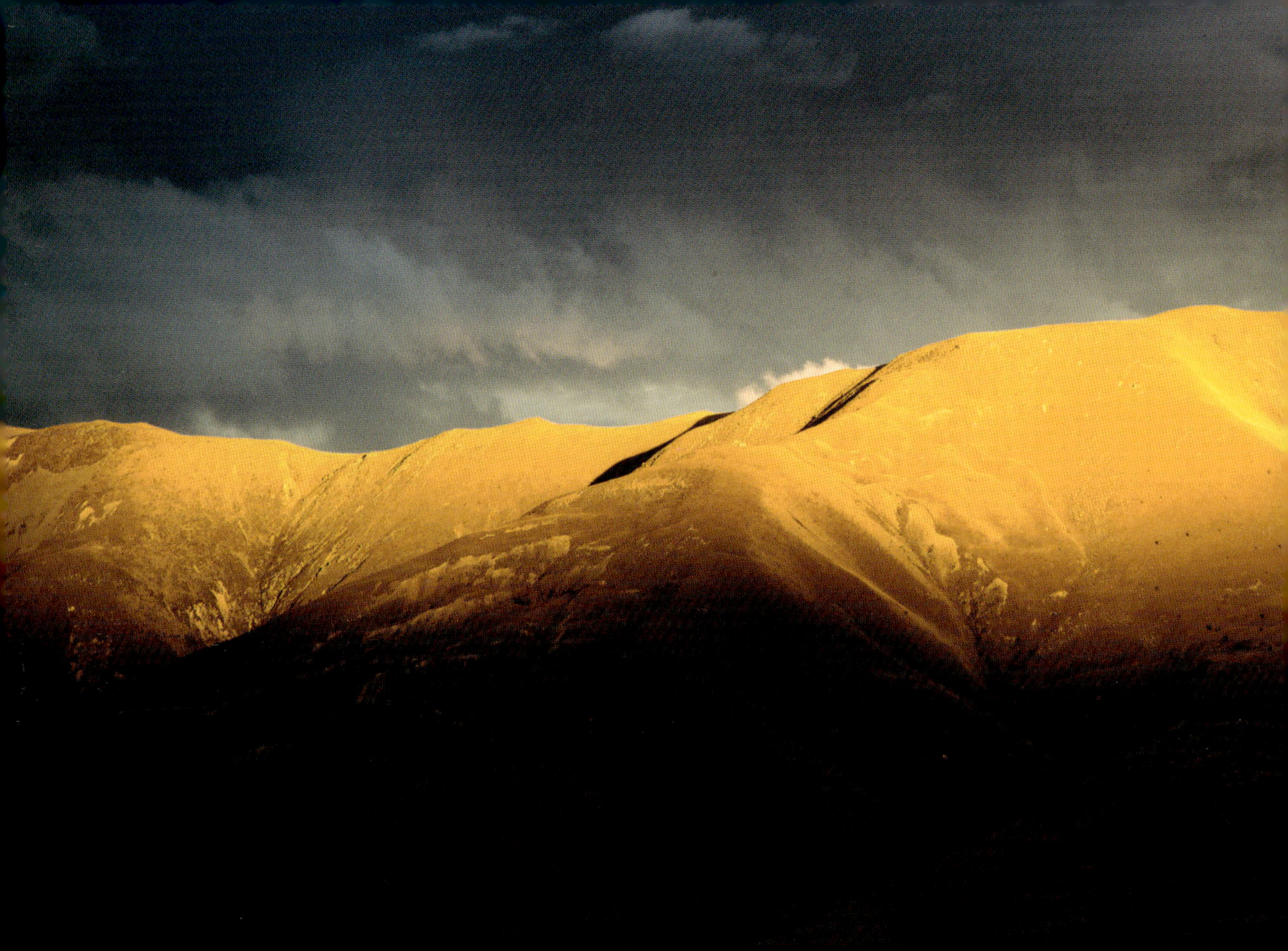

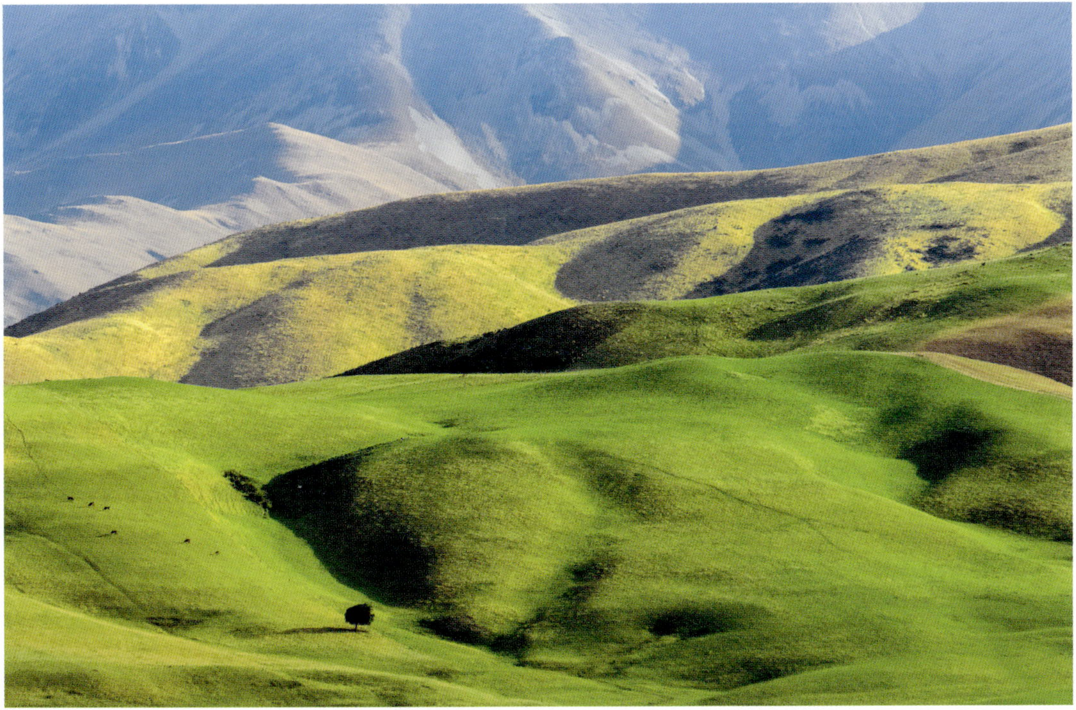

Pastures at the foothills of the Hawkdun Mountains, near Ranfurly, Central Otago.
opposite: Sunlight in the Kakanui Mountain Range, Ranfurly.

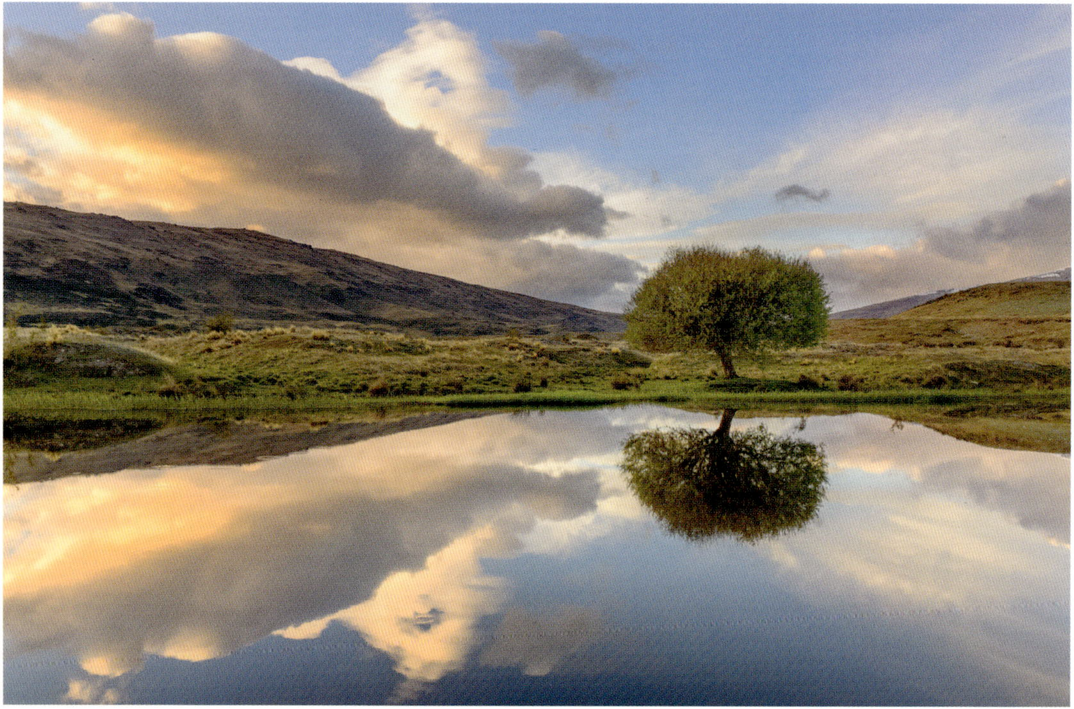

A willow sits by on old sluicing pond, Lower Nevis Valley, Central Otago.
opposite: Pink morning skies over the Blue Lake, St Bathans.

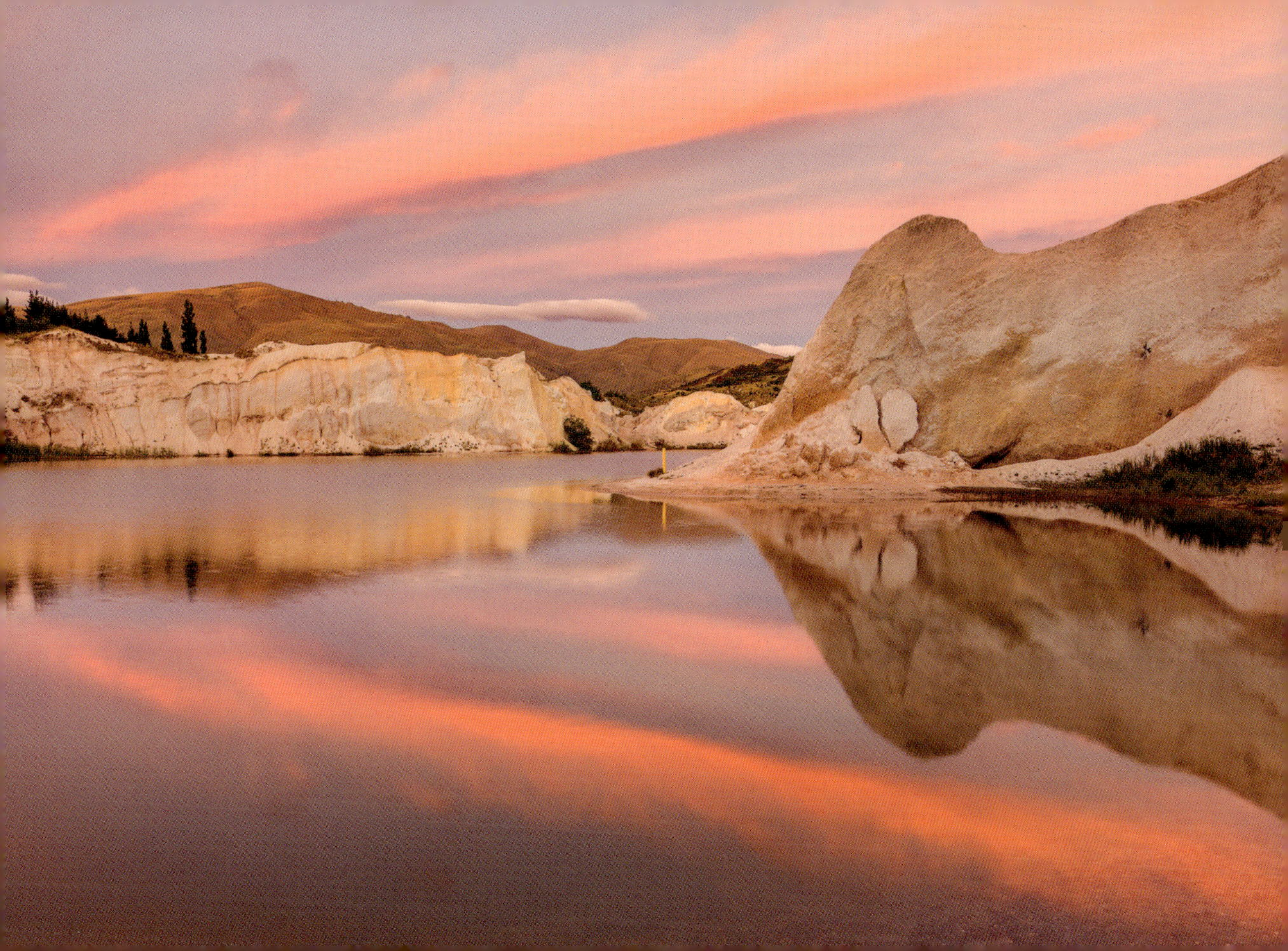

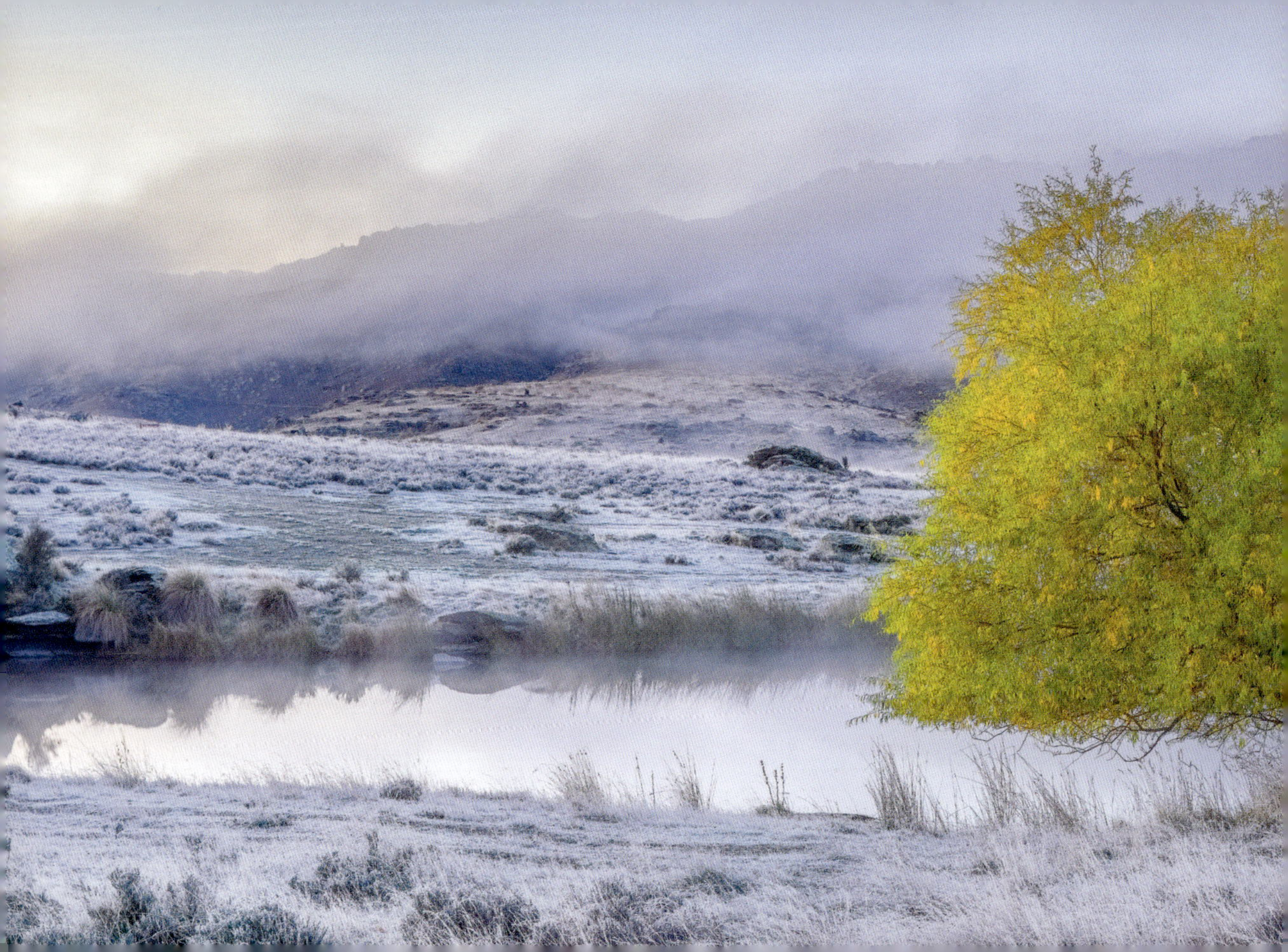

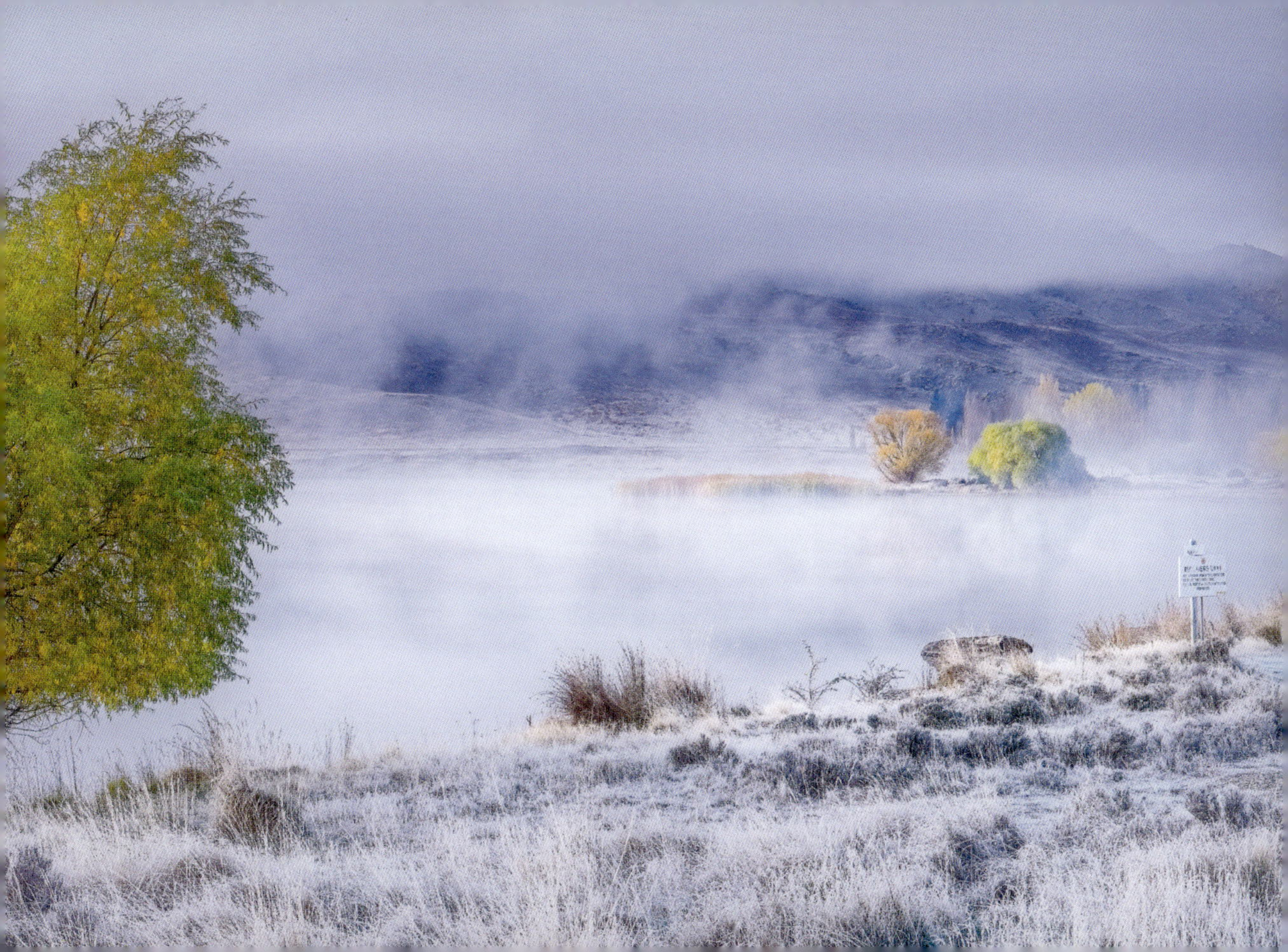

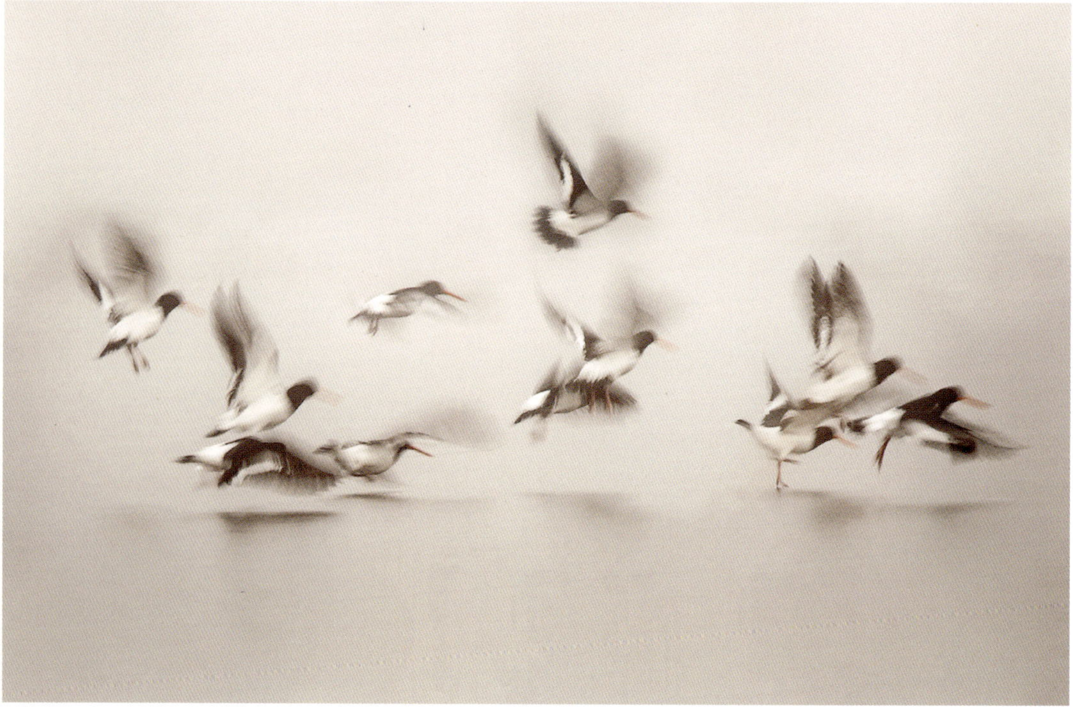

Oystercatchers take flight, Butchers Dam, Alexandra.
previous: A frosty misty winters morning at Butchers Dam.

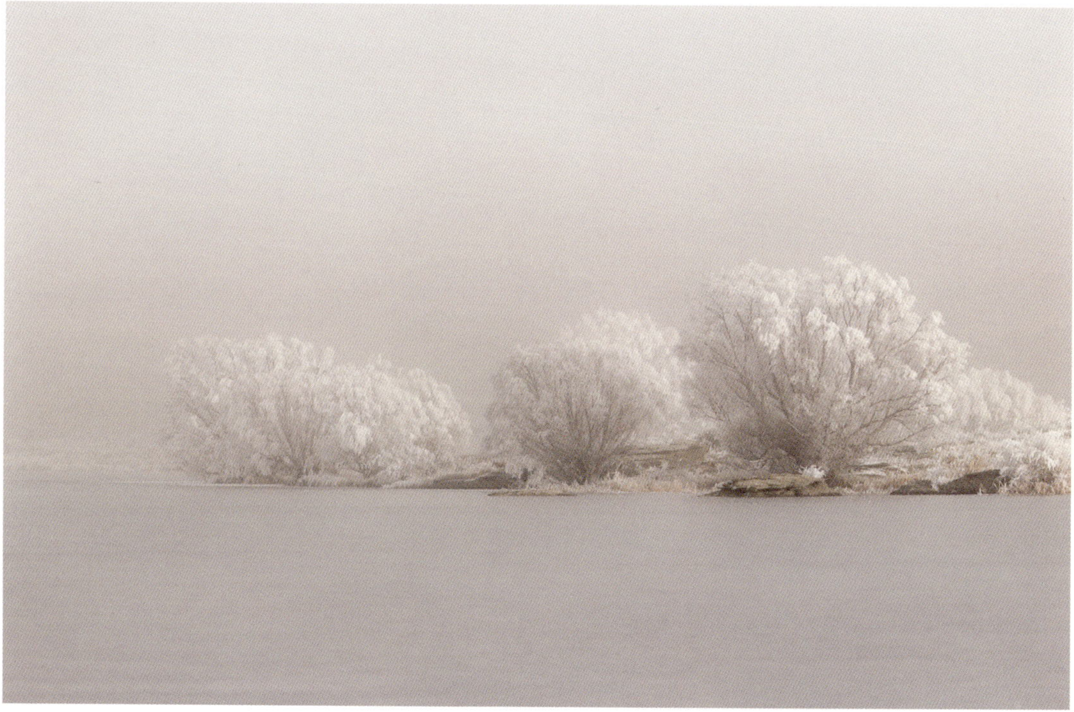

Hoar frost in the willows, at the frozen over Butchers Dam, Alexandra.

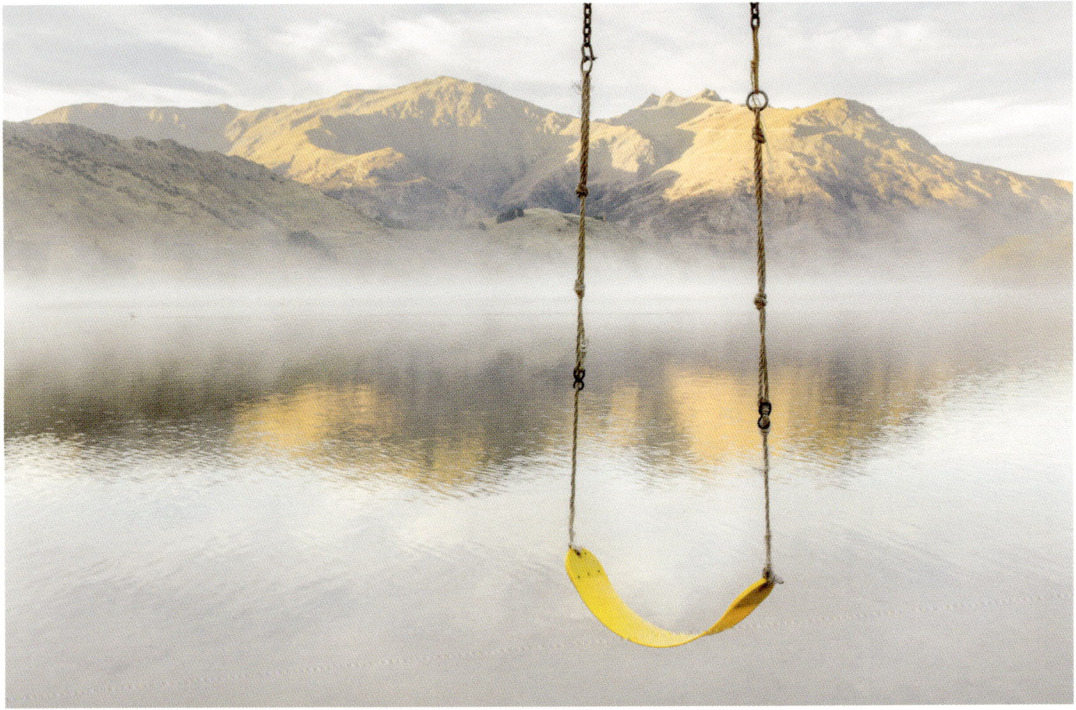

Sit, wait and contemplate, morning mist at Lake Hayes, Central Otago.

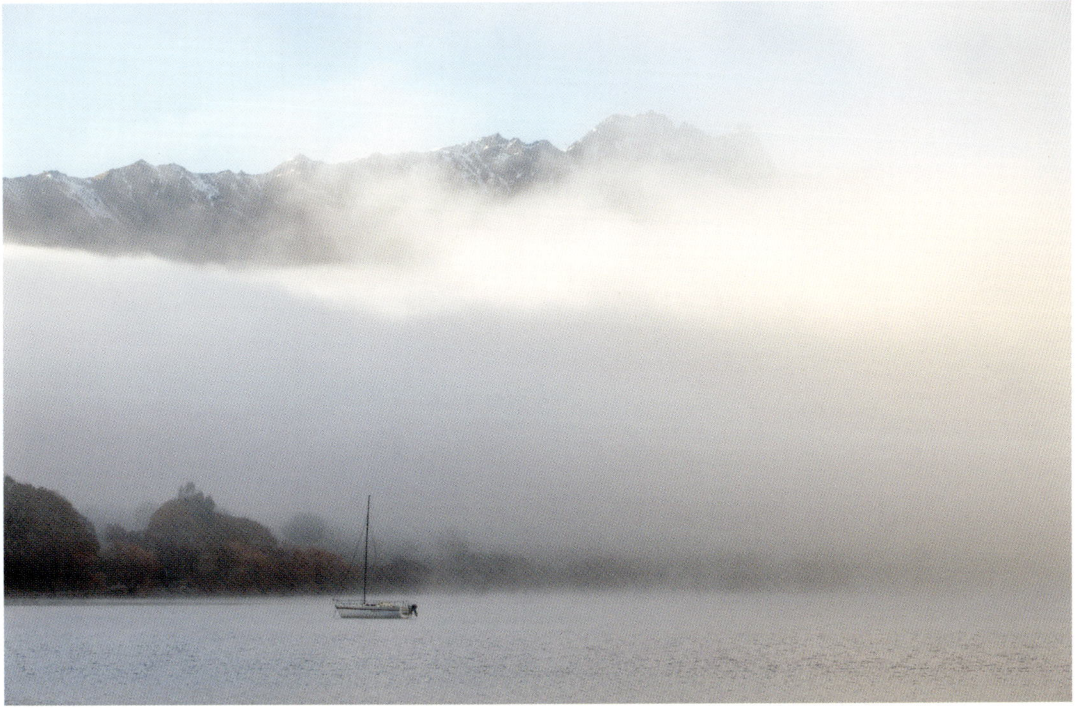

Mist on the waters, Frankton Arm, Lake Wakatipu, Frankton.
overleaf: Last light on the snow capped Remarkables, Queenstown.

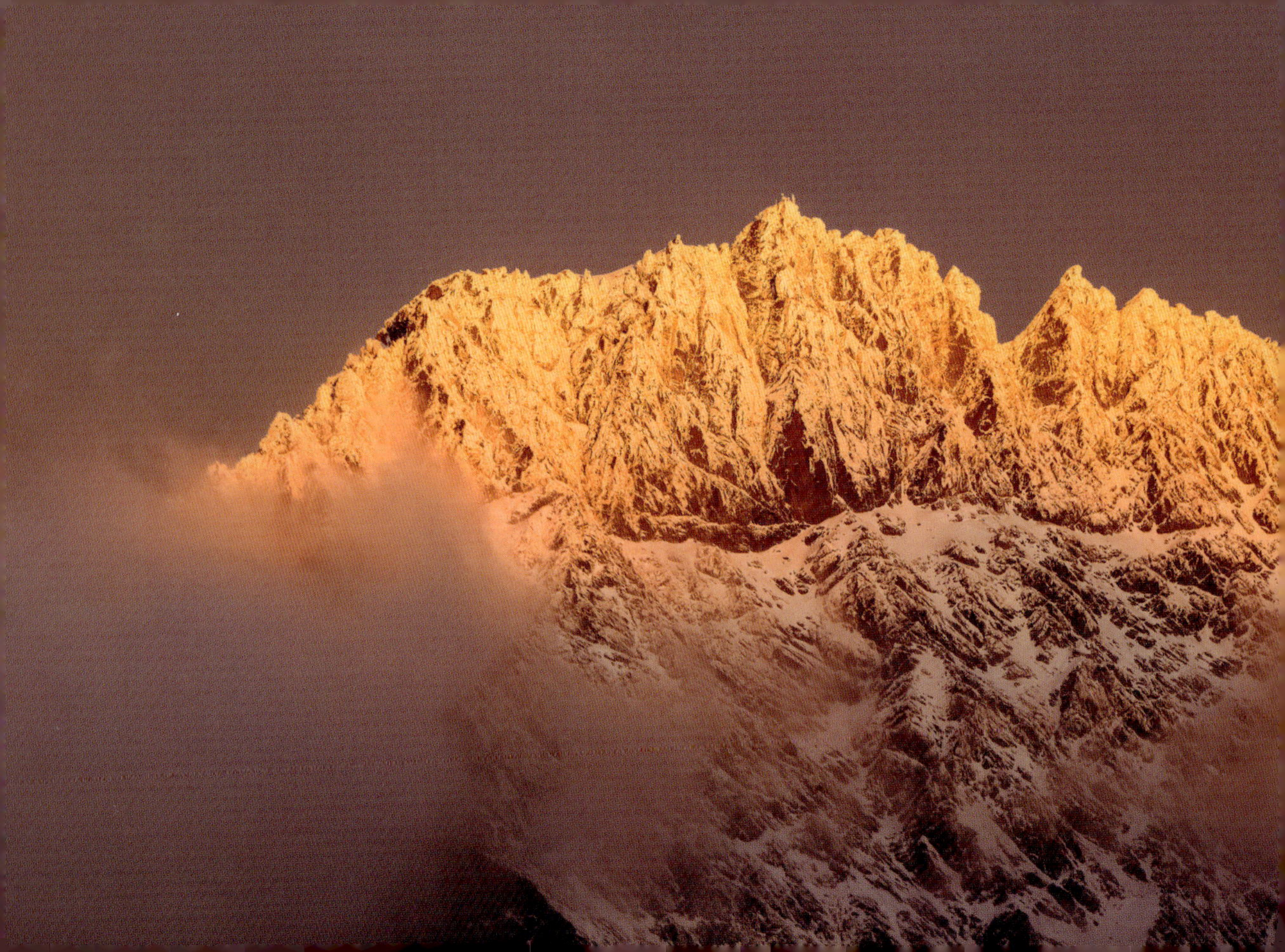

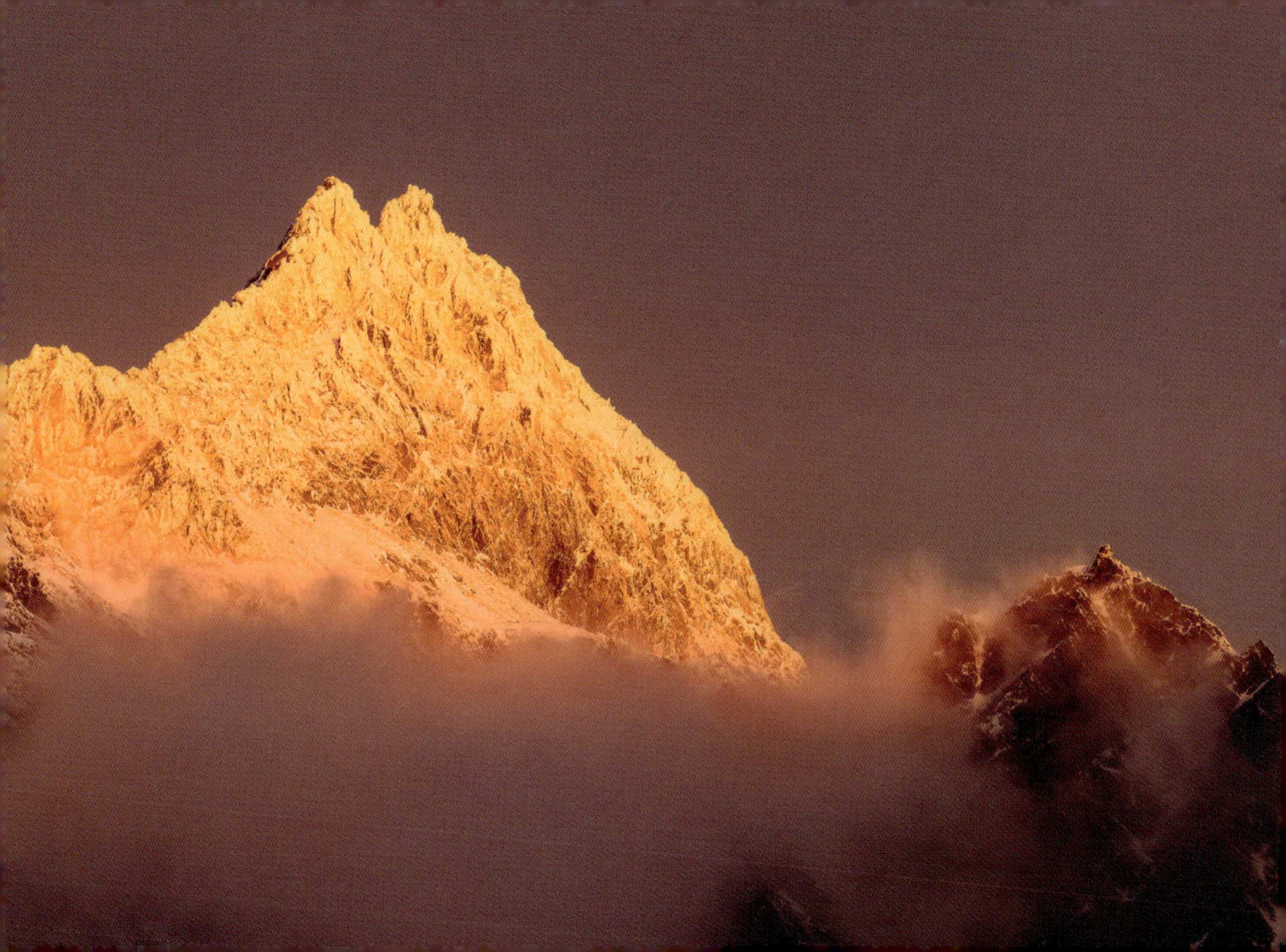

"The Remarkable Remarkables"

The view from the Remarkables over Lake Wakatipu, Queenstown.

The Remarkables mountain range in Queenstown are something special to behold. I have spent countless hours photographing this unique mountain range in all seasons and I never get tired of watching the interplay of light and cloud on its craggy peaks or the way the mountains' personalities change when their winter coats come out on show.

Home of one of Queenstown's two ski fields, in the wintertime locals and tourists spend their days running the slopes of The Remarkables ski field enjoying the fantastic facilities on offer. I, however, would rather travel at a slower pace, away from the crowds and with my camera at hand. For me, a snow day is one where photographic opportunities take priority over anything else, and with fresh snow in the Wakatipu Basin these are the rare opportunities I must make the most of.

Queenstown is a vastly interesting place to live, it offers a lot in terms of night life, shops, tourist activities and extreme sports. My Queenstown however does not exist in those realms; my Queenstown is one of solitude and freedom, where access to the outdoors is plentiful and Mother Nature's remarkable handiwork is on show for all to see. Whilst Queenstown relies on tourism and business to keep the area afloat, it is amongst the mountains and at the lake shore that I choose to spend my time. This place provides for all, but we must not lose sight of what is truly remarkable about this area, for it is Mother Nature who is the one that truly provides for us here.

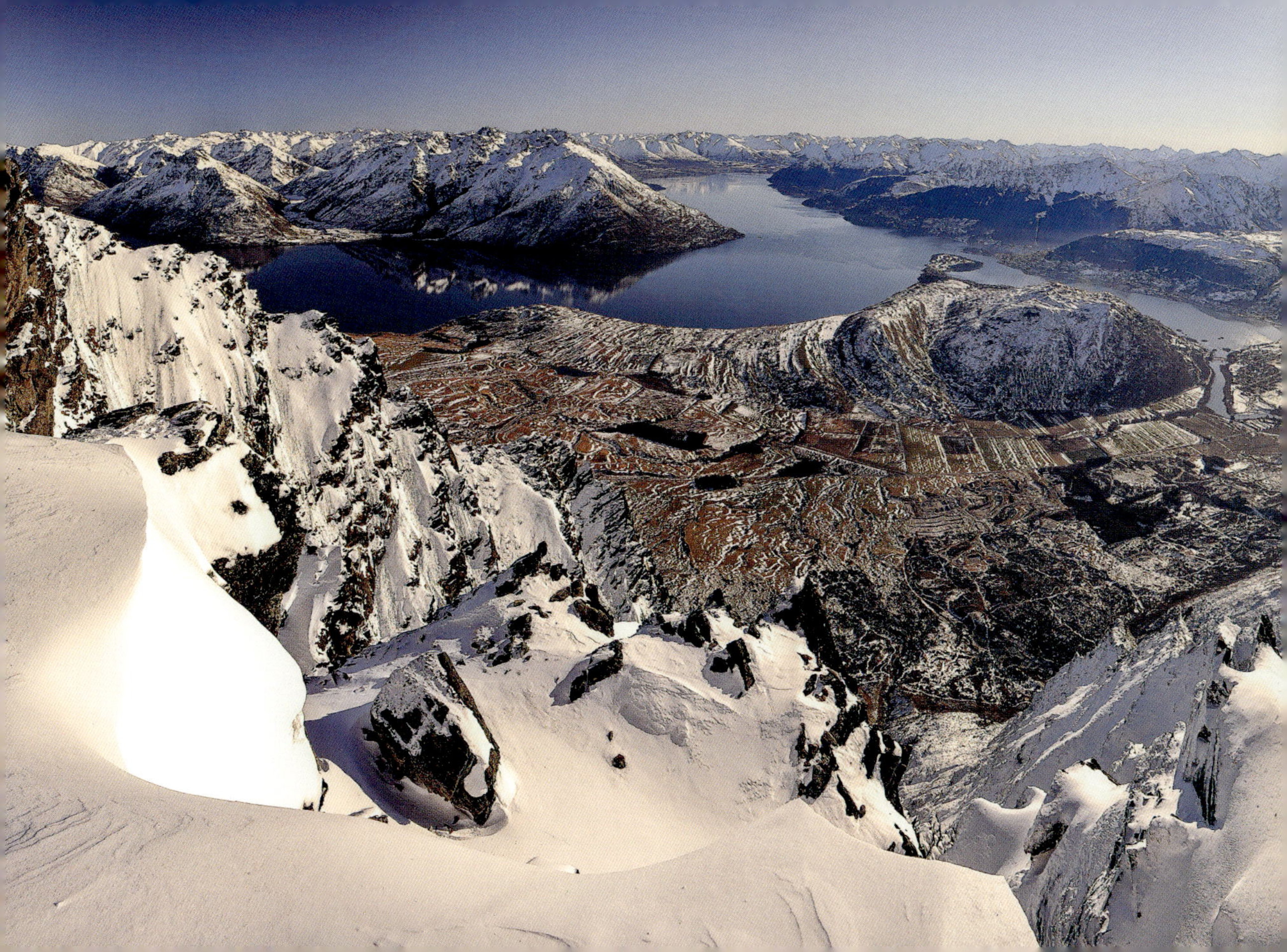

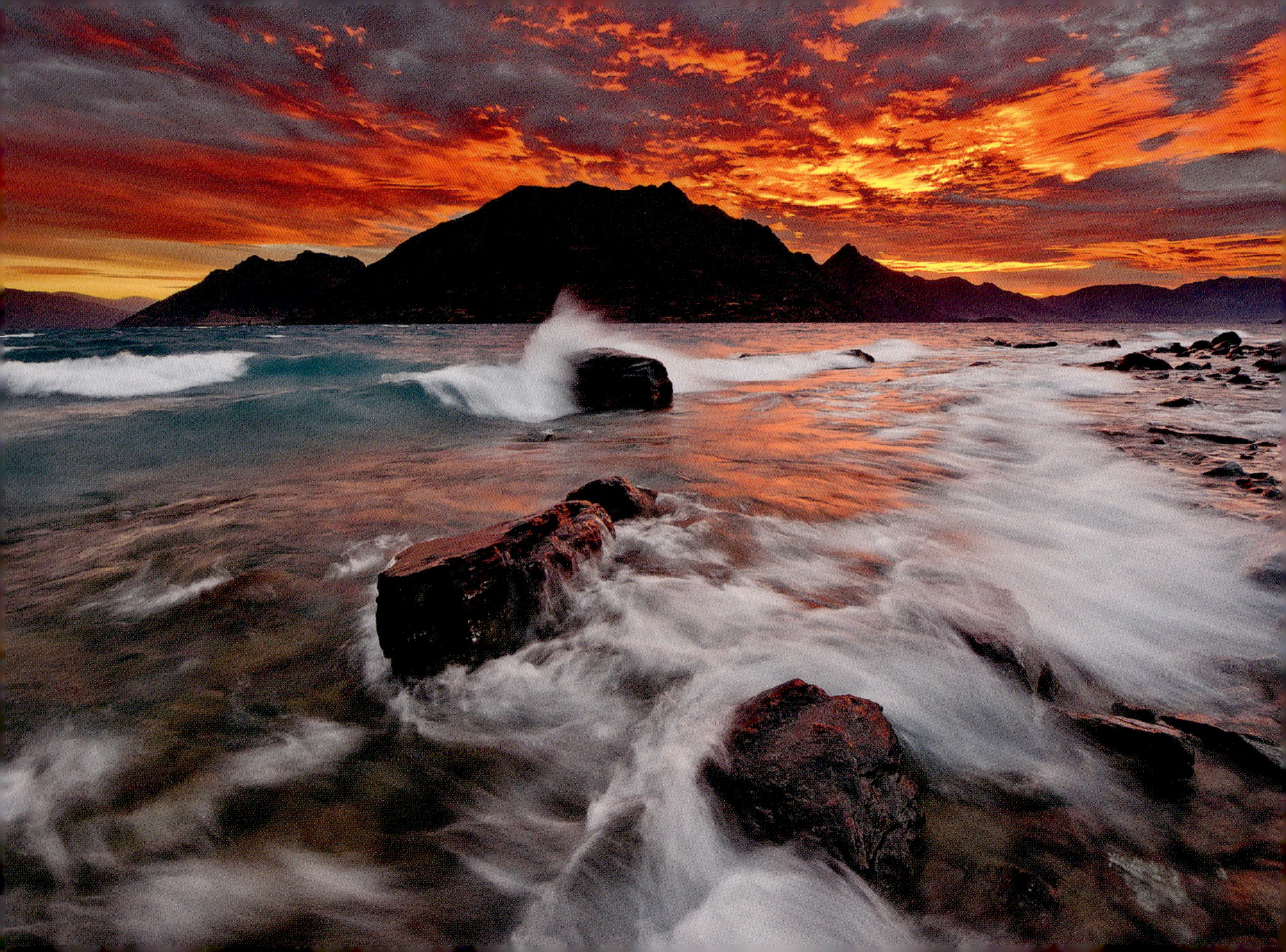

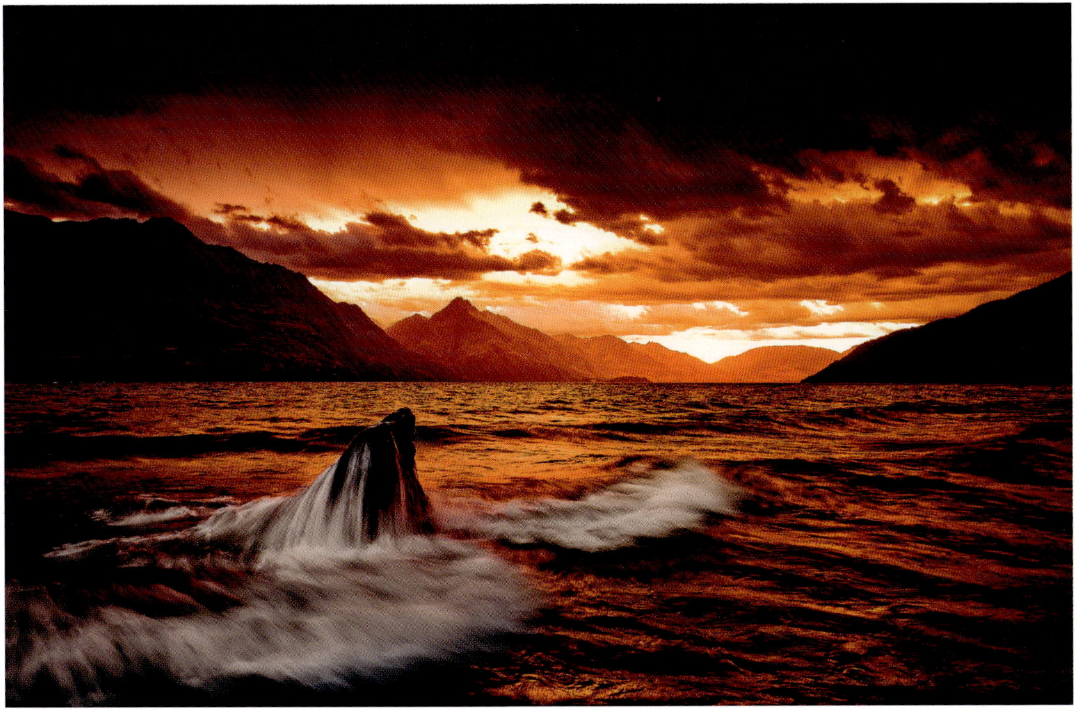

Stormy sunset over Lake Wakatipu, Queenstown.
opposite: Sky on fire over Cecil and Walter Peaks, Lake Wakatipu.

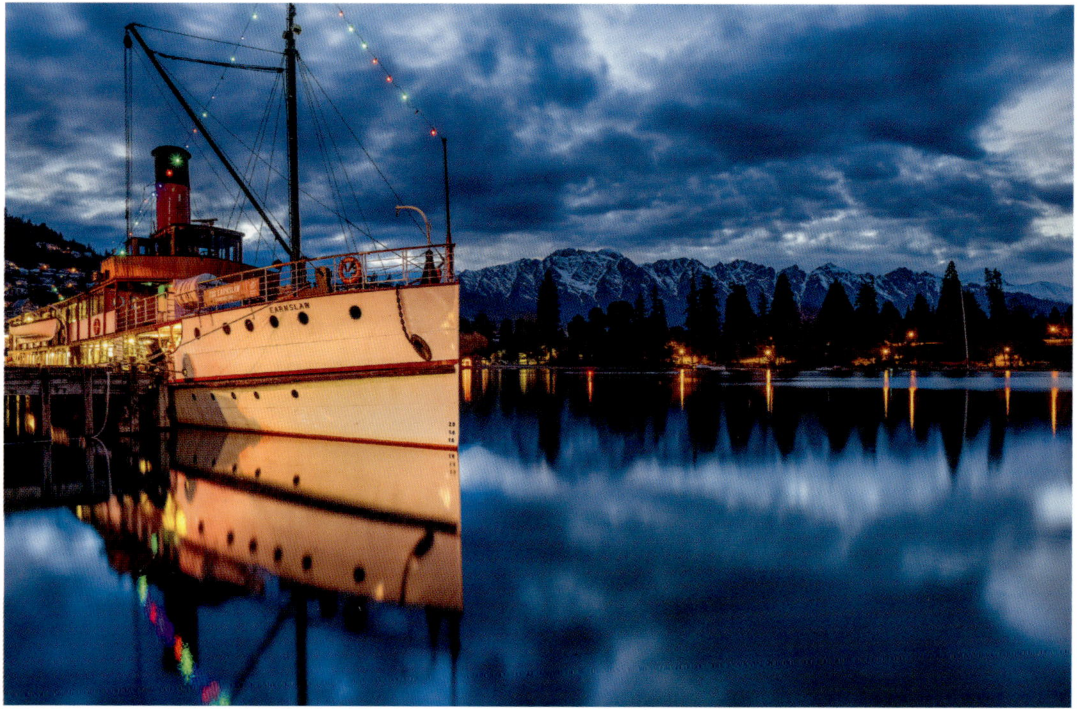

The glow of town lights on TSS Earnslaw at dock at dawn, Lake Wakatipu.
opposite: Winter night lights after the snow storm clears, Queenstown.

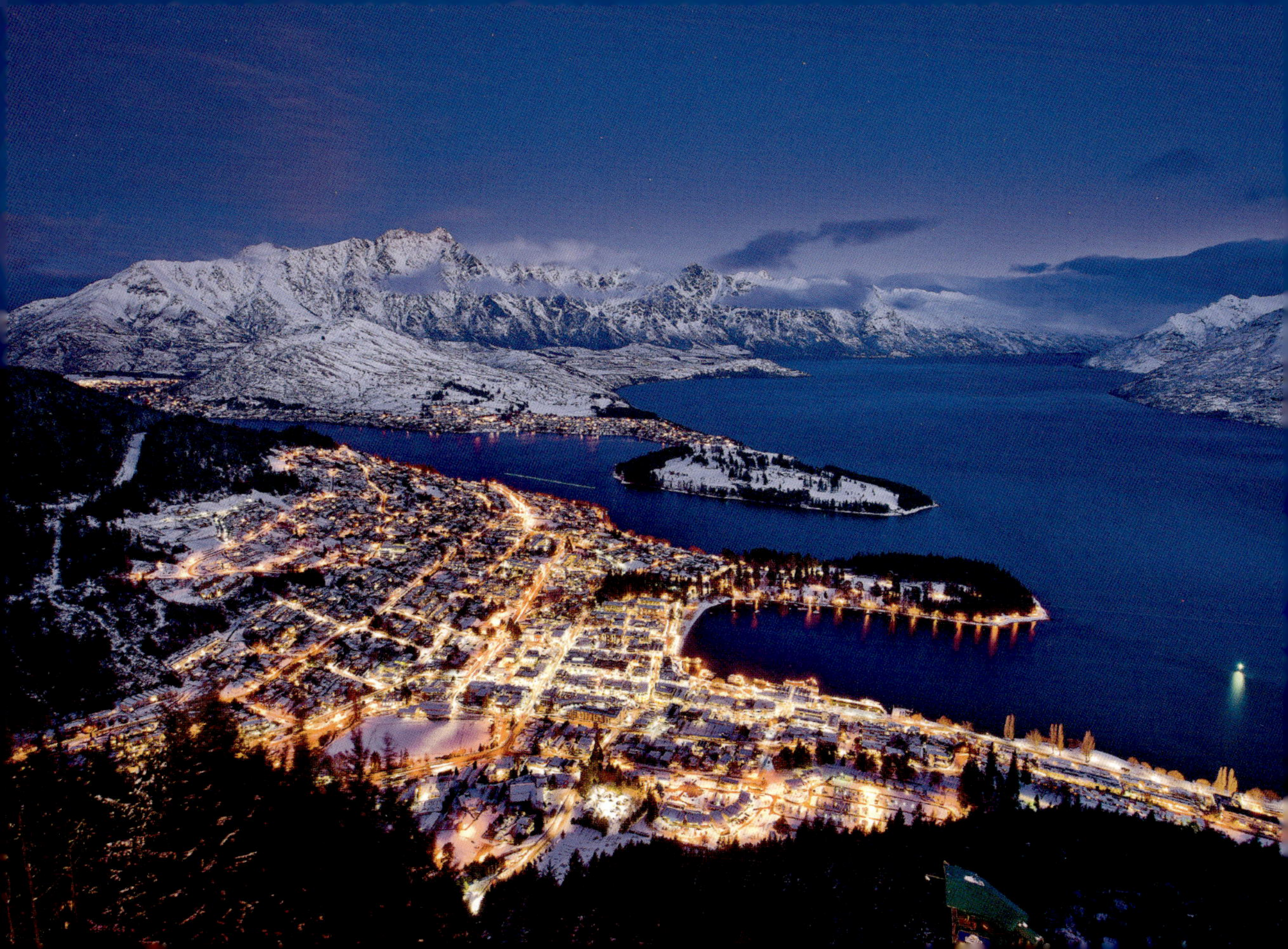

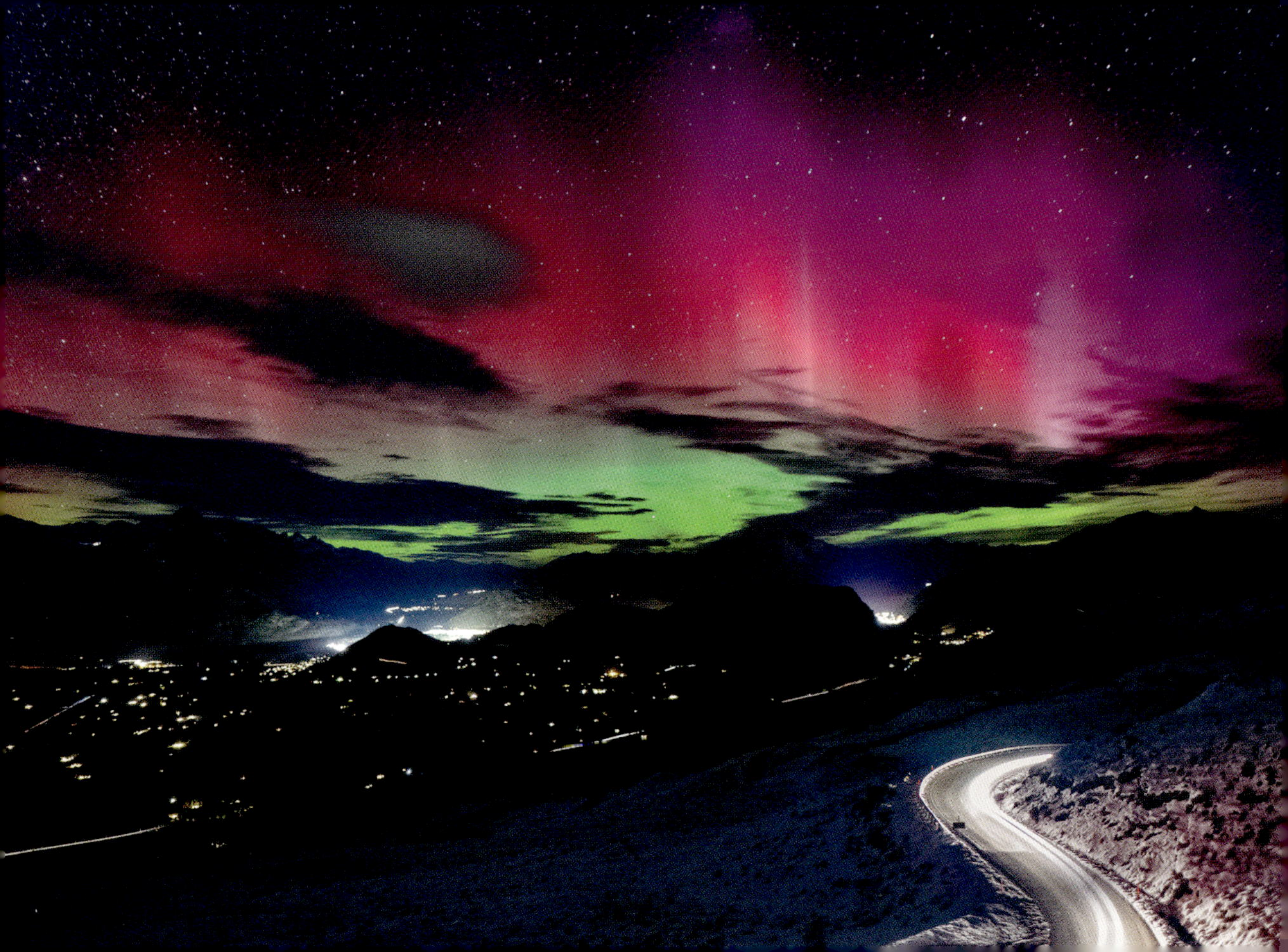

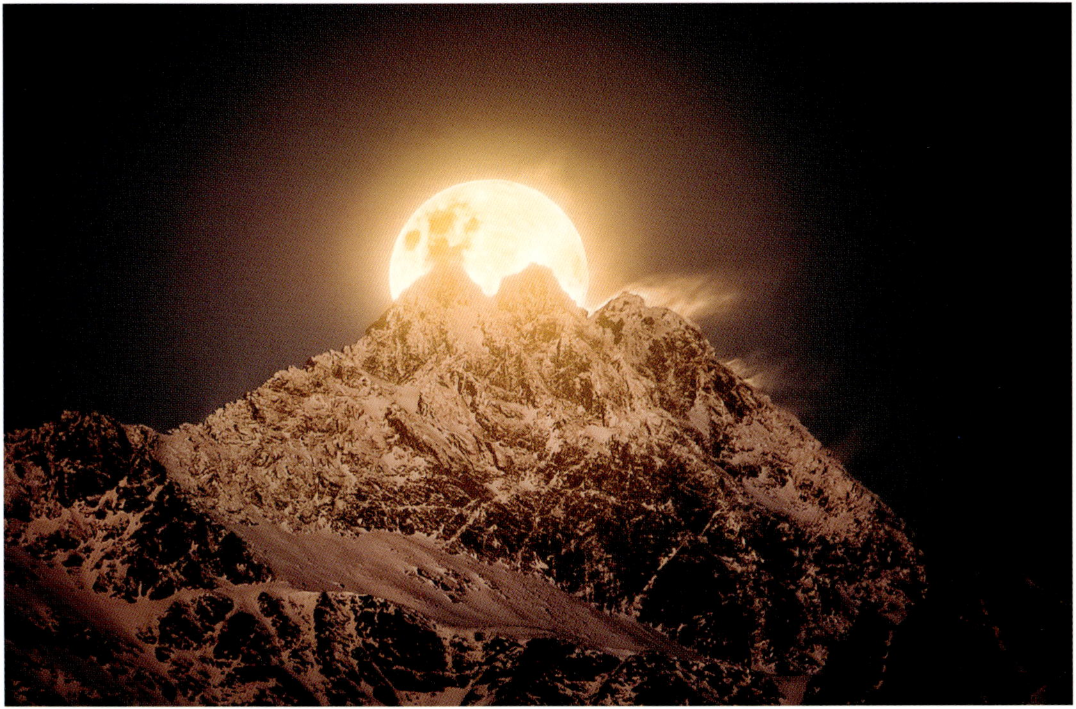

Moonrise over the Remarkables, Queenstown.
opposite: The Southern Lights over the Wakatipu Basin, Central Otago.

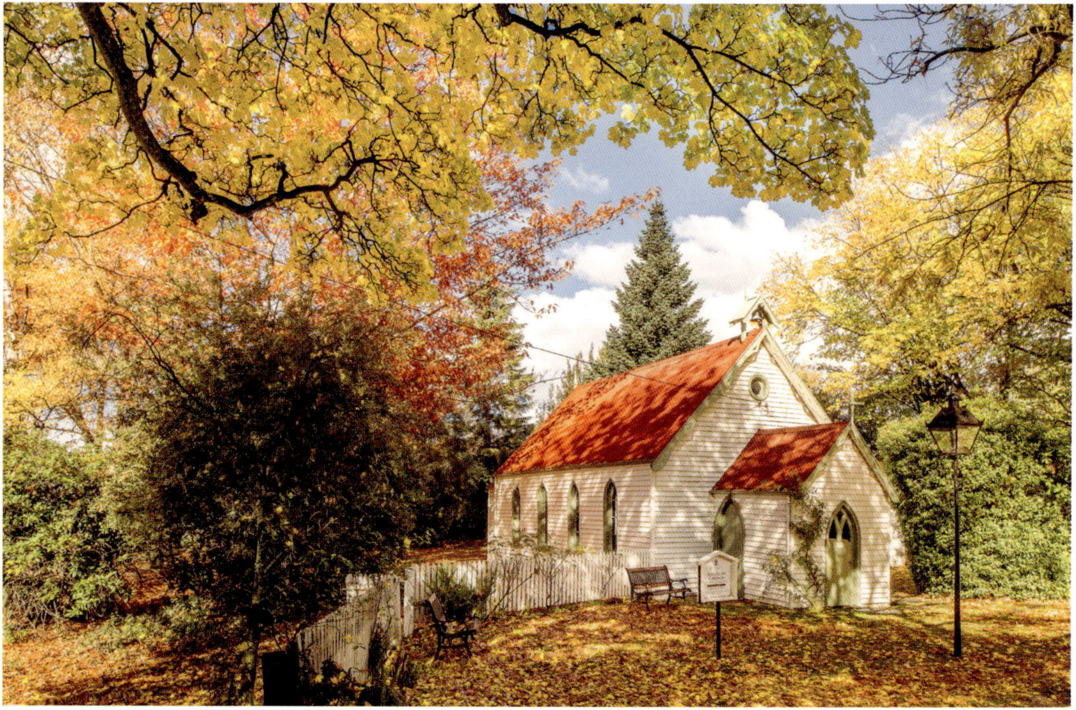

St Paul's Anglican Church, Arrowtown, Central Otago.

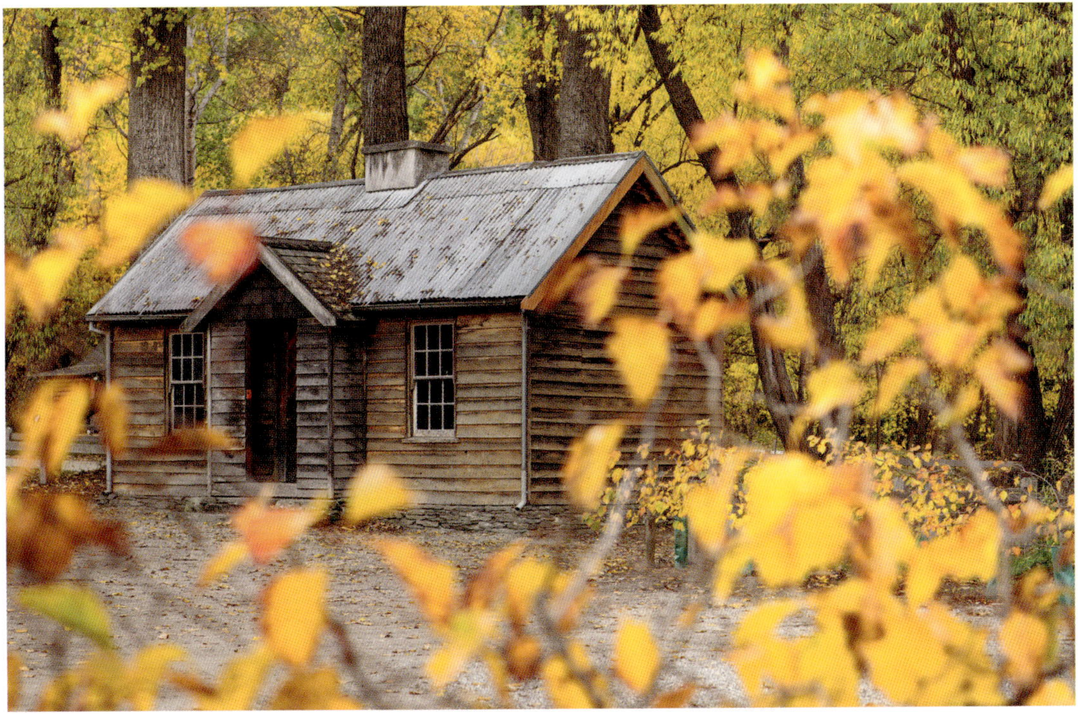

Old police cottage in autumn, Butlers Green, Arrowtown.
overleaf: An autumn morning at Macetown, Central Otago.

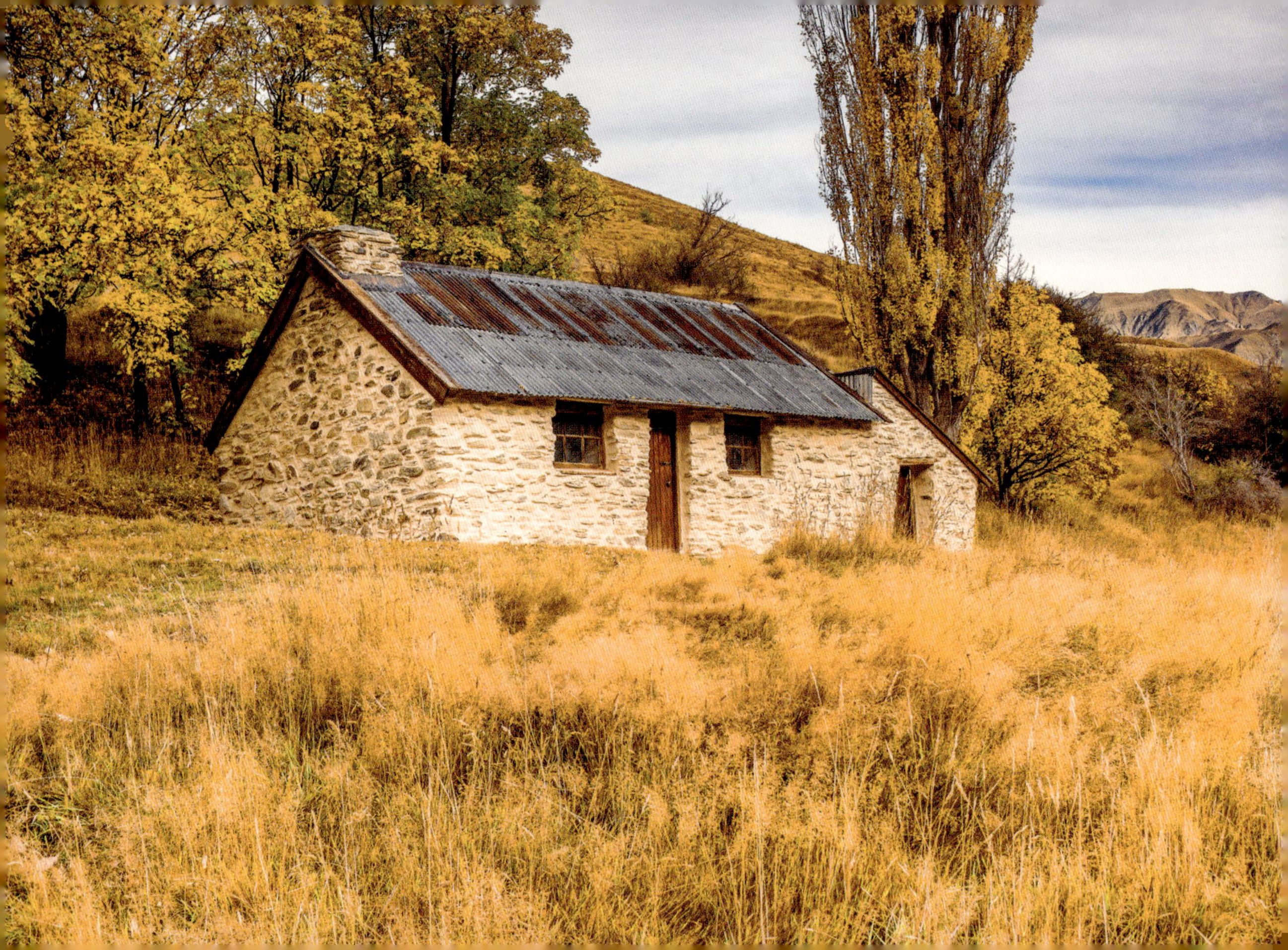

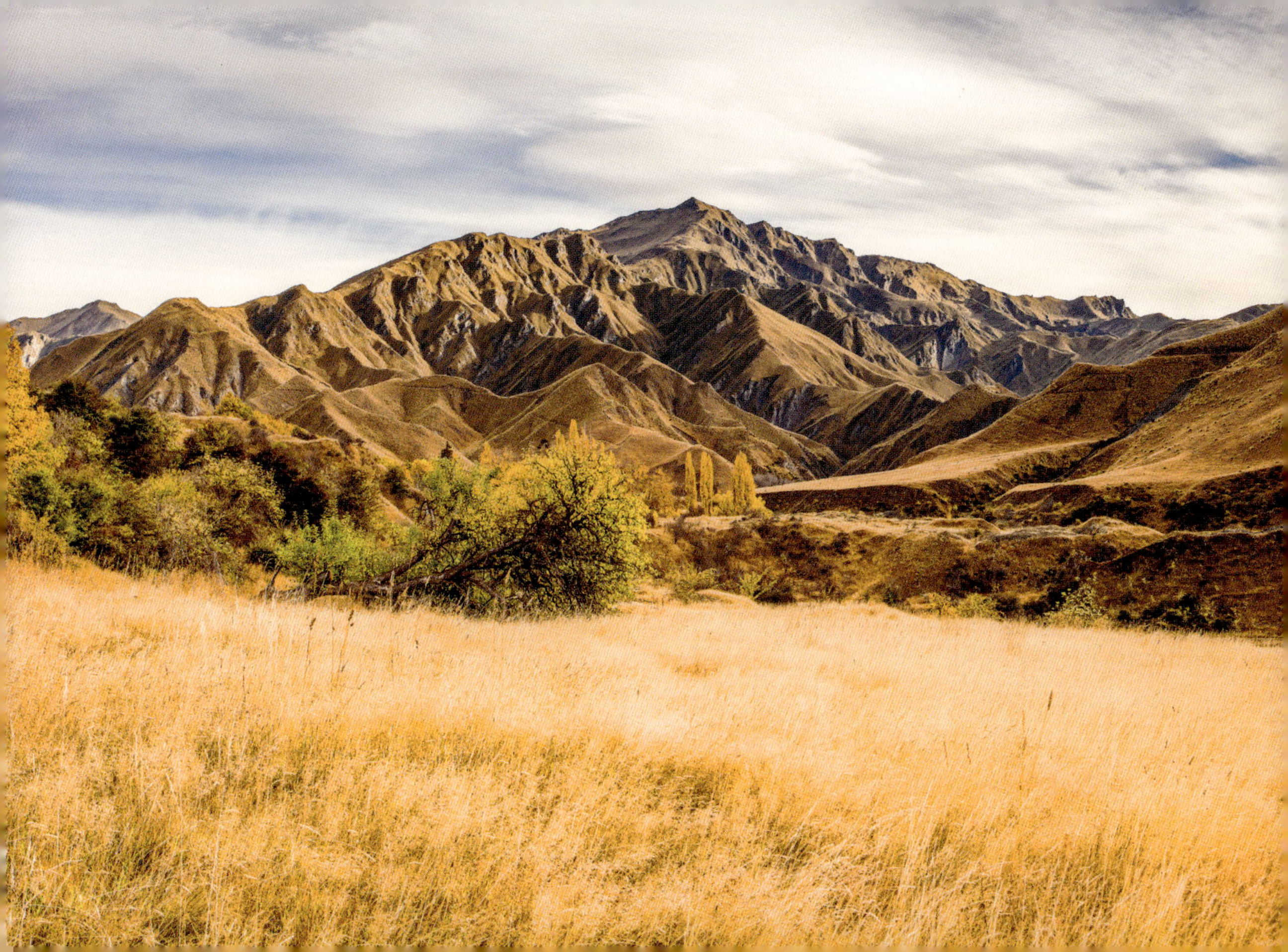

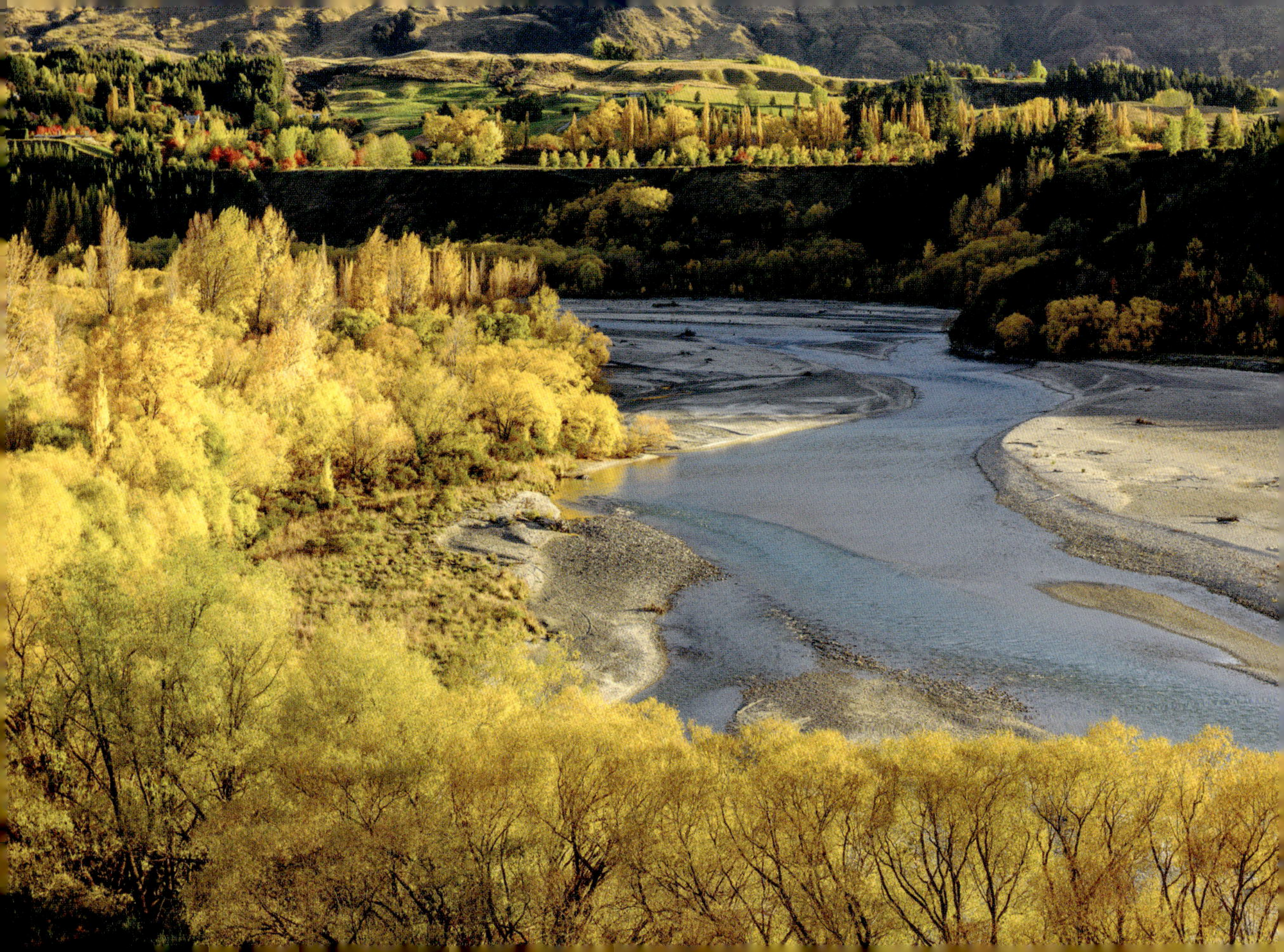

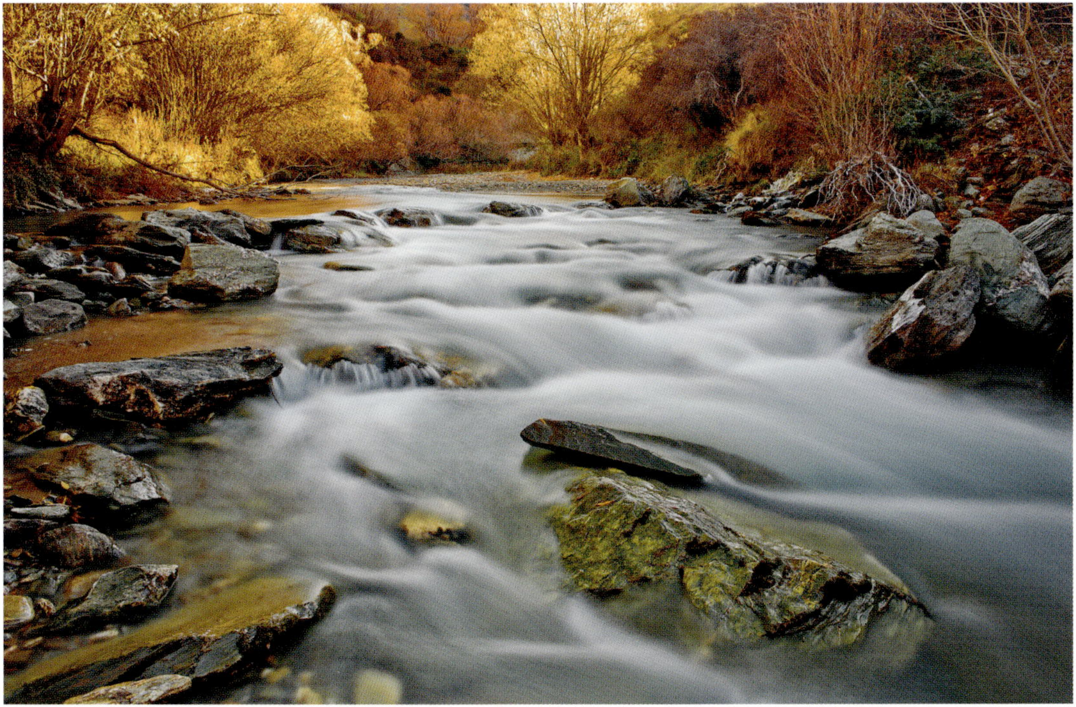

Afternoon autumn glow in the willow trees on the Arrow River near Macetown.
opposite: Morning light on the Shotover River near Queenstown.

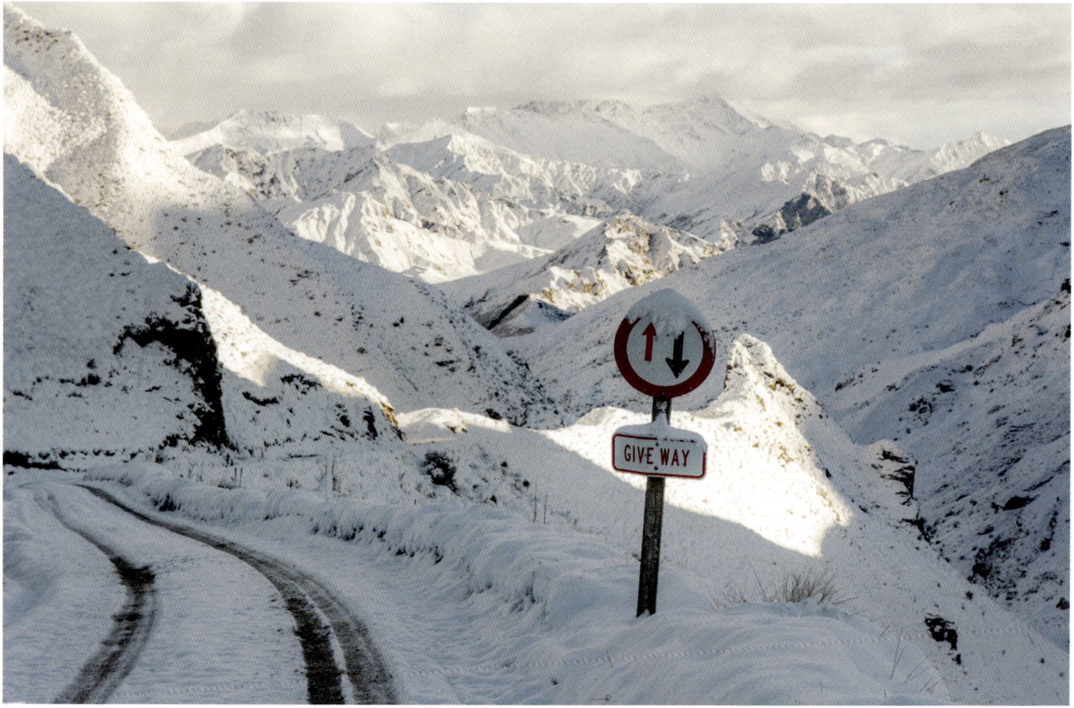

Slippery slide into Skippers Canyon, Central Otago.
opposite: Blustery Bennetts Bluff, Lake Wakatipu.

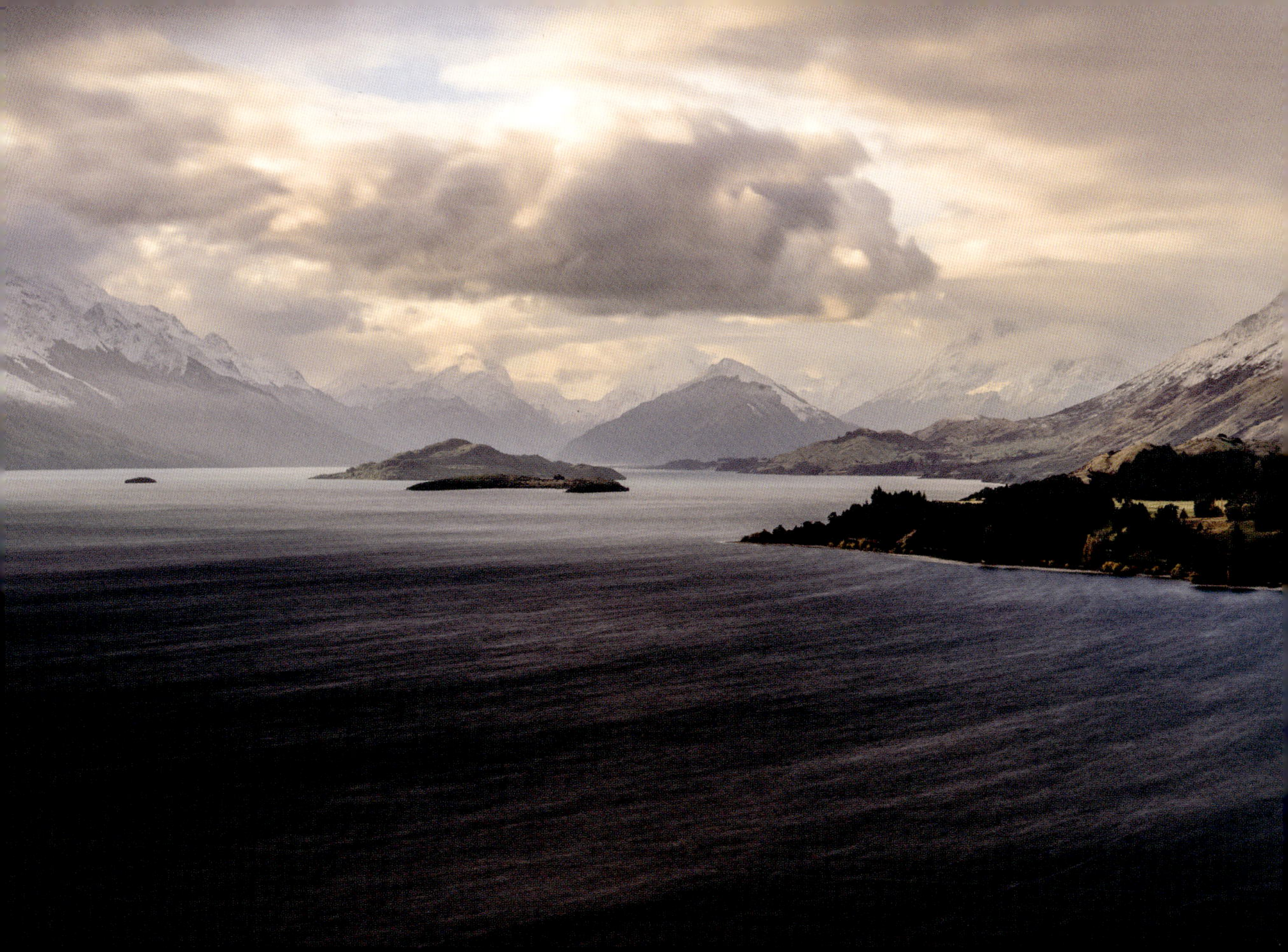

"Gateway to Paradise"

The wharf at the head of Lake Wakatipu, Glenorchy.

At the head of Lake Wakatipu lies a sleepy town called Glenorchy. This little community sits outside the rapidly growing metropolis of Queenstown, nestled between the mountains and the waters of Lake Wakatipu.

Glenorchy is the Gateway to Paradise; it is the last stop before adventurers head into Mt Aspiring National Park to climb peaks, trek the famous Routeburn Track or explore the Dart and Rees Valleys on foot.

I eagerly woke very early one morning in Glenorchy to find the winter's storm from the previous night had eased, leaving fresh snow on the mountain tops. The rain had stopped so I ventured out around the lakeside.

I walked out onto the famous Glenorchy wharf by the Boat Shed to see this scene; the lamp light at the end glowing bright in the early dawn, no wind, just a crisp chill to the air. I took a few exposures, and just stood there, looking around me. The stillness, the peace, the balance between man's creation and the land; it was special. The light then went out and it was time for me to journey into paradise, or perhaps I was already there.

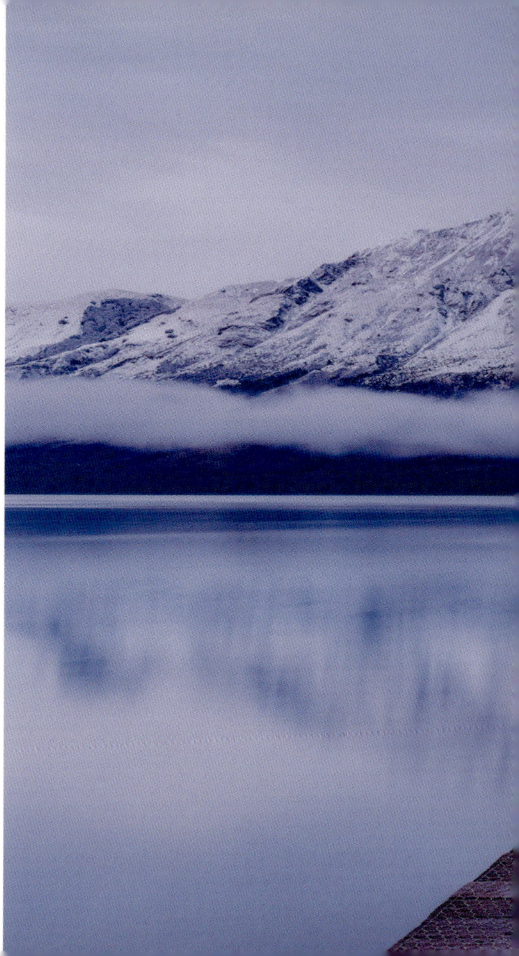

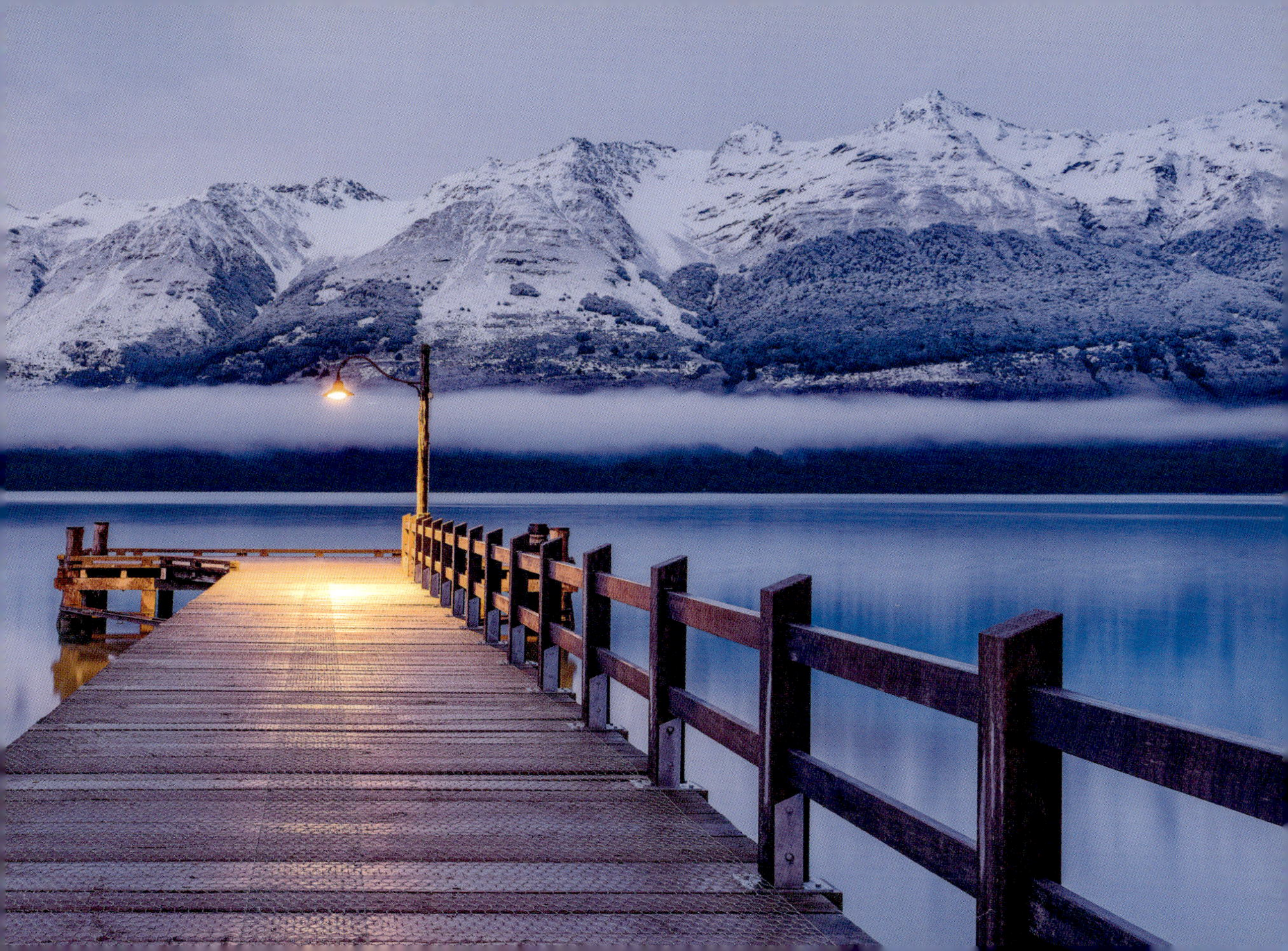

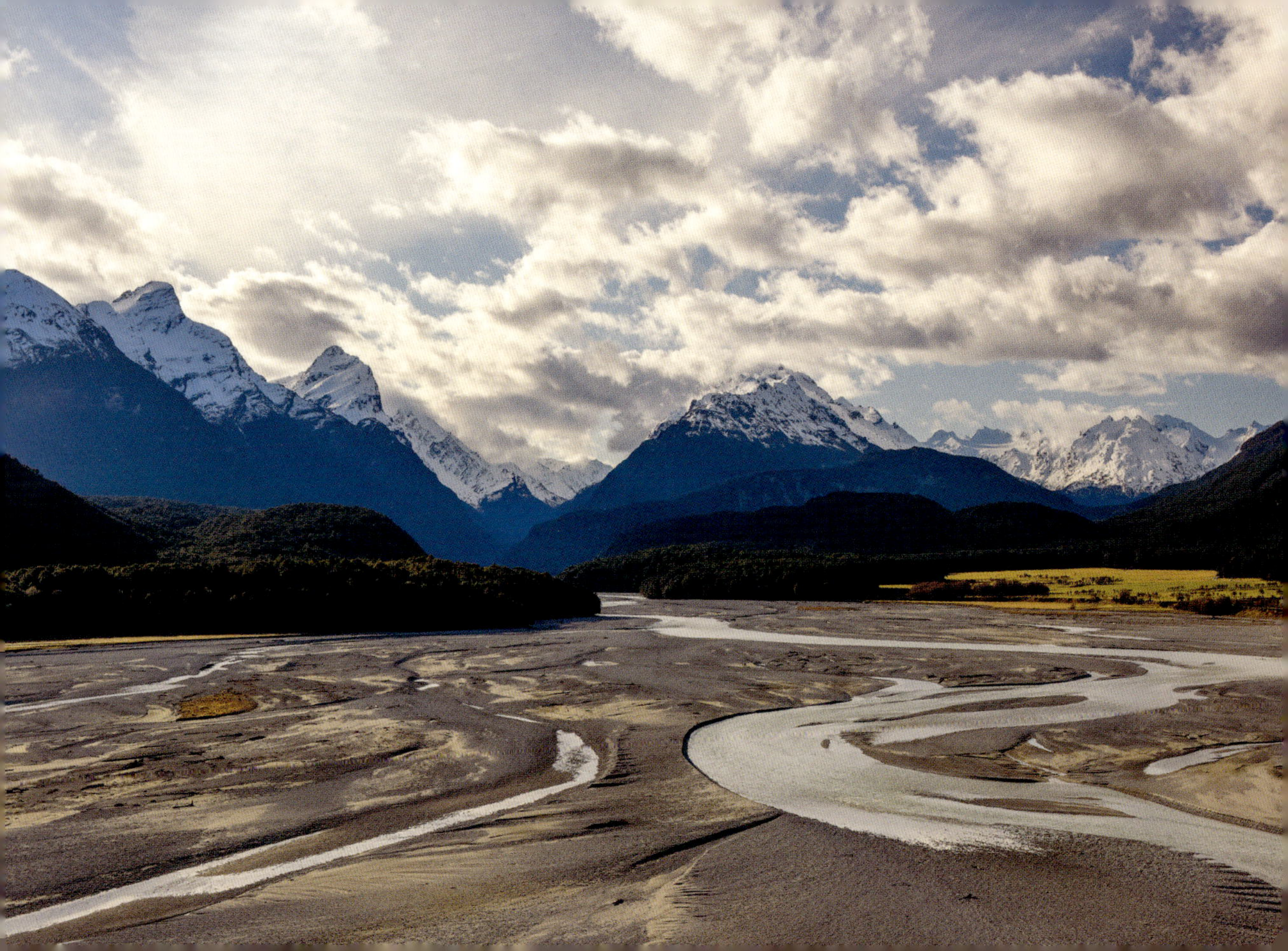

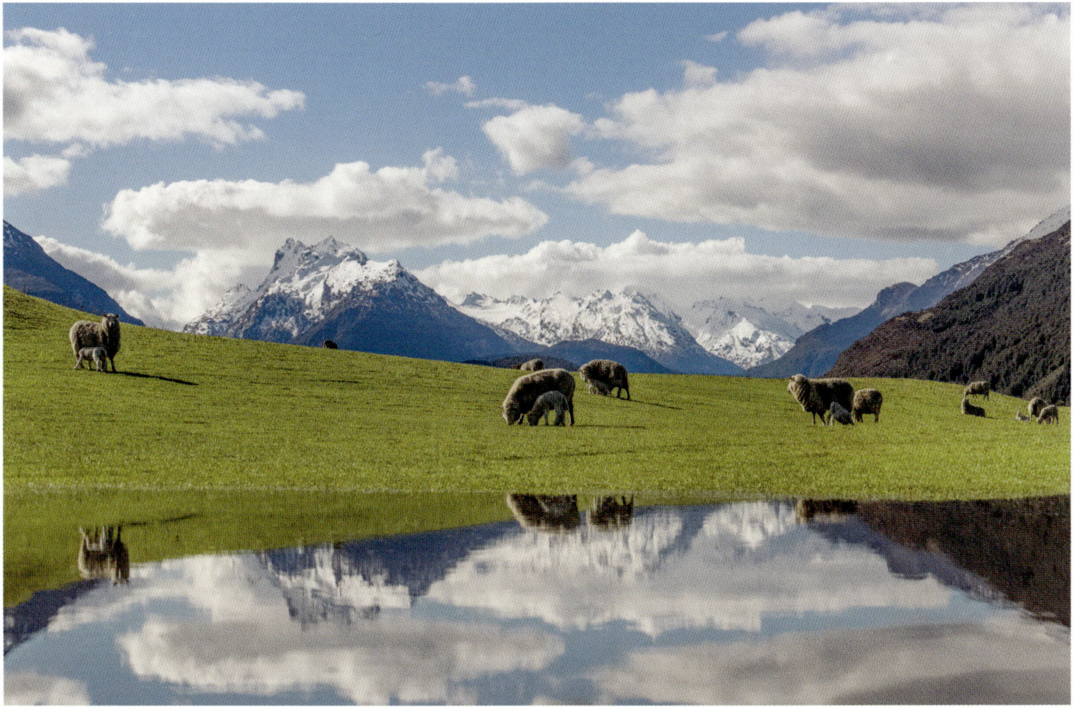

A sheep's paradise, near Glenorchy, Central Otago.
opposite: Overlooking the Dart River and Mt Aspiring National Park, Paradise.
overleaf: Mt Earnslaw through the clouds, Glenorchy.

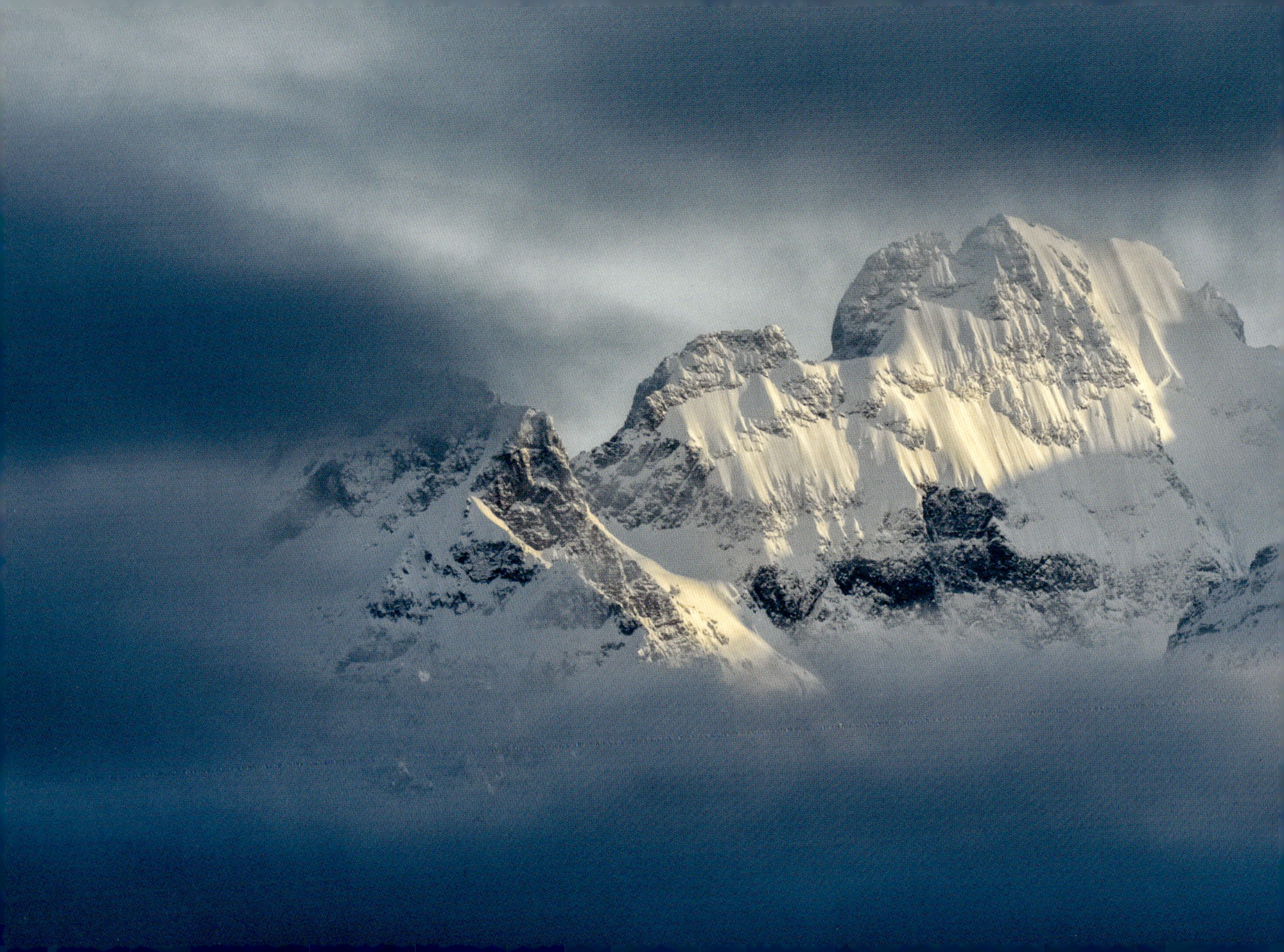

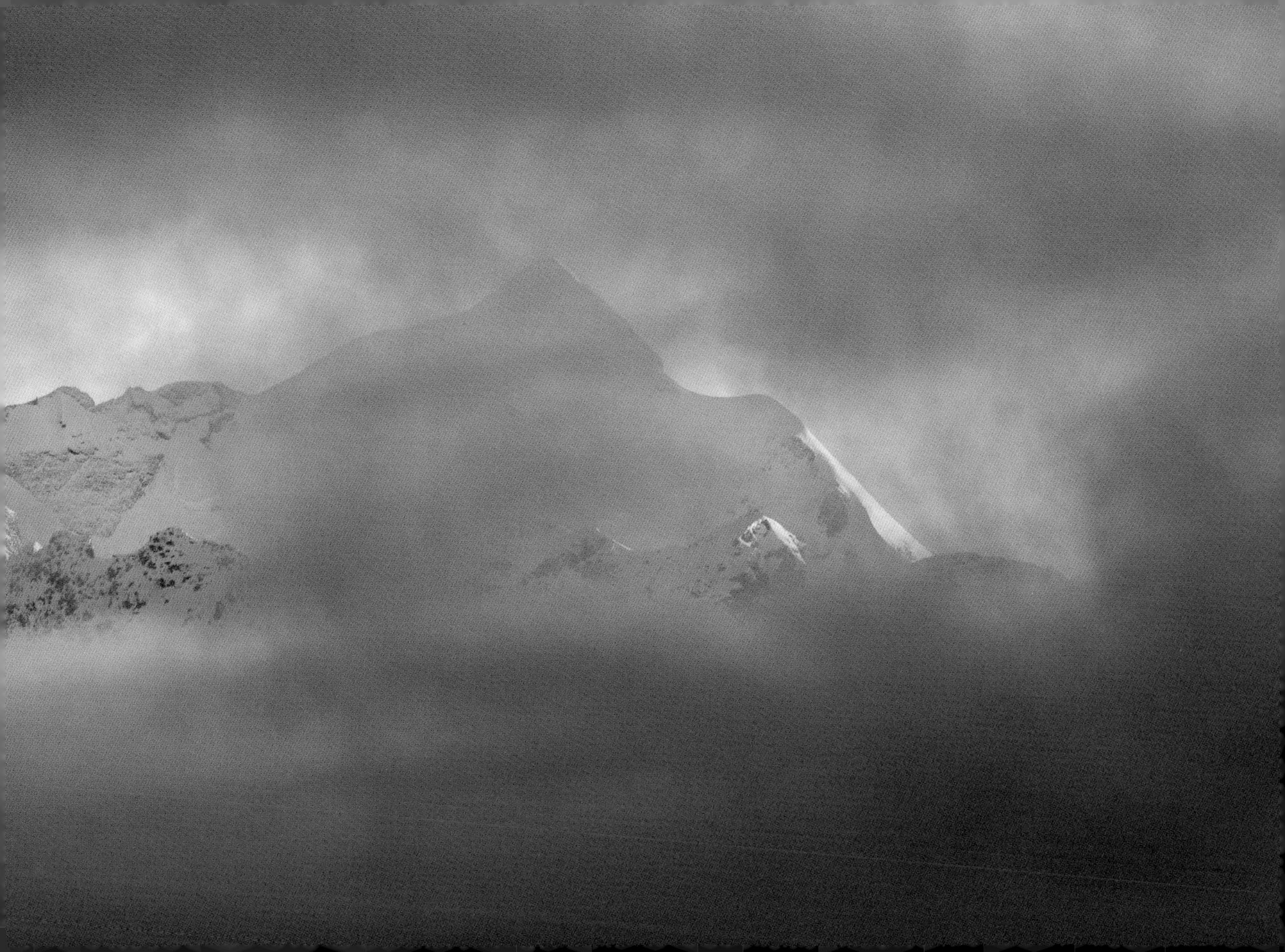

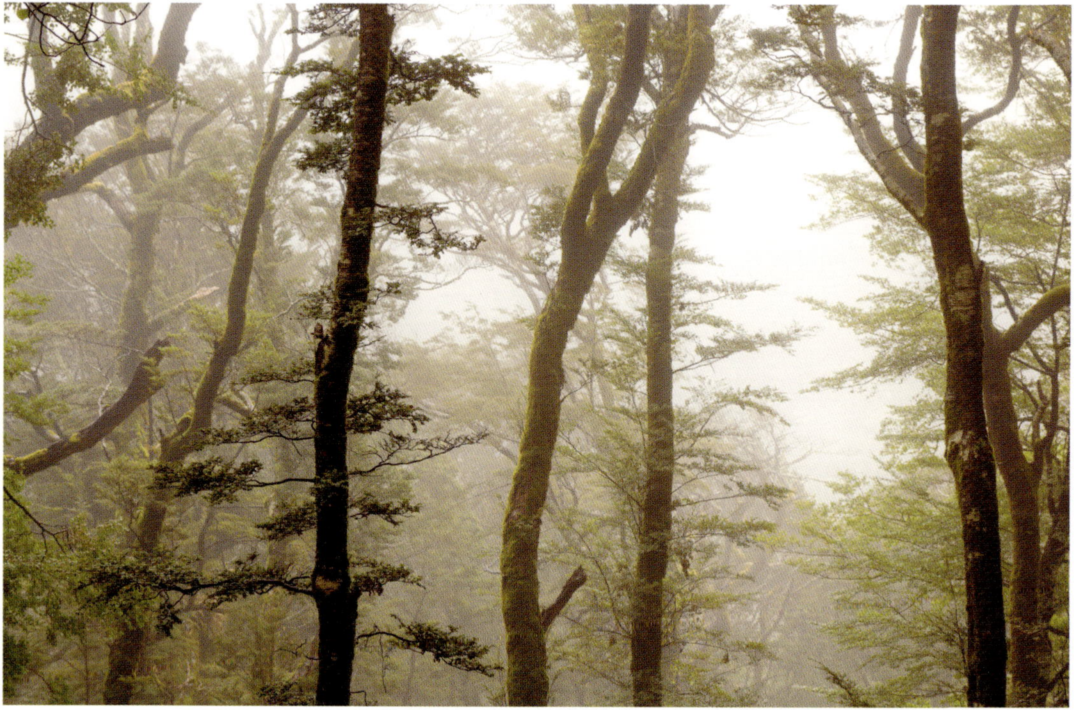

Forest in the mist, Routeburn Track, Mt Aspiring National Park.

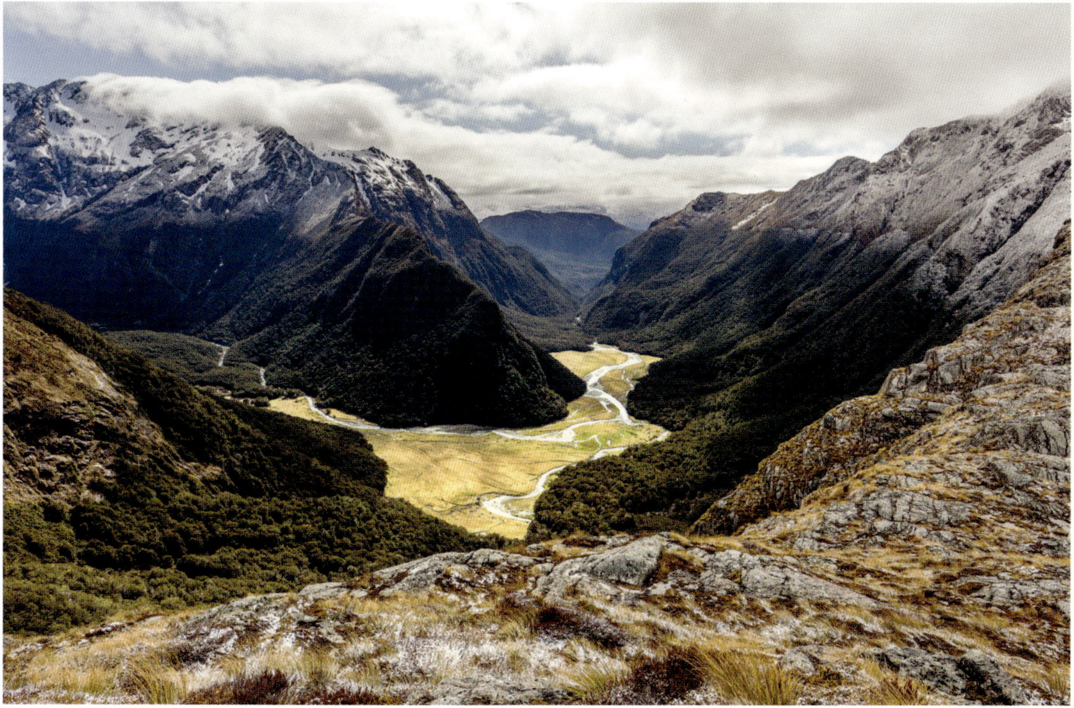

Overlooking the Routeburn Flats, Routeburn Track, Mt Aspiring National Park.

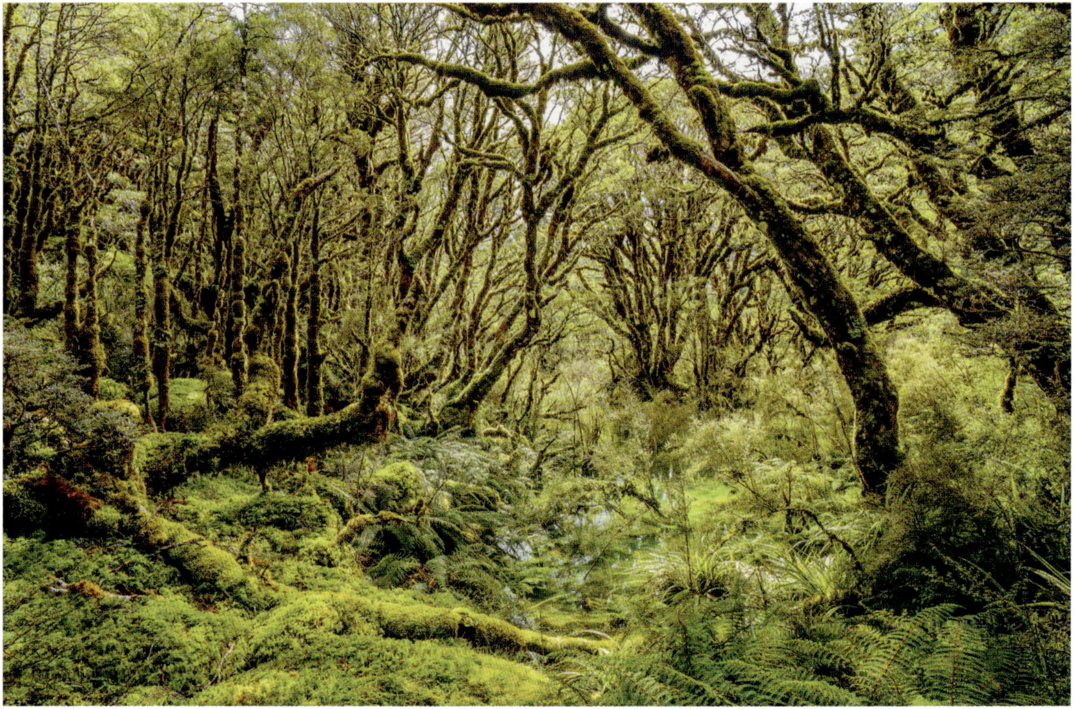

Native beech forest on the Routeburn Track, Fiordland National Park.
opposite: Morning cloud at Key Summit, Routeburn Track.

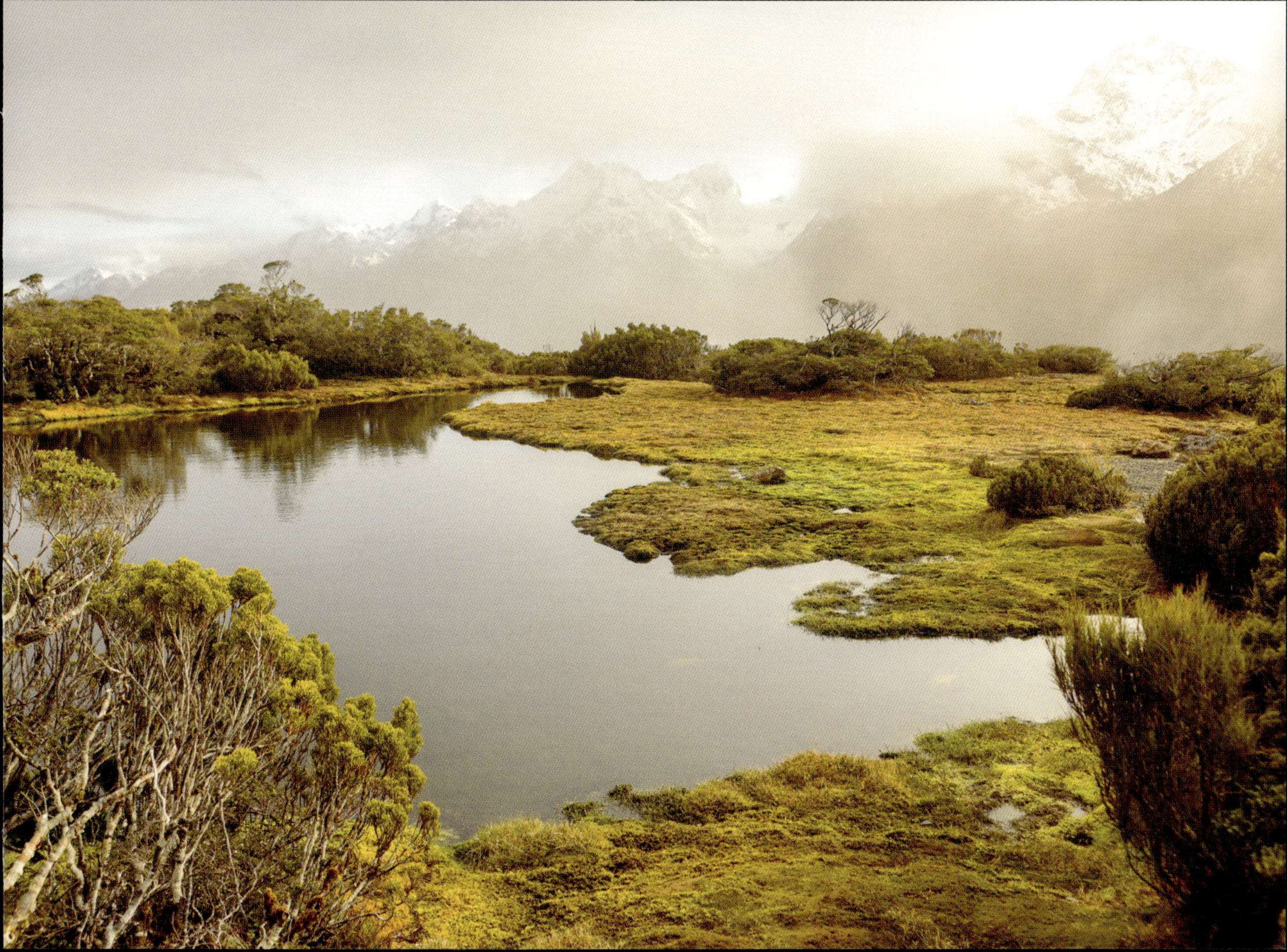

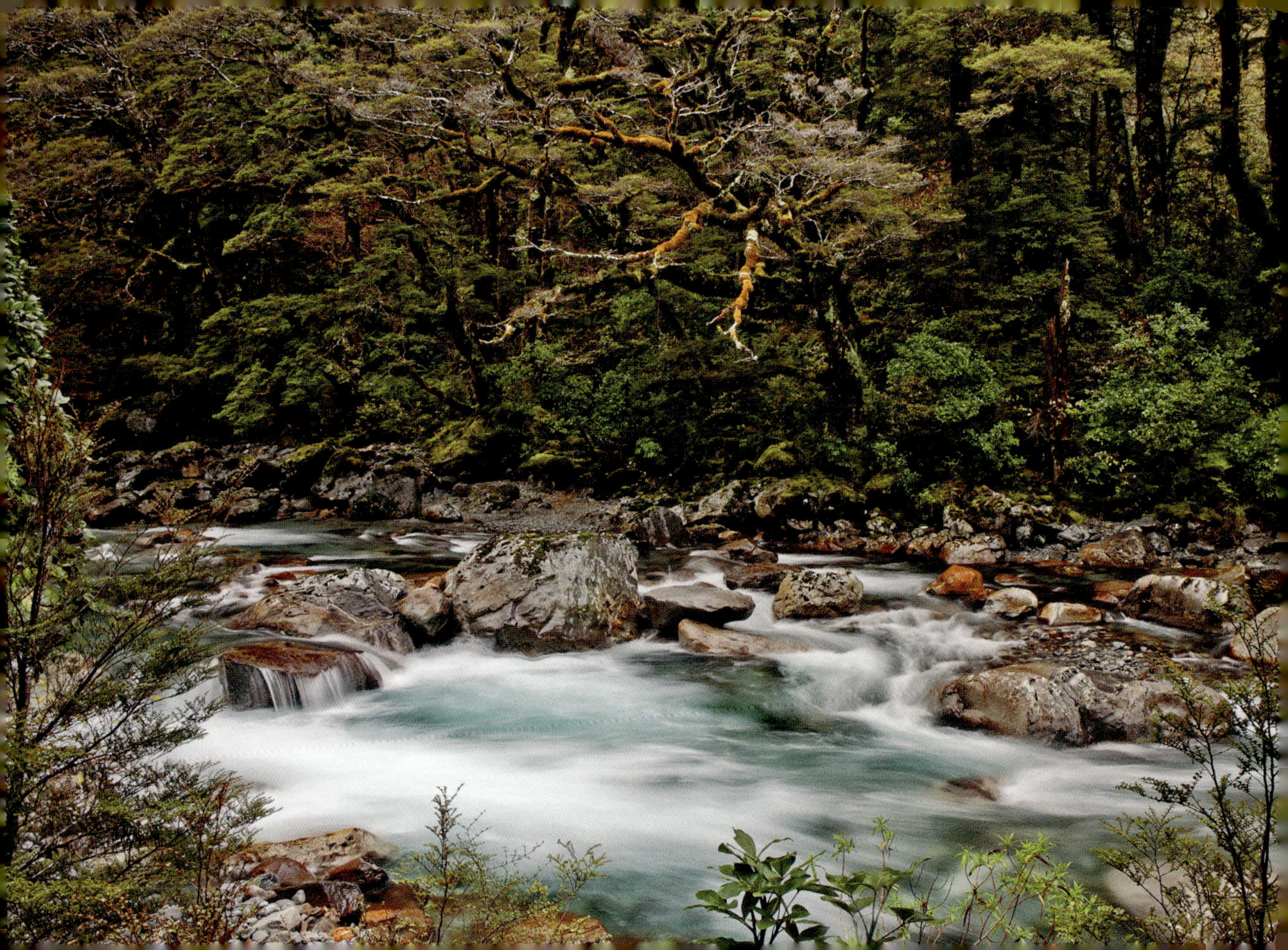

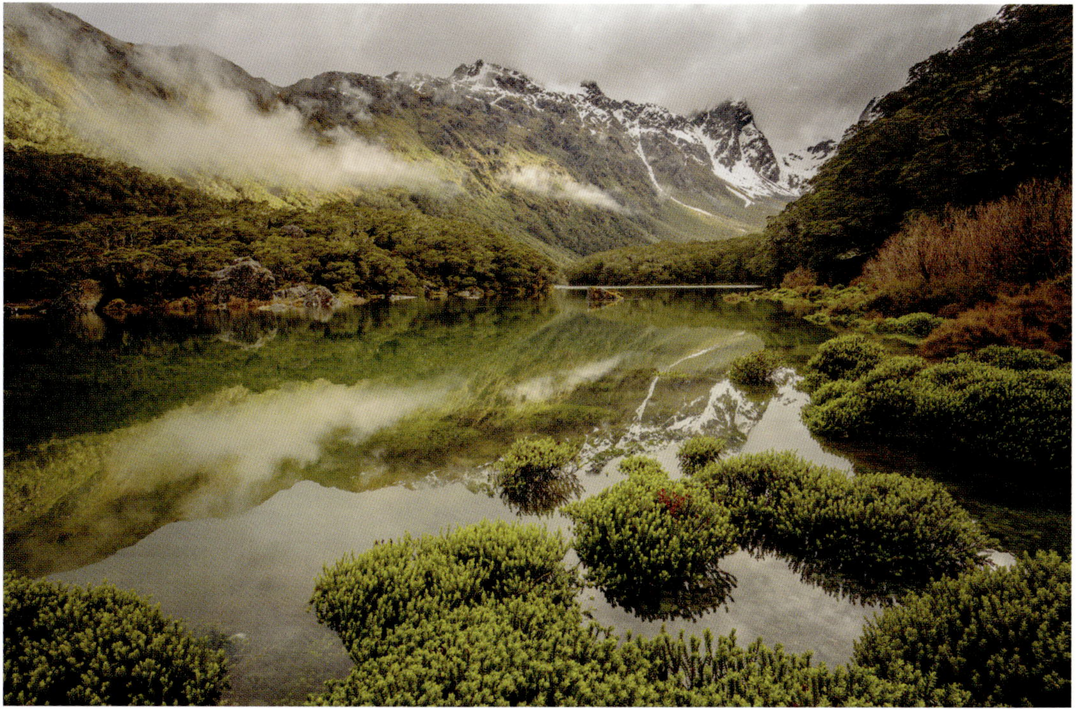

Morning at Lake Mackenzie on the Routeburn Track, Fiordland.
opposite: Native beech forest by the Hollyford River, Fiordland.

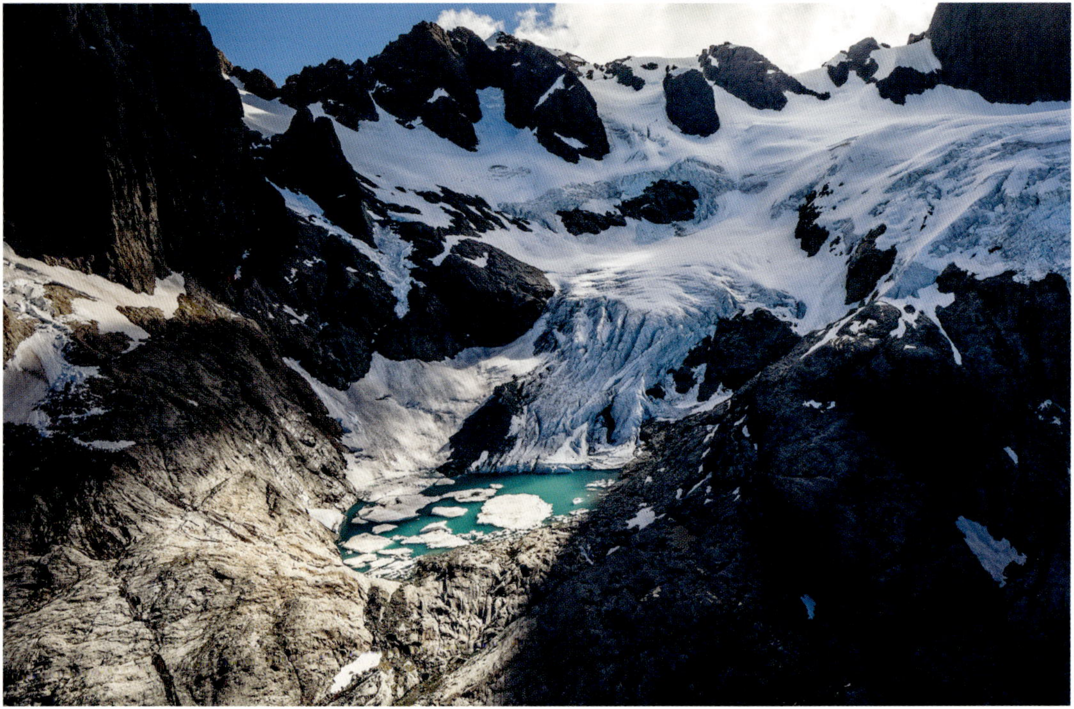

The Te Puoho Glacier and Boulder Lake on the way to Milford Sound, Fiordland.
opposite: Stella Falls, Wilmot Pass, Doubtful Sound, Fiordland.

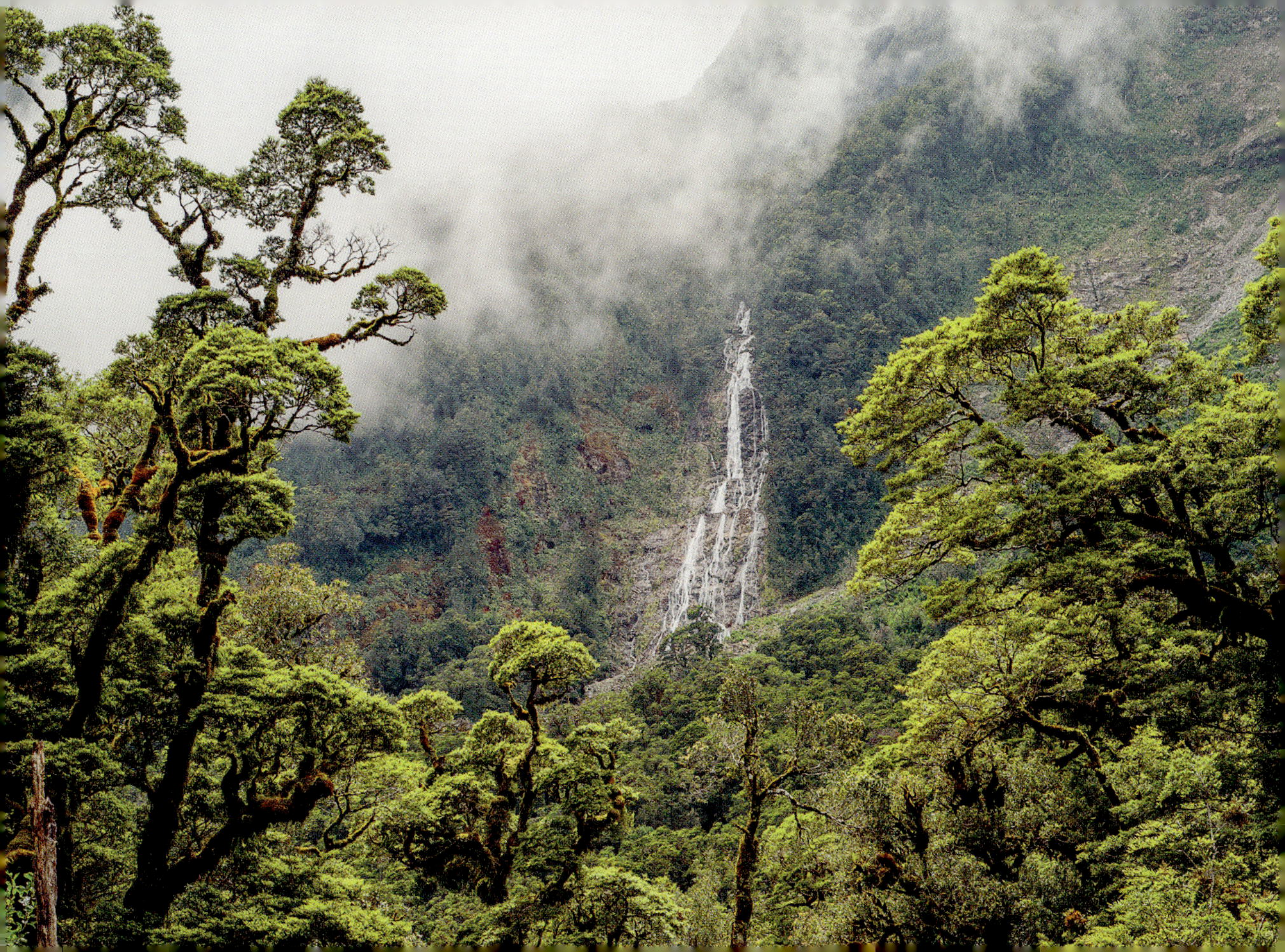

"A Search for Simplicity"

Ripples on the foreshore at Milford Sound, Fiordland.

The air was thick with heavy fog early one morning as I walked to the water's edge at the shore of Milford Sound. Milford is a place that never disappoints; every day is ripe with unique photographic opportunities. On this morning as I stood looking out into an abyss of white, the towering Mitre Peak's invisible presence beyond, I knew this was special.

Shortly upon my arrival to the scene I noticed a faint darkening, a line on the horizon appearing in the form of a ripple. The sun was already up providing just enough light to bounce off the cliff faces, lending a beautiful tonal quality to the scene.

I framed up a small rock on the shoreline as I anticipated the little ripples coming ashore and I took three exposures just as the ripples made the shoreline. Not long after this shot was taken, the first Milford cruise boat started heading out, the wind picked up, and the serenity of the scene was quickly turned into a wash of waves.

Moments like these, so simple and pure, hold so much meaning for me. These are the genuine moments of simple natural beauty I seek to find and share; the search for simplicity continues.

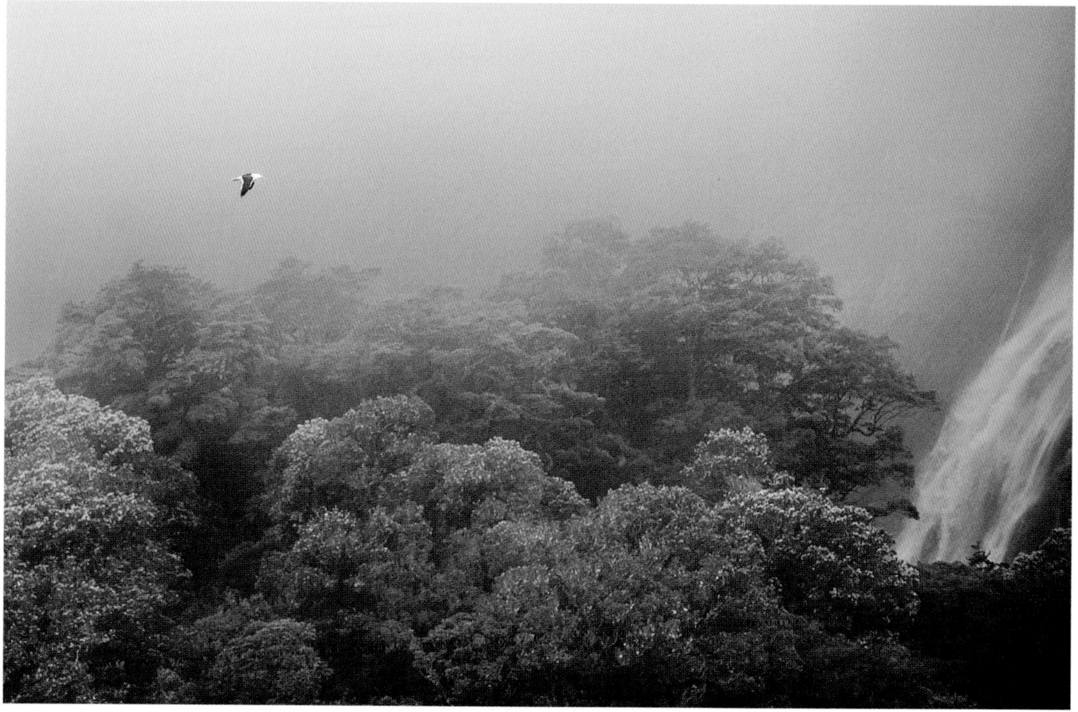

Seagull in flight through the mist, Milford Sound, Fiordland.
opposite: Rainbow in the aptly named Fairy Falls, Milford Sound.

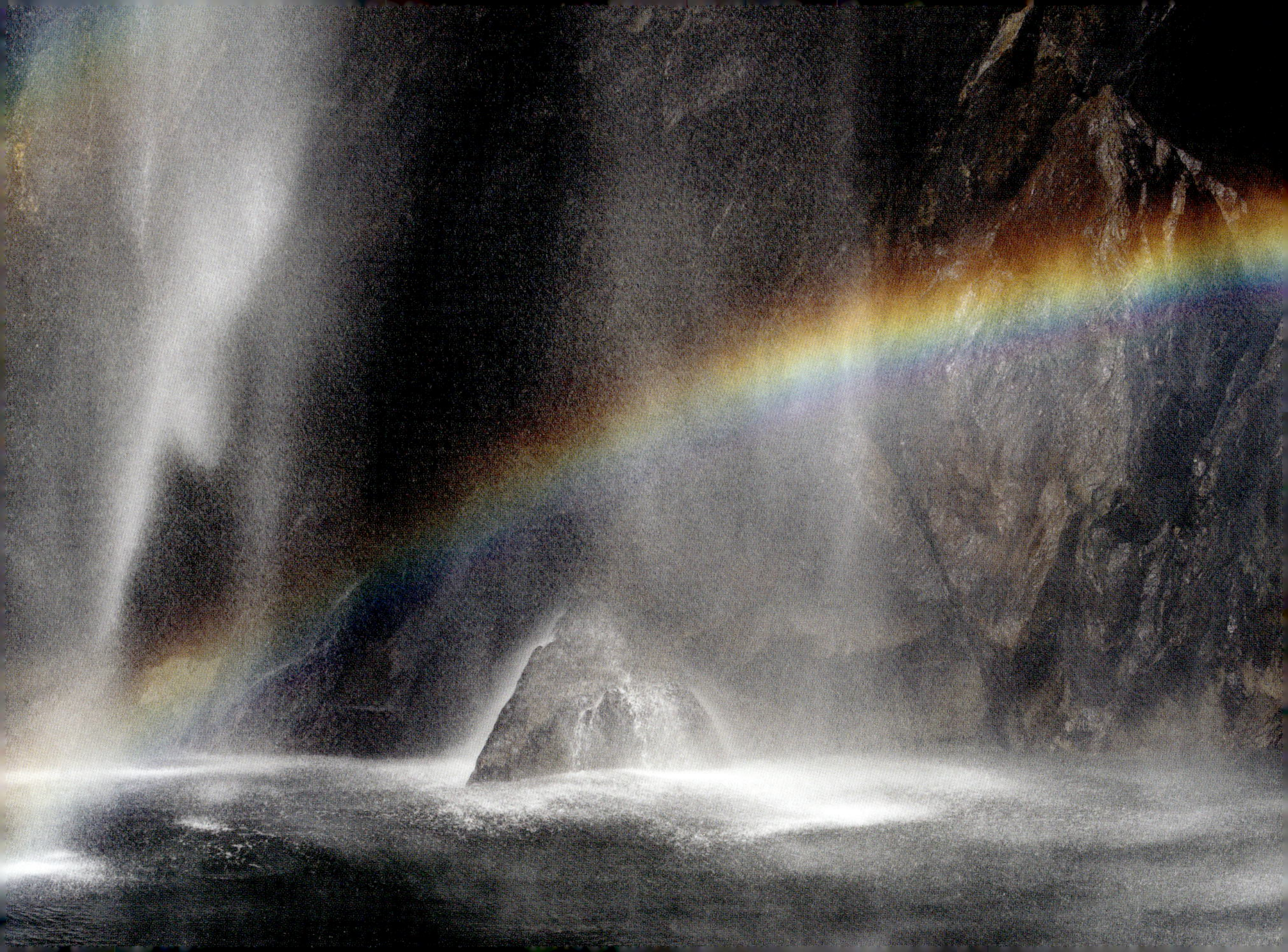

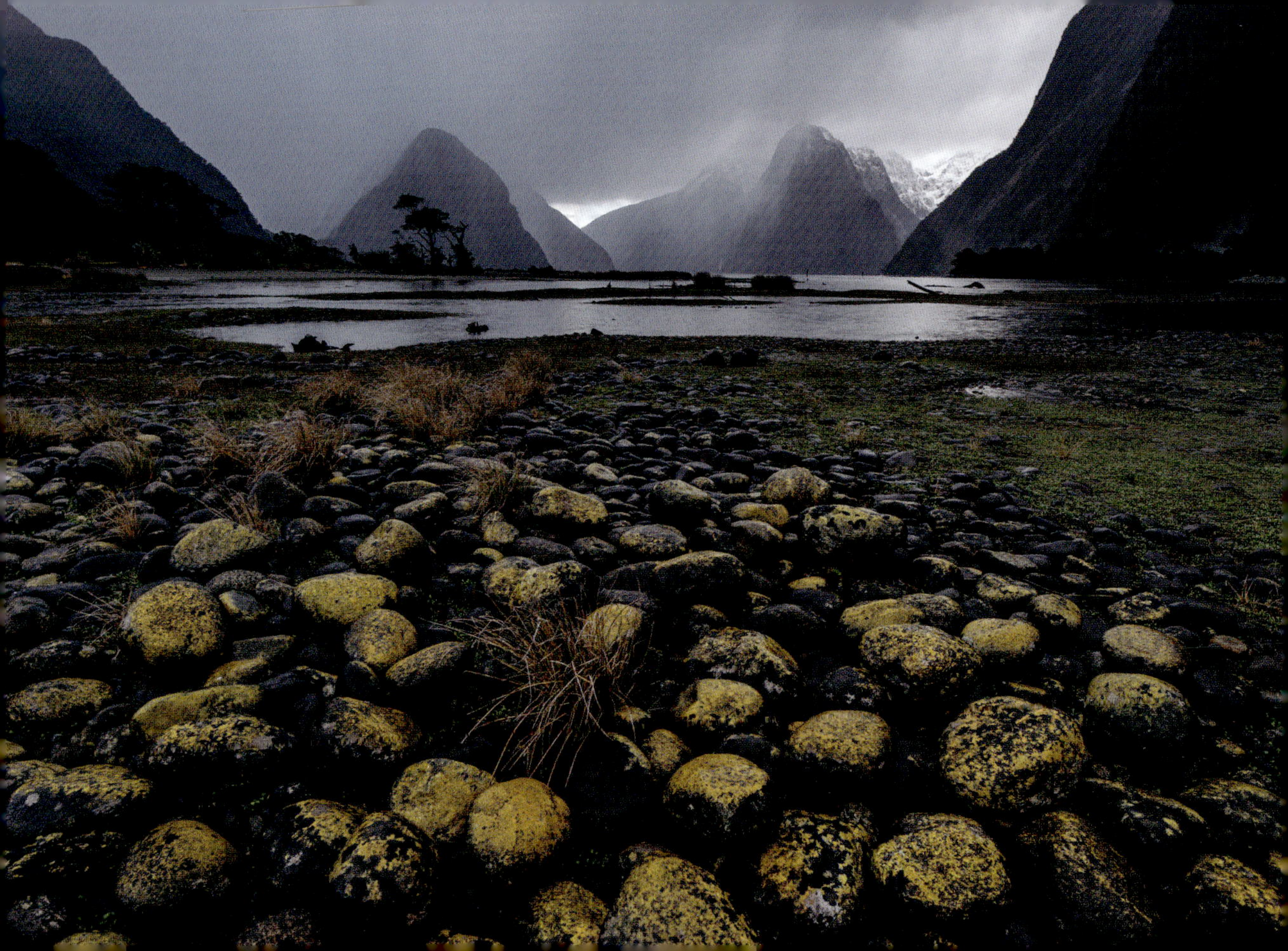

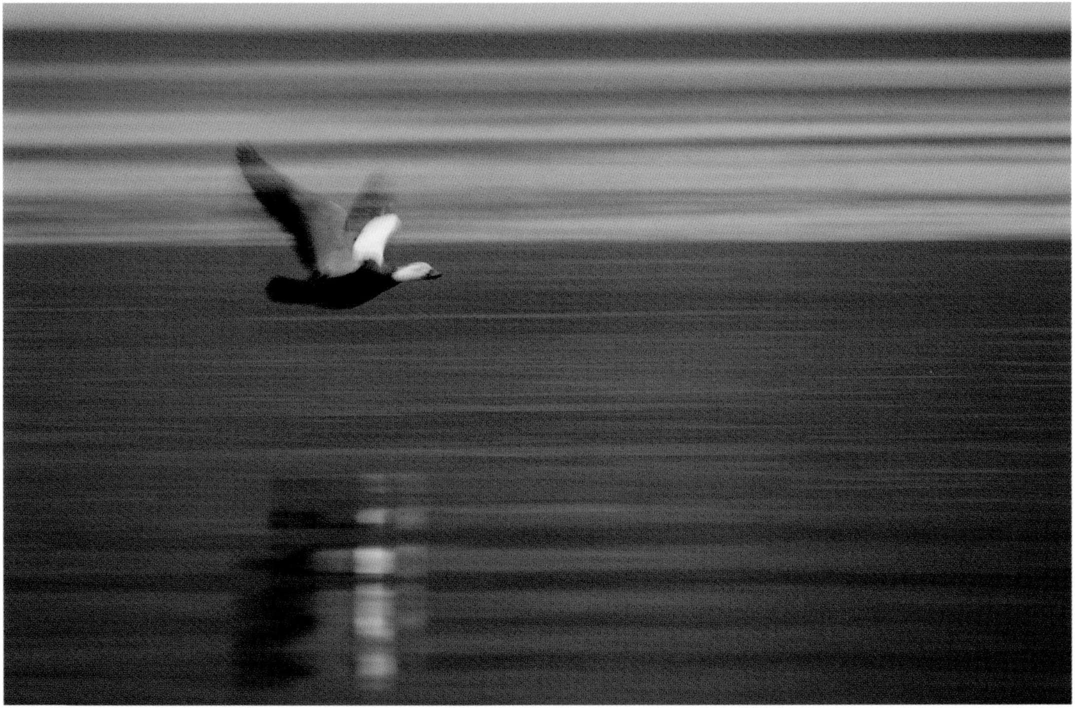

A Paradise duck flies by on the foreshore, Milford Sound, Fiordland.
opposite: Lichen clad stones on the foreshore at Milford Sound.

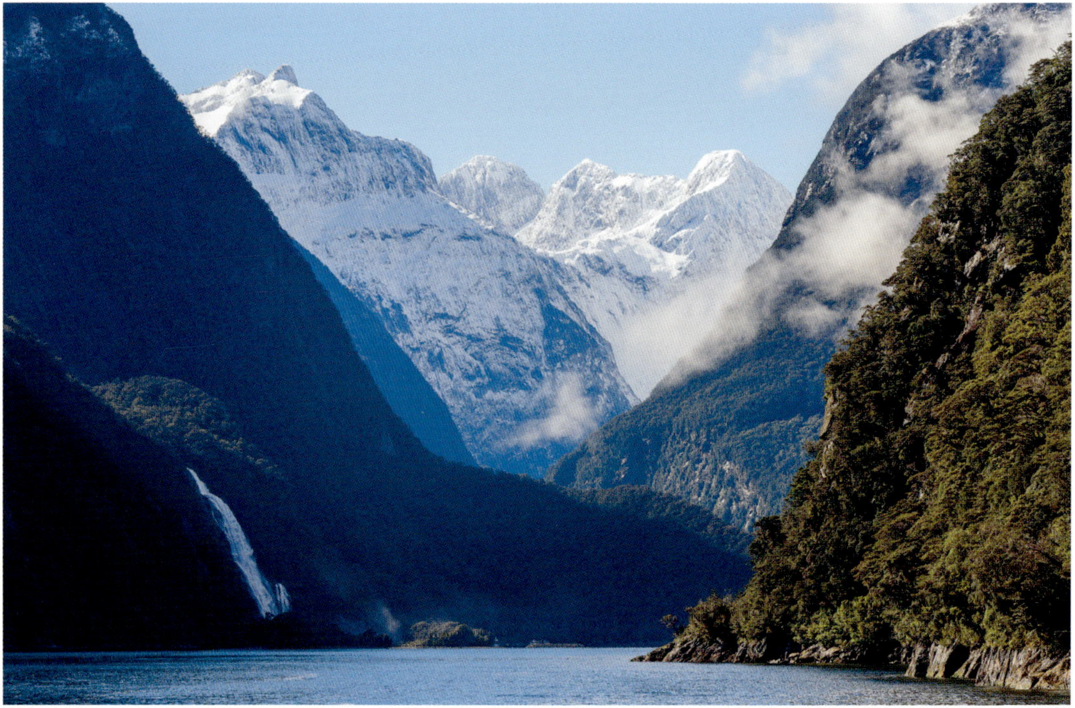

Taking a morning discovery cruise in Milford Sound, Fiordland.
opposite: Fresh snow on Mitre Peak in the morning, Milford Sound.

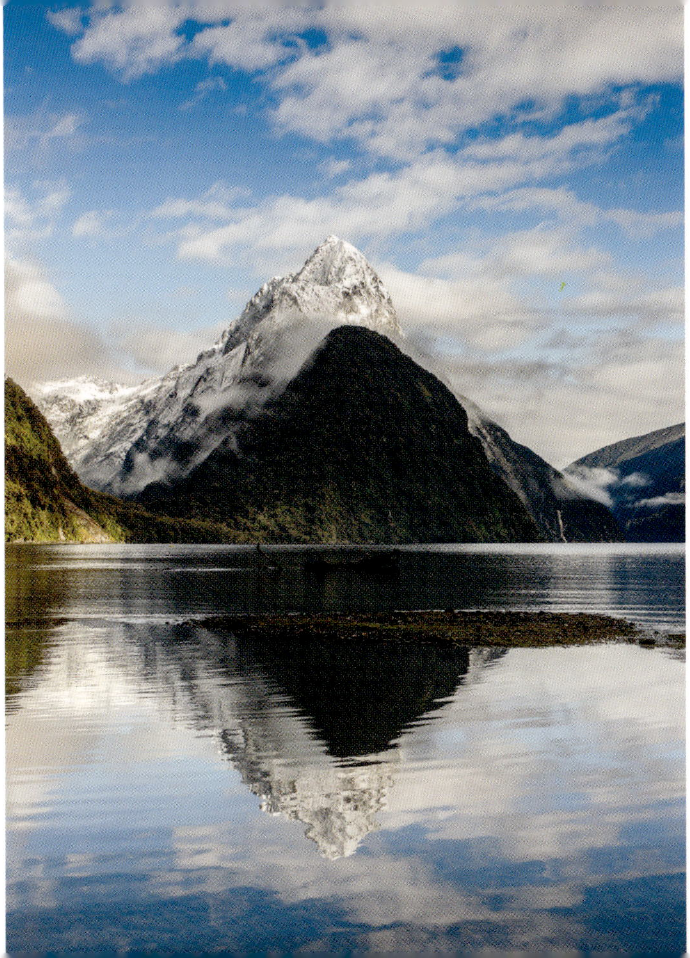

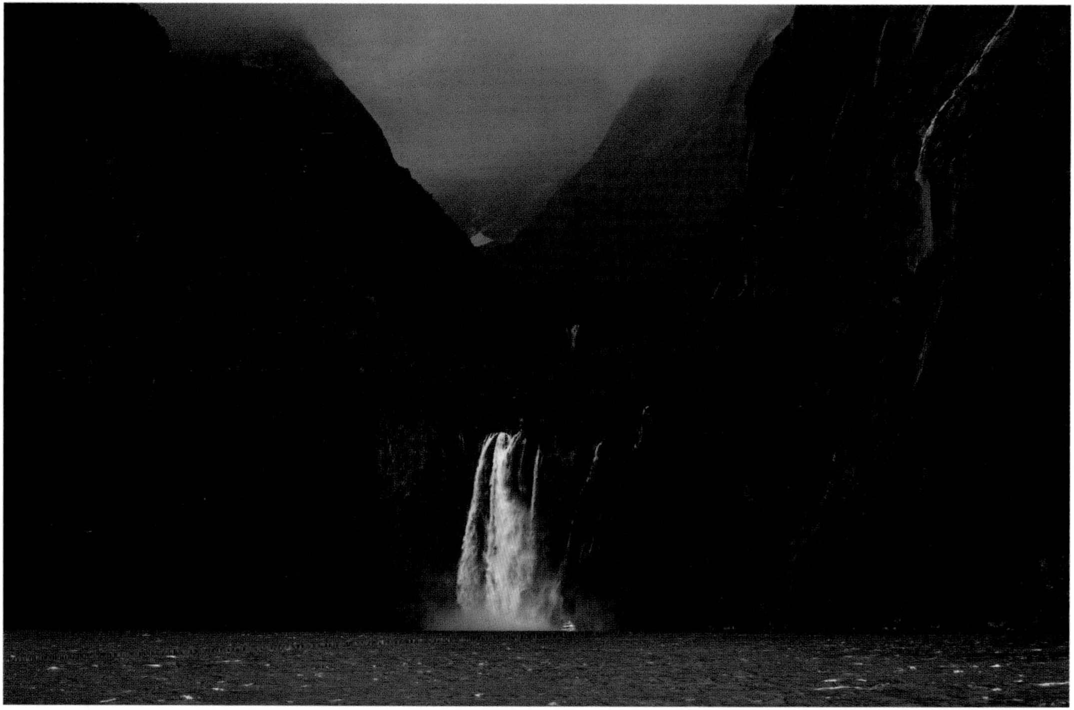

Cruise boat dwarfed by Stirling Falls, Milford Sound, Fiordland.
opposite: Light breaks through on a dark evening over Mitre Peak.

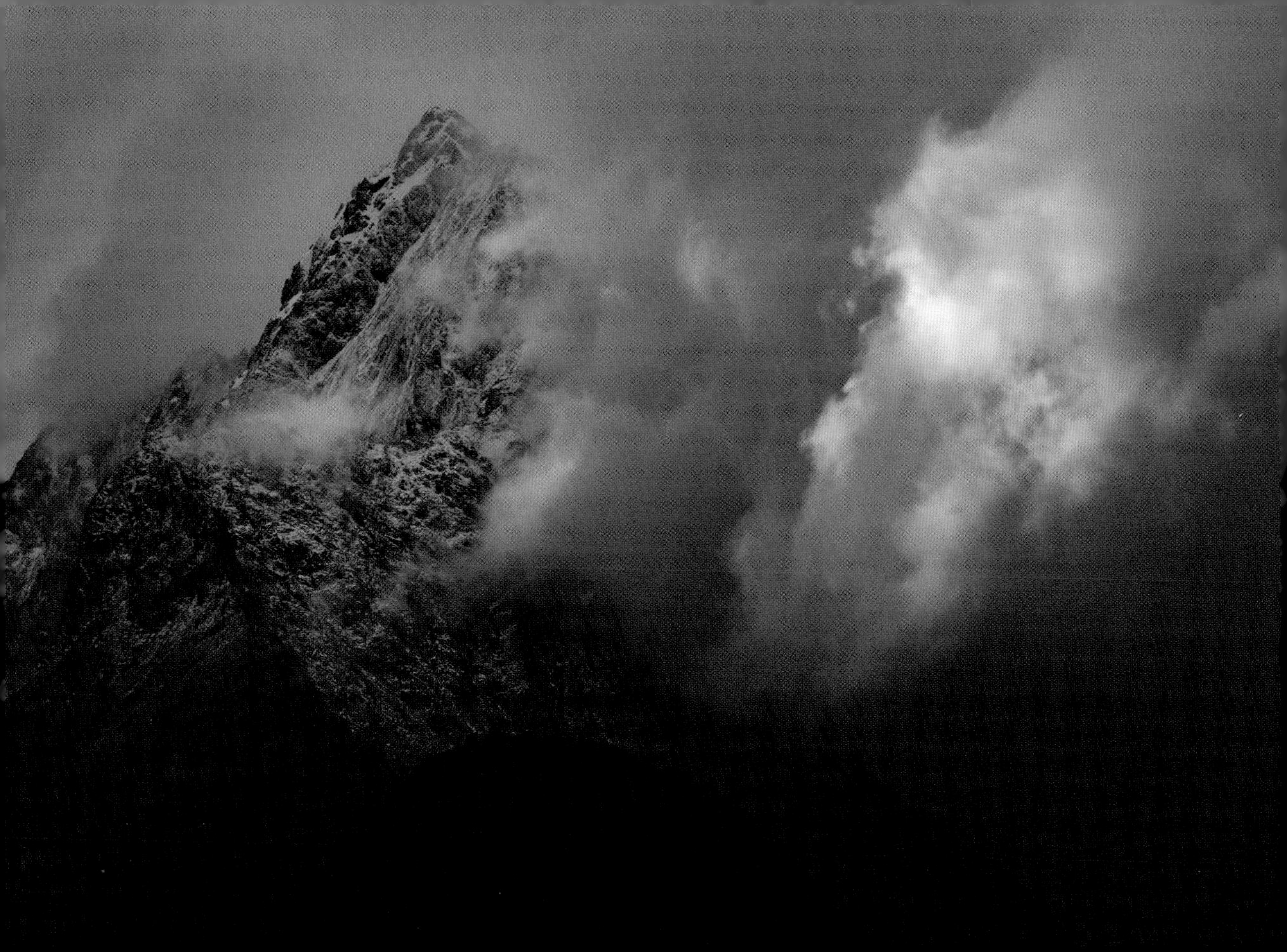

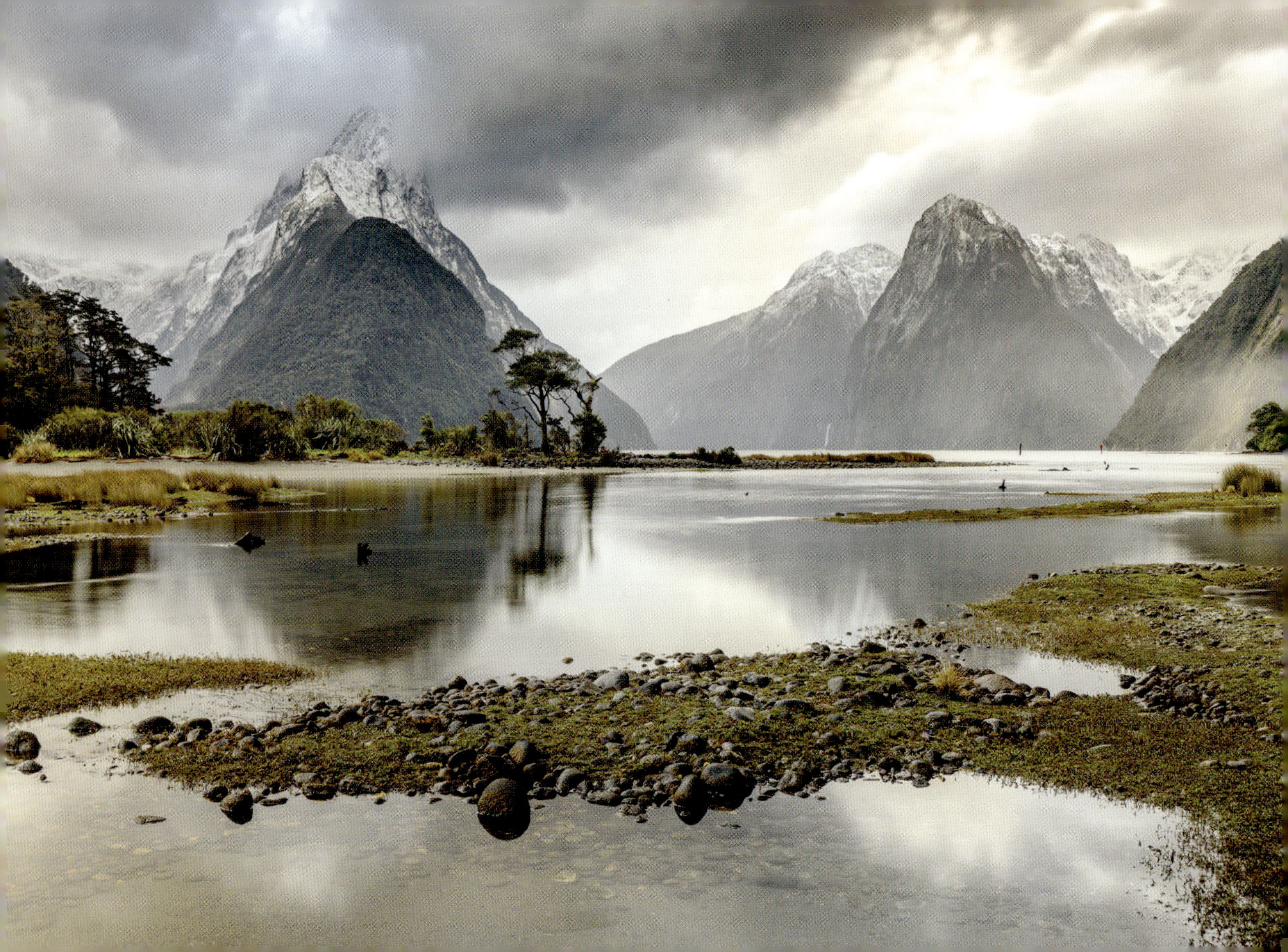

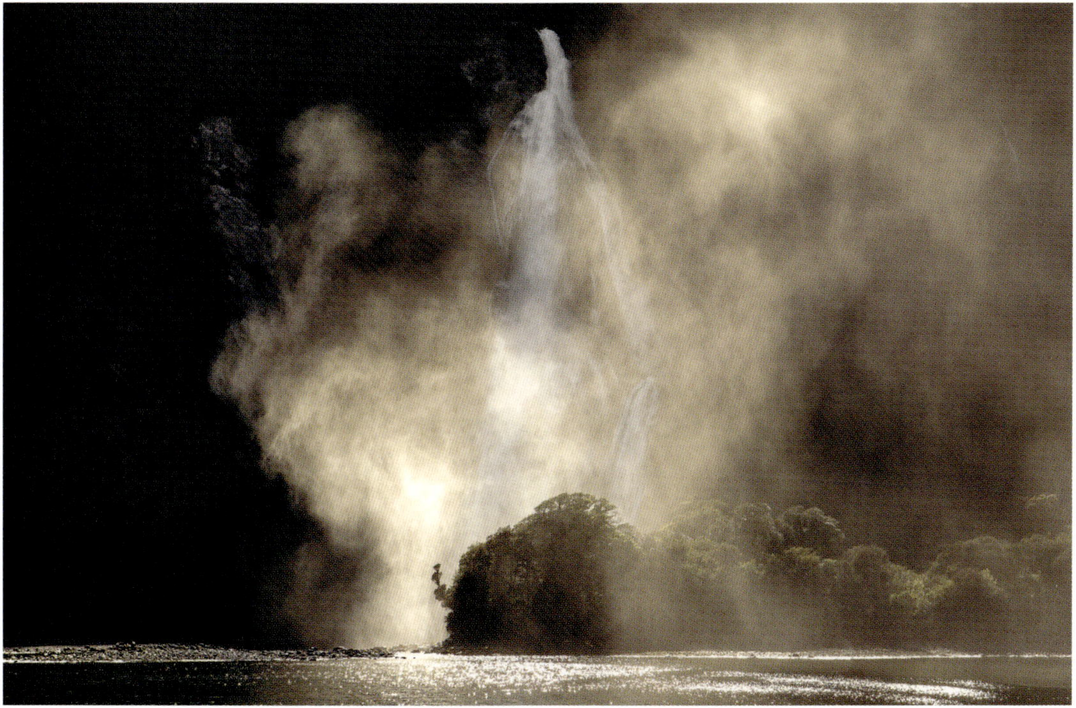

Spray from Lady Bowen Falls in the morning sunlight, Milford Sound.
opposite: Foreshore on an incoming tide, Milford Sound.

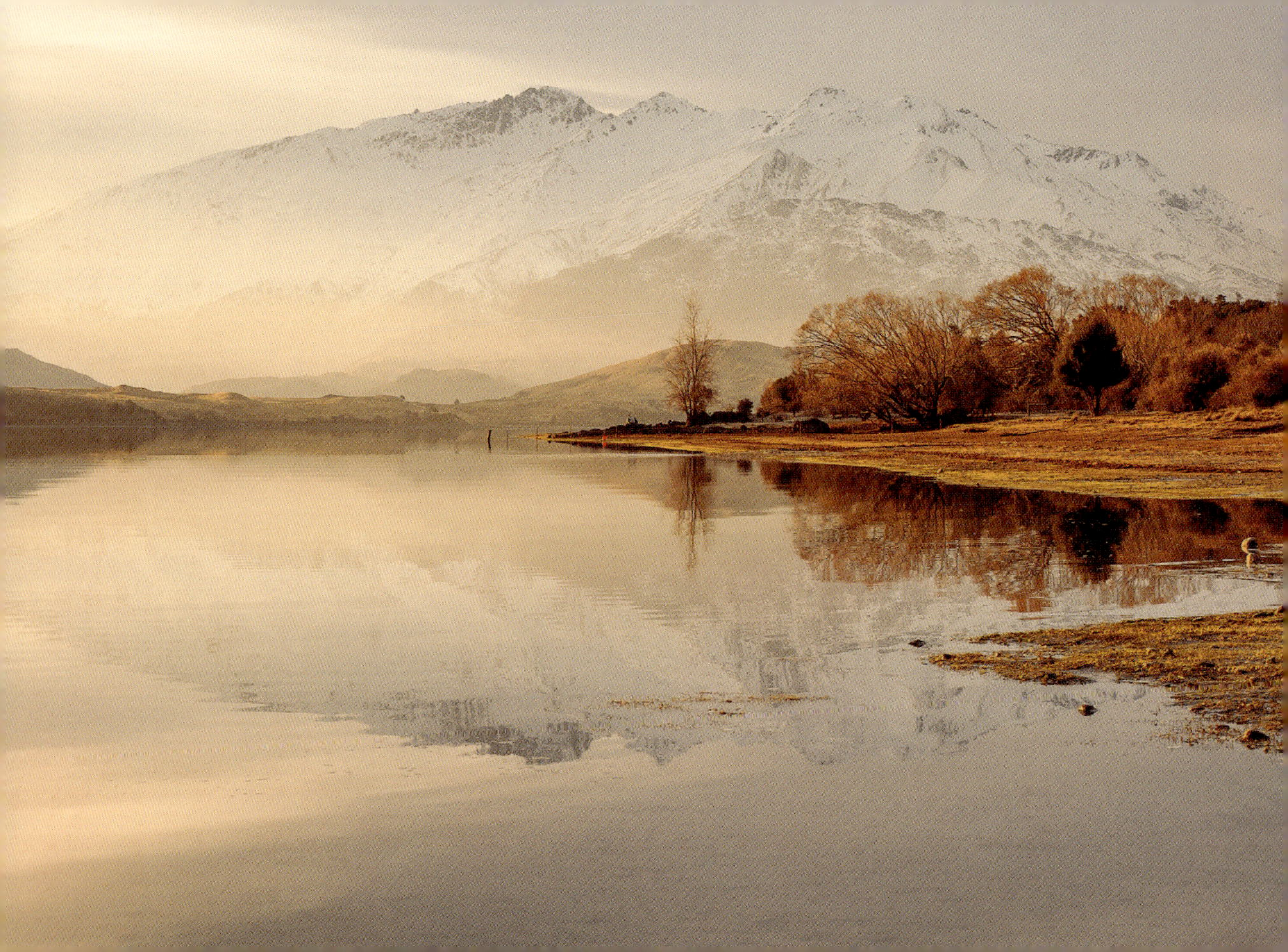

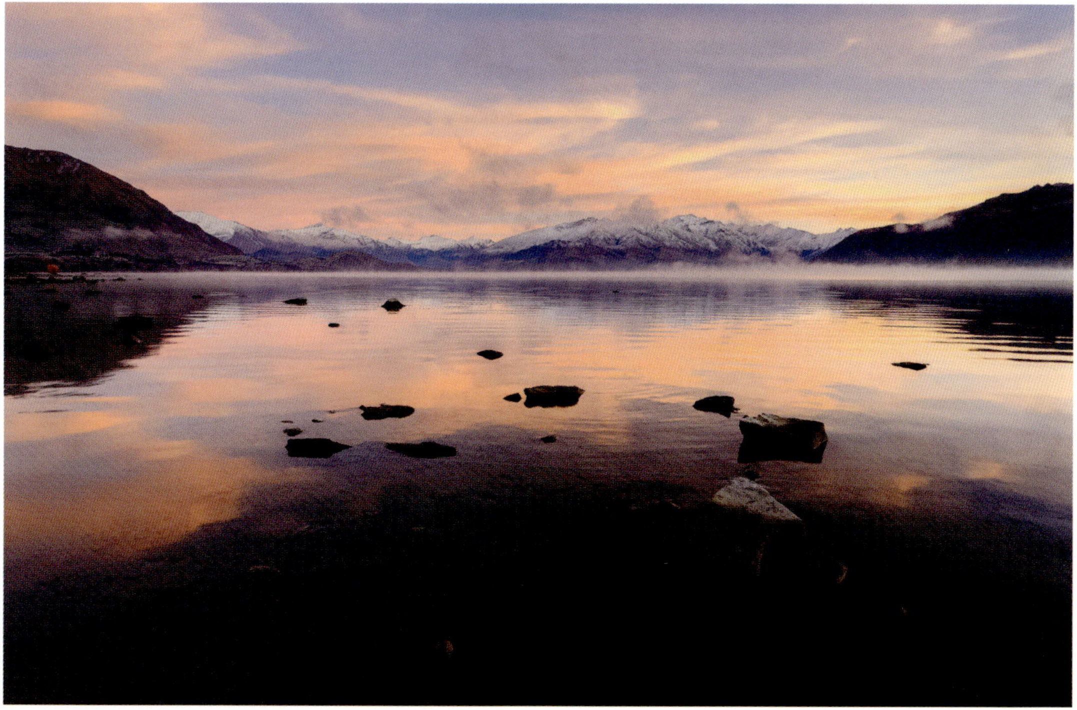

Dawn at Bremner Bay, Lake Wanaka, Central Otago.
opposite: Afternoon sunlight on the shore at Glendhu Bay, Lake Wanaka.

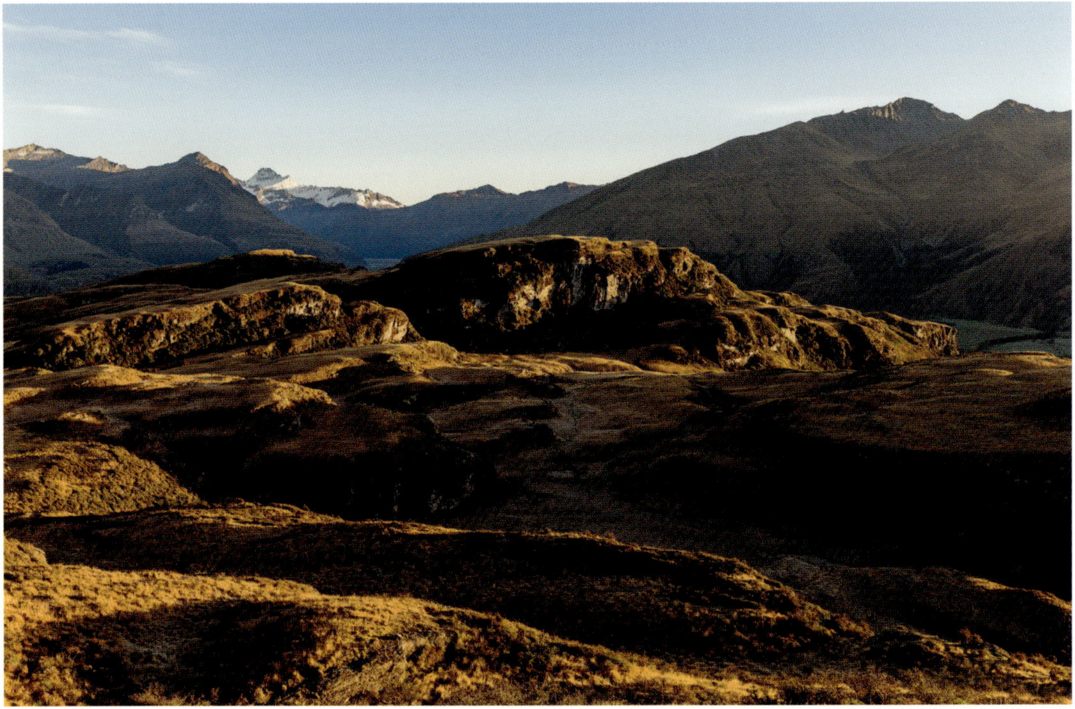

Mt Aspiring and the Matukituki Valley from Rocky Mountain, Wanaka.
opposite: Overlooking Roys Peak and Glendhu Bay, Lake Wanaka.

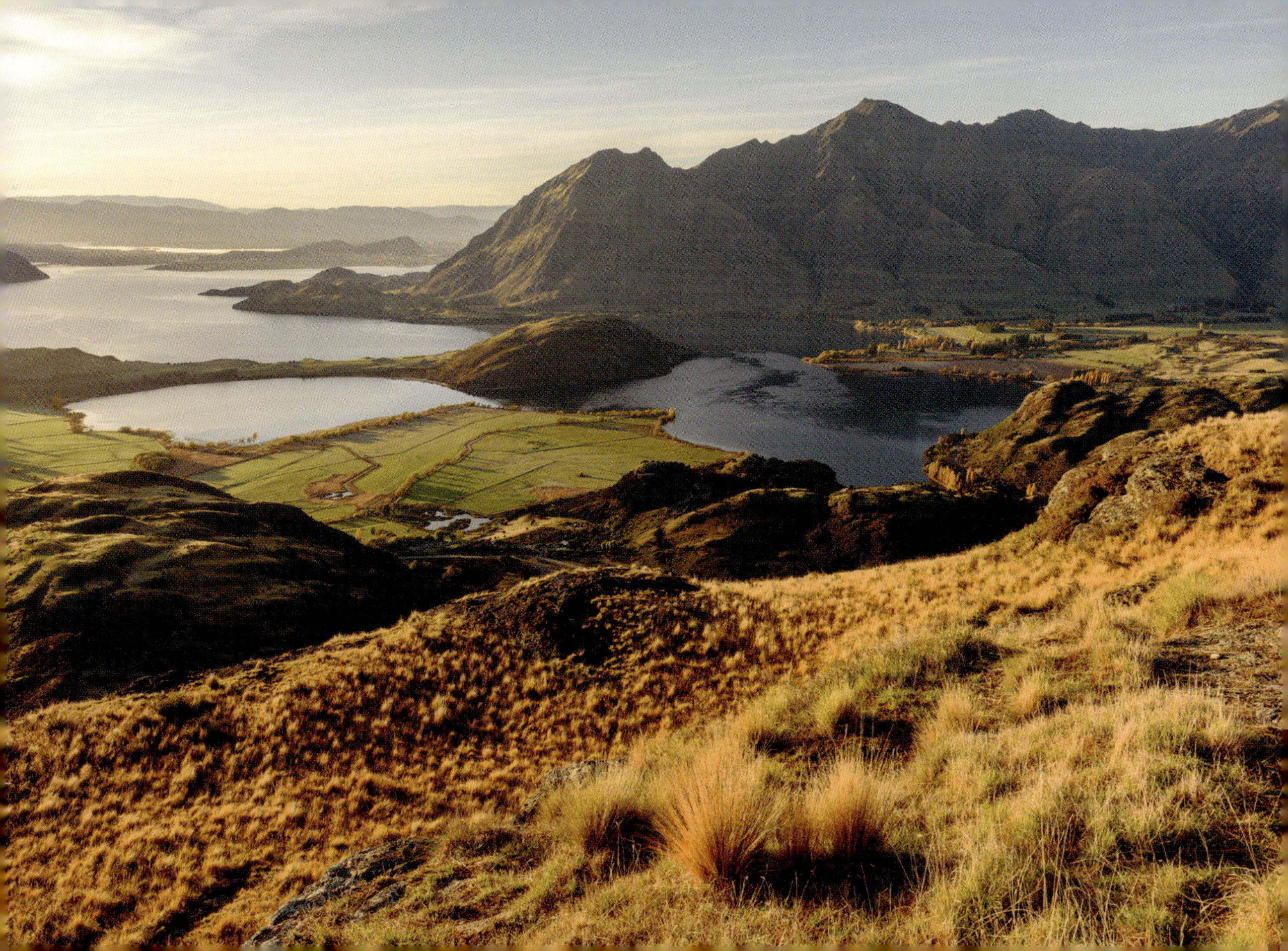

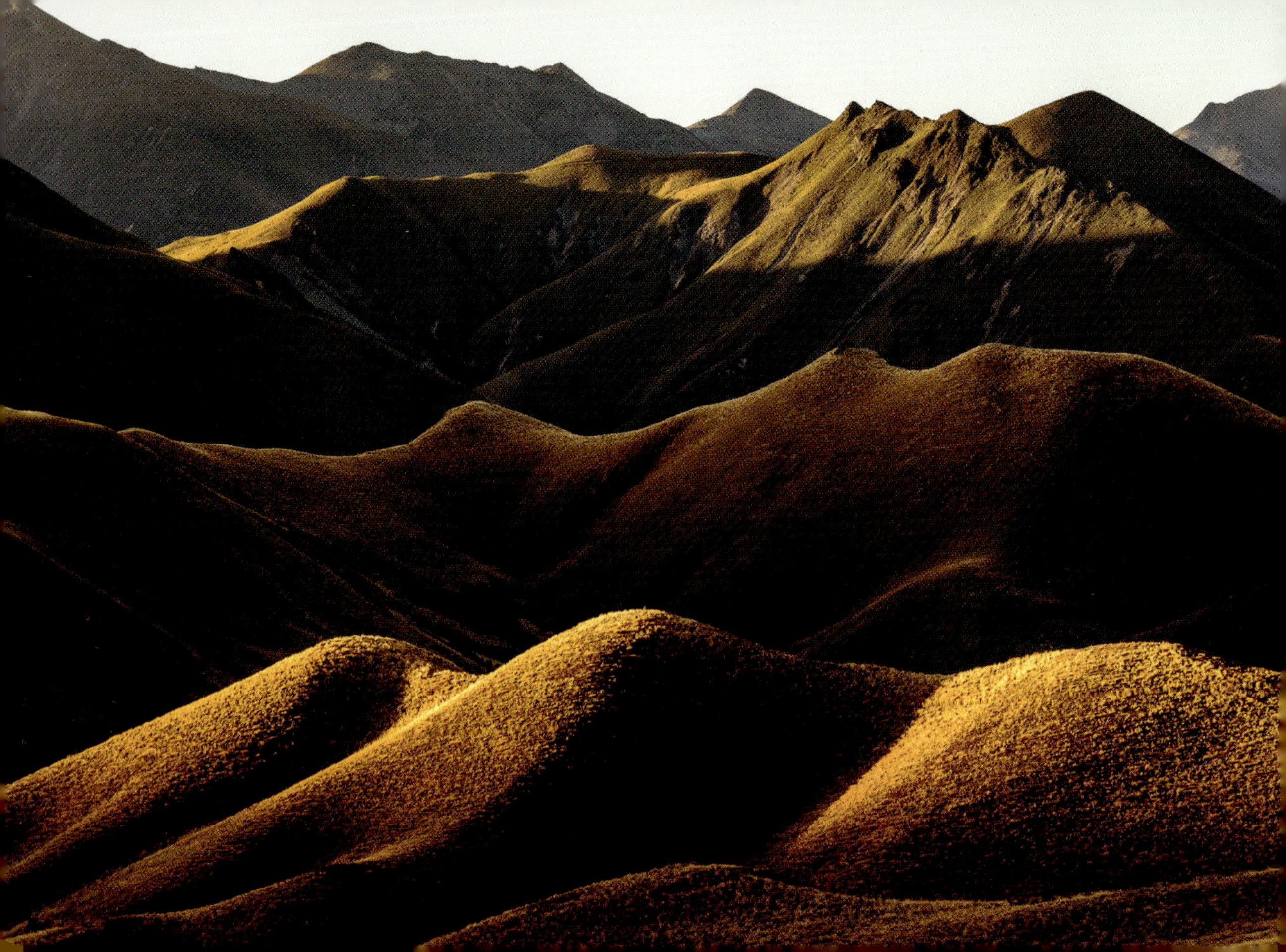

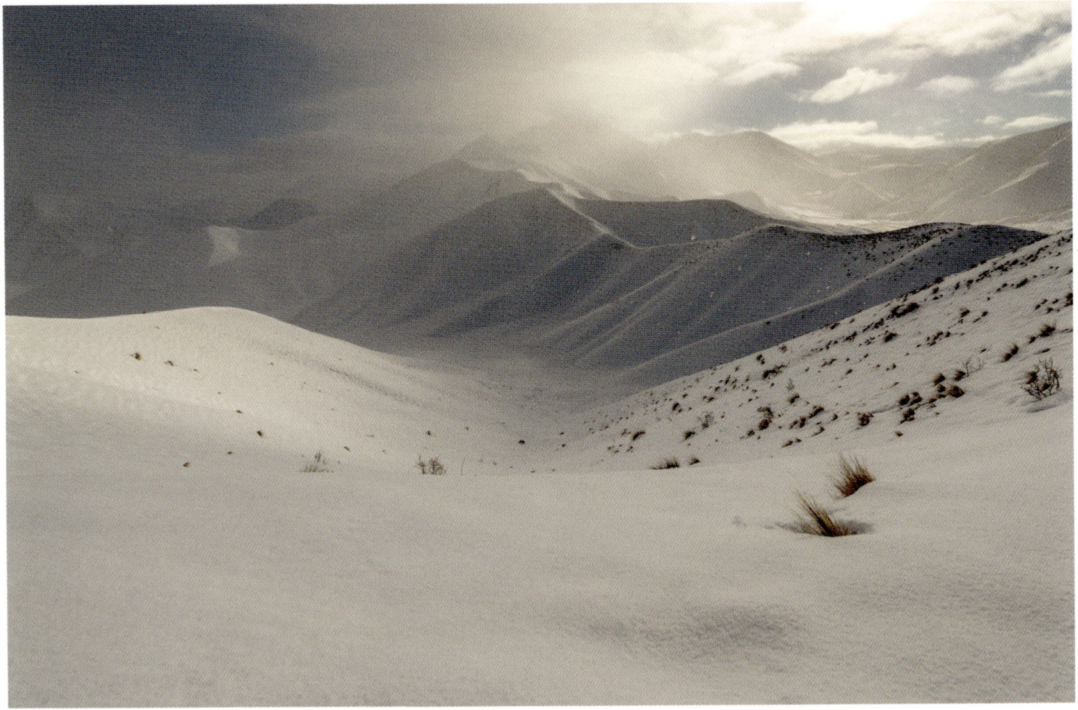

Clearing snow storm from the top of the Lindis Pass, Central Otago.
opposite: Last light on the land, Lindis Pass.

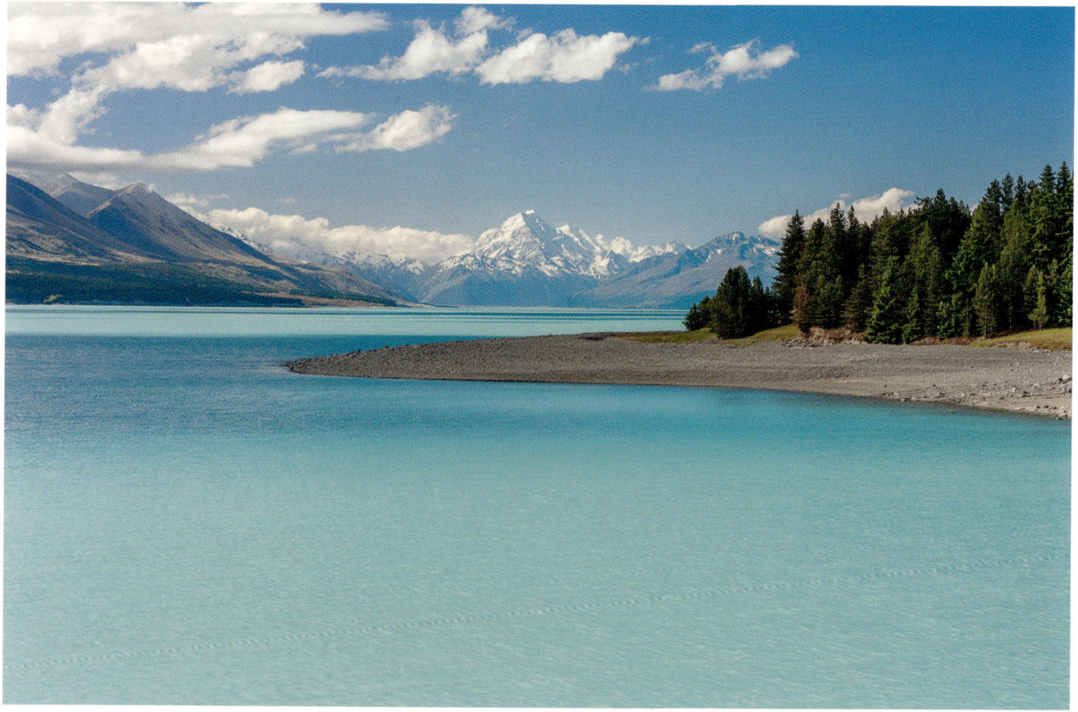

Shadows over Lake Pukaki and Mt Cook, Mackenzie Basin.

opposite: Icebergs at dawn, Tasman Lake, Aoraki/Mt Cook National park.

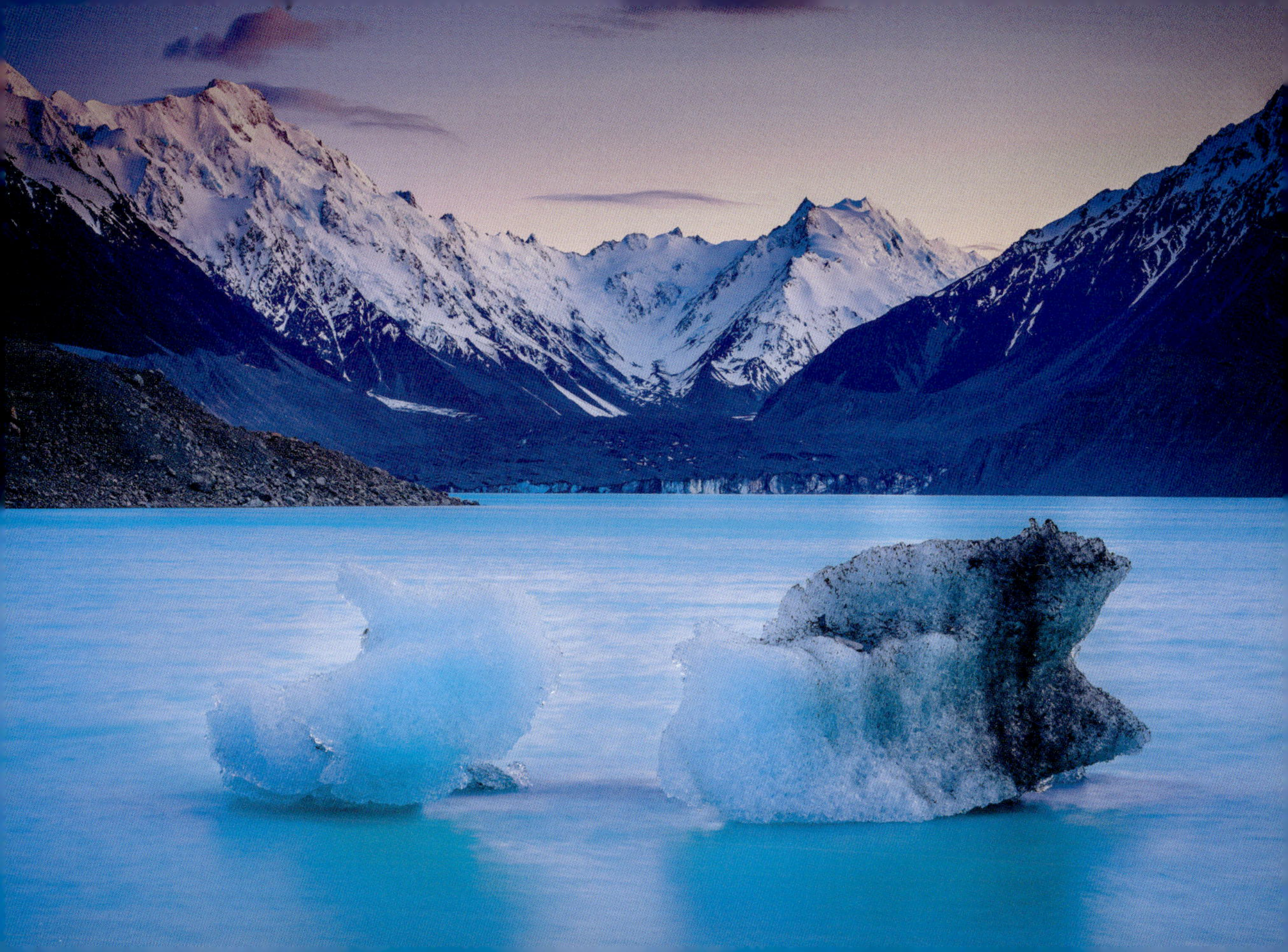

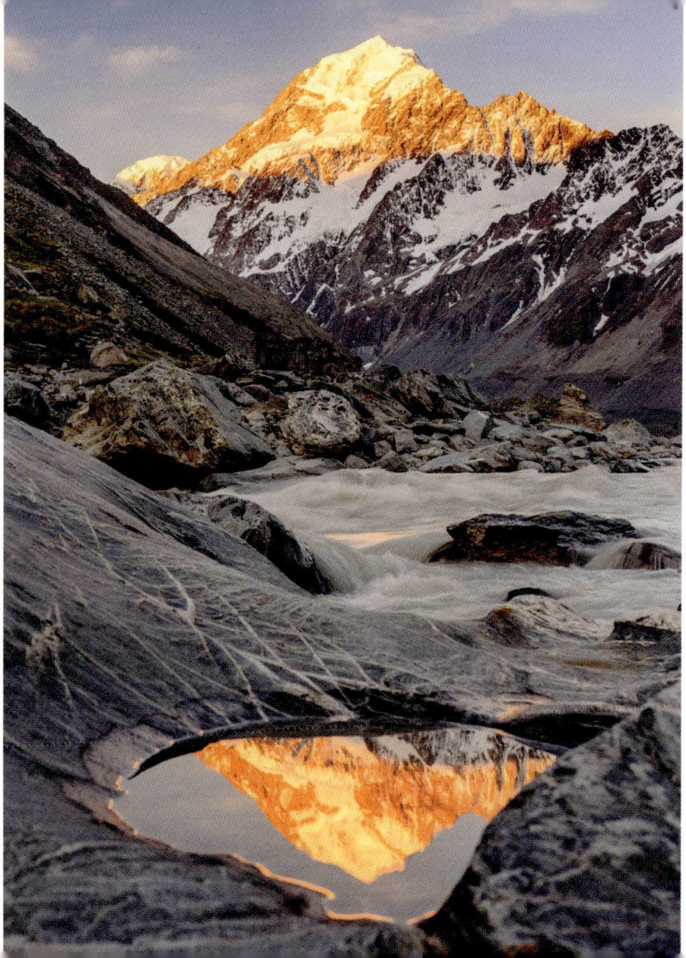

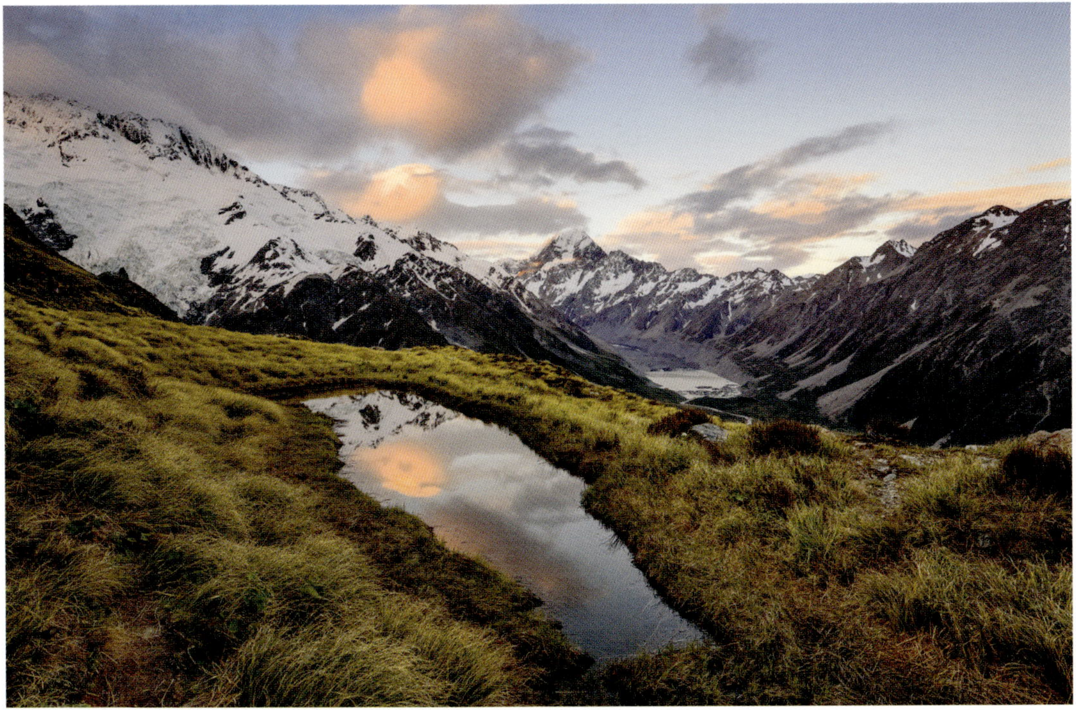

Sunset from the Sealy Tarns, Aoraki/Mt Cook National Park.
opposite: Reflection of Mt Cook in a small rock pool, Hooker Lake.

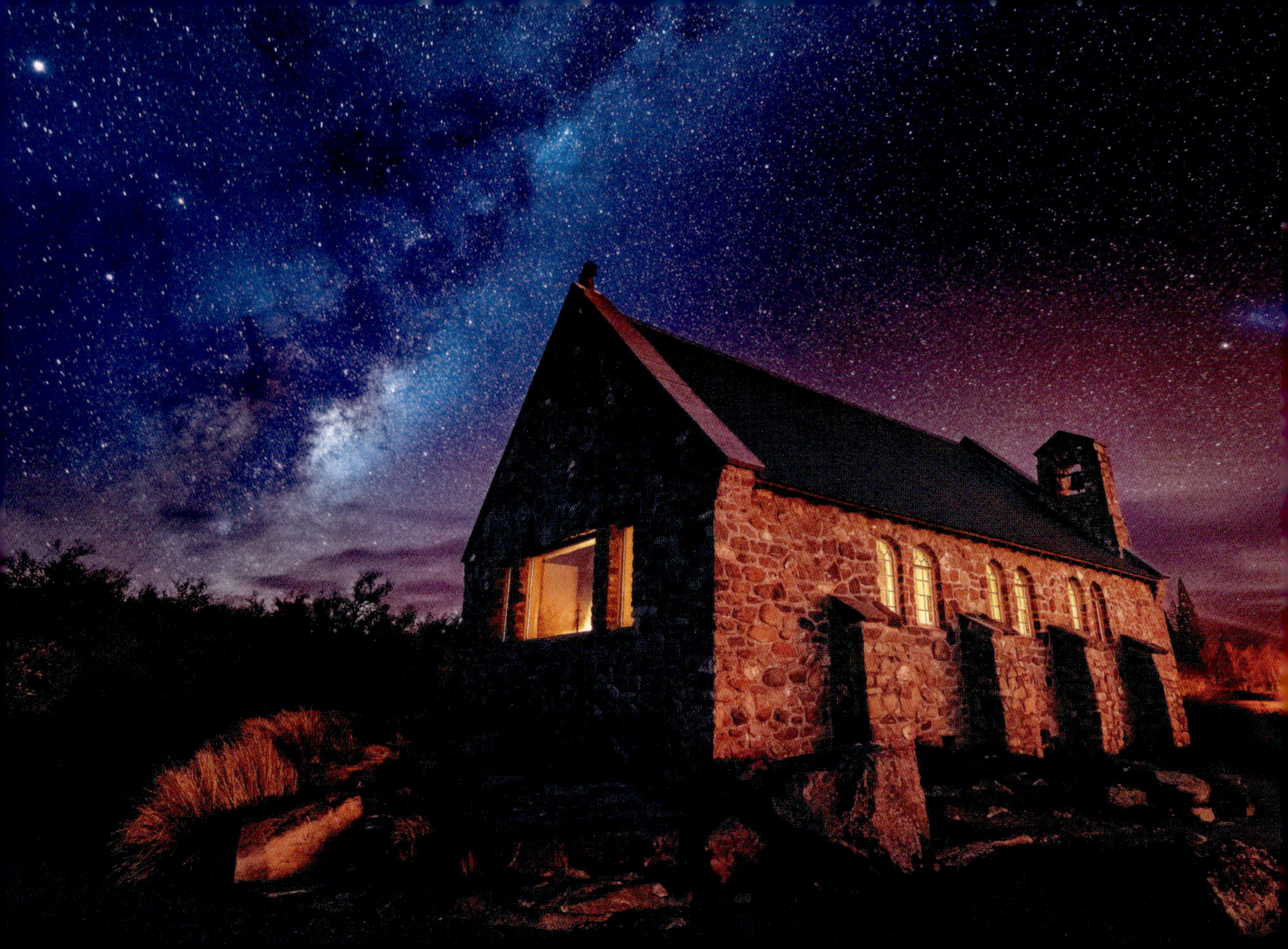

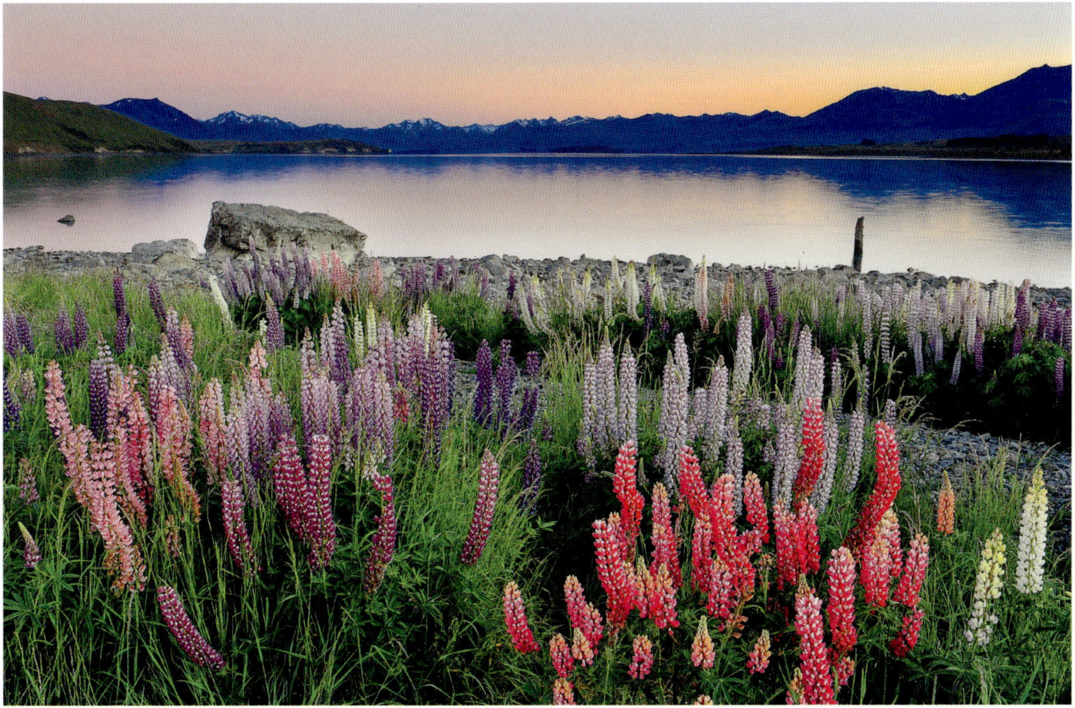

Summertime lupins at dawn, Lake Tekapo, Mackenzie Country.
opposite: The ever popular Church of the Good Shepherd under the rising Milky Way, Lake Tekapo, Mackenzie Country.

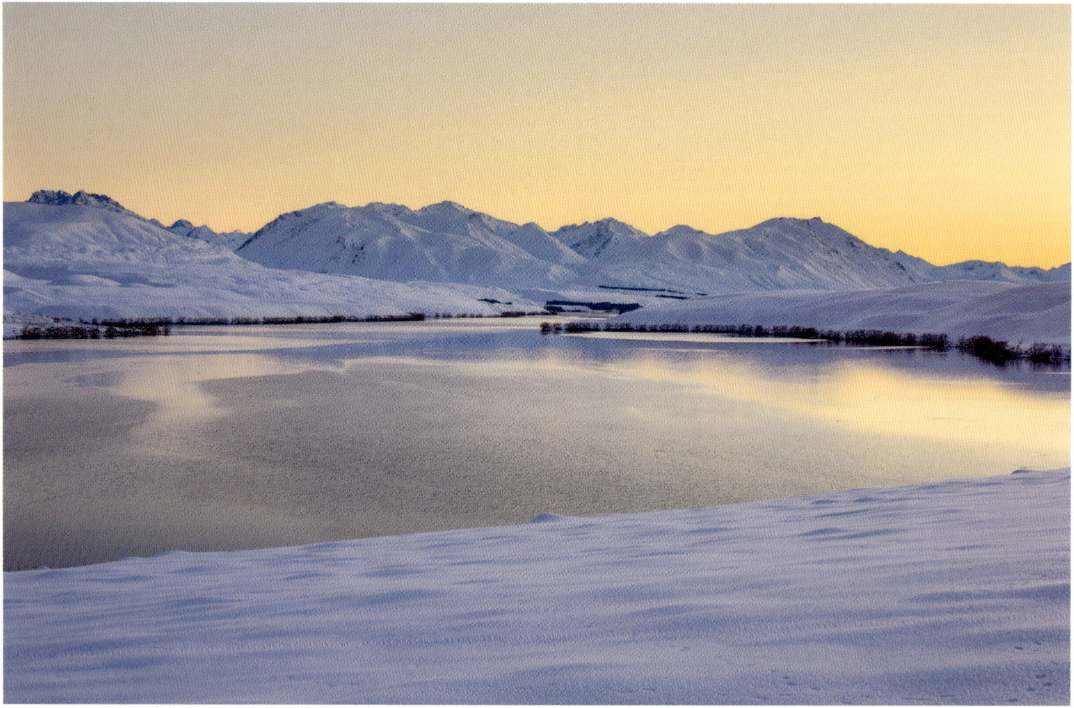

Lake Alexandrina at dawn, Mackenzie Country.
opposite: Row boats under fresh snow fall at Lake Alexandrina.

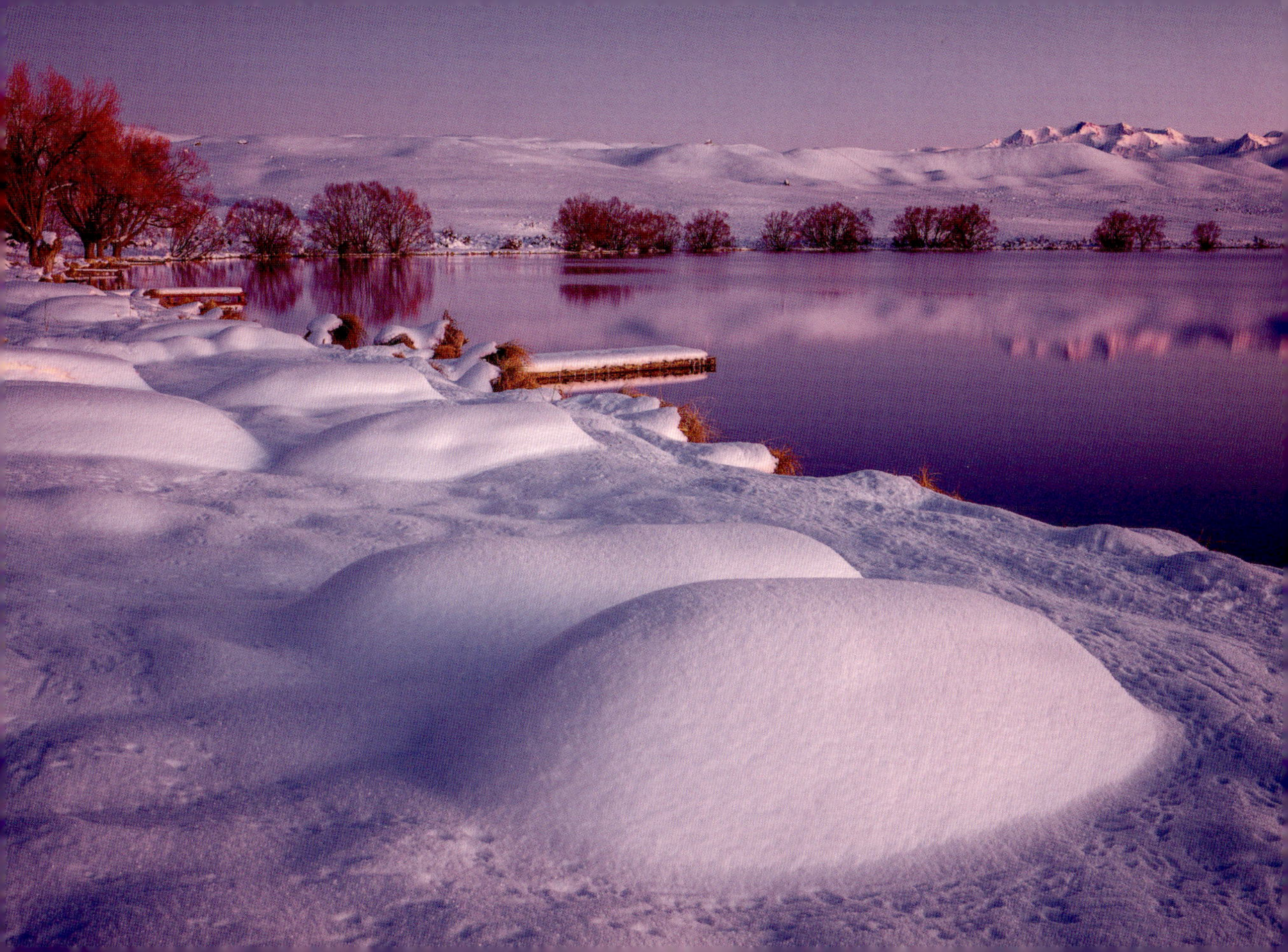

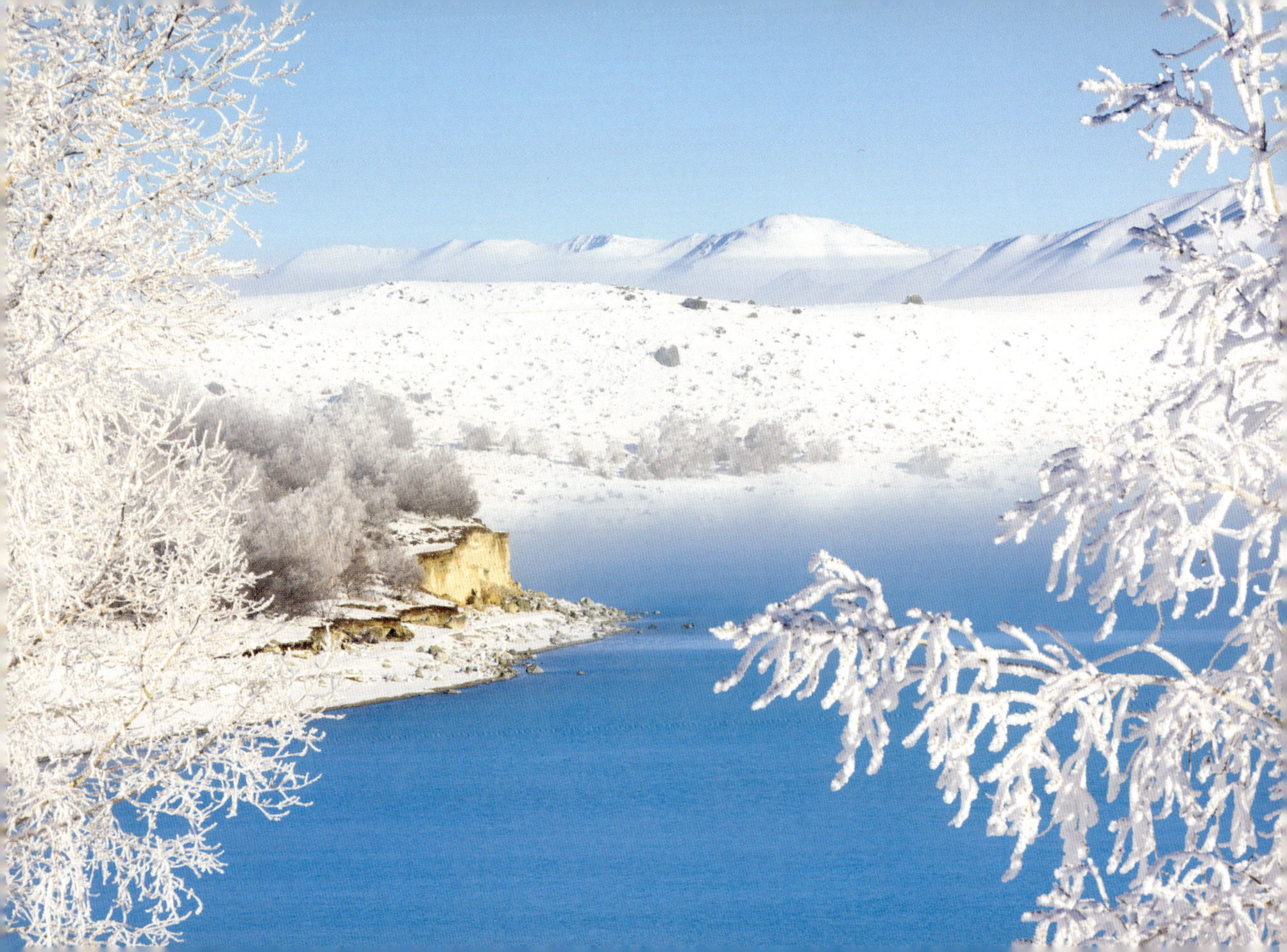

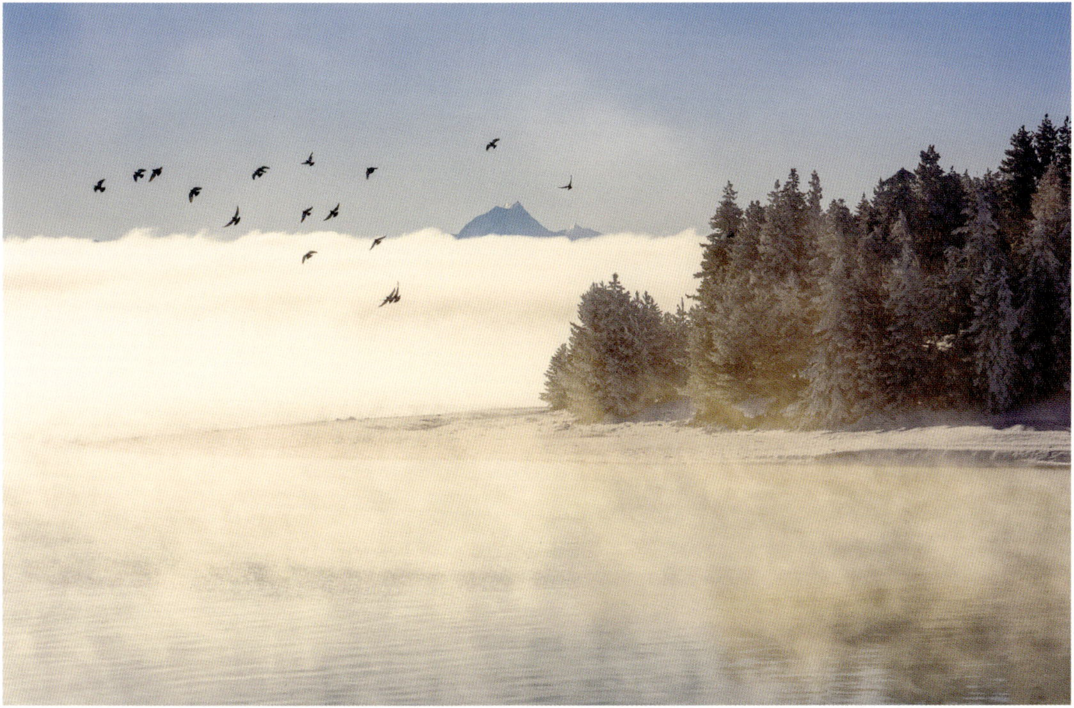

Pigeons take flight over Lake Pukaki, Mt Cook in the distance above the clouds.
opposite: A winter paradise on the shores of Lake Pukaki, Mackenzie Basin.

"The Heart of Haast"

Mist in the Haast Pass, Mount Aspiring National Park.

The beginnings of every lengthy journey are always filled with apprehension, with that feeling of emptiness as you leave the familiar behind and head into the unknown. It is a feeling I have grown to love; life springs into awareness as you empty your mind and open yourself up to possibilities. I left Queenstown on a blue sky day, the truck packed with gear ready for my longest trip about the South Island, which was long overdue as I hadn't been out exploring with my camera in hand for quite a while. As I left the Southern Lakes District ultimately destined for Golden Bay at the very top of the South Island, little did I know that I was heading into two weeks of near solid rain on the West Coast.

Haast greeted me with the first sign of this dampness, so absolute it hugged everything with great weight. Driving through the mist I caught a glimpse of the scene you now see; so breathtaking I had to turn my truck around for another look.

As I stood on the side of the road, watching the mist flow through the valley, photographing various compositions for over an hour, I felt the sense of being such a small thing amongst all encompassing wilderness. I thought about the two travellers who were recently tragically lost near this place in a landslide, and how precious our time is in this land.

The mist gradually thickened as the sun fell toward the horizon and the temperature began to drop. It was time for me to continue, feeling that this land was alive, breathing and watching me. This is the Heart of Haast, an untamable place where nature rules and man can only wonder at its grandeur.

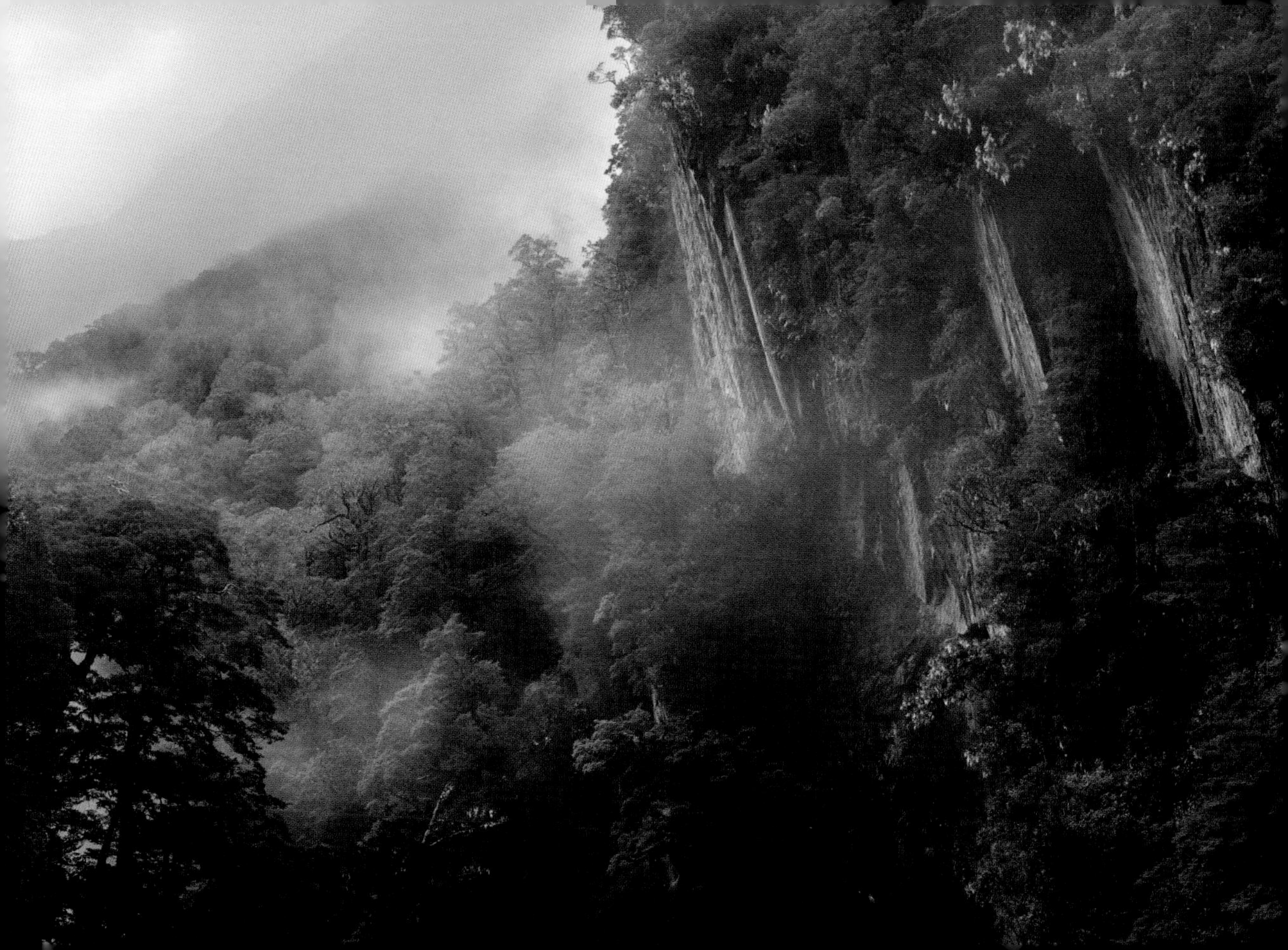

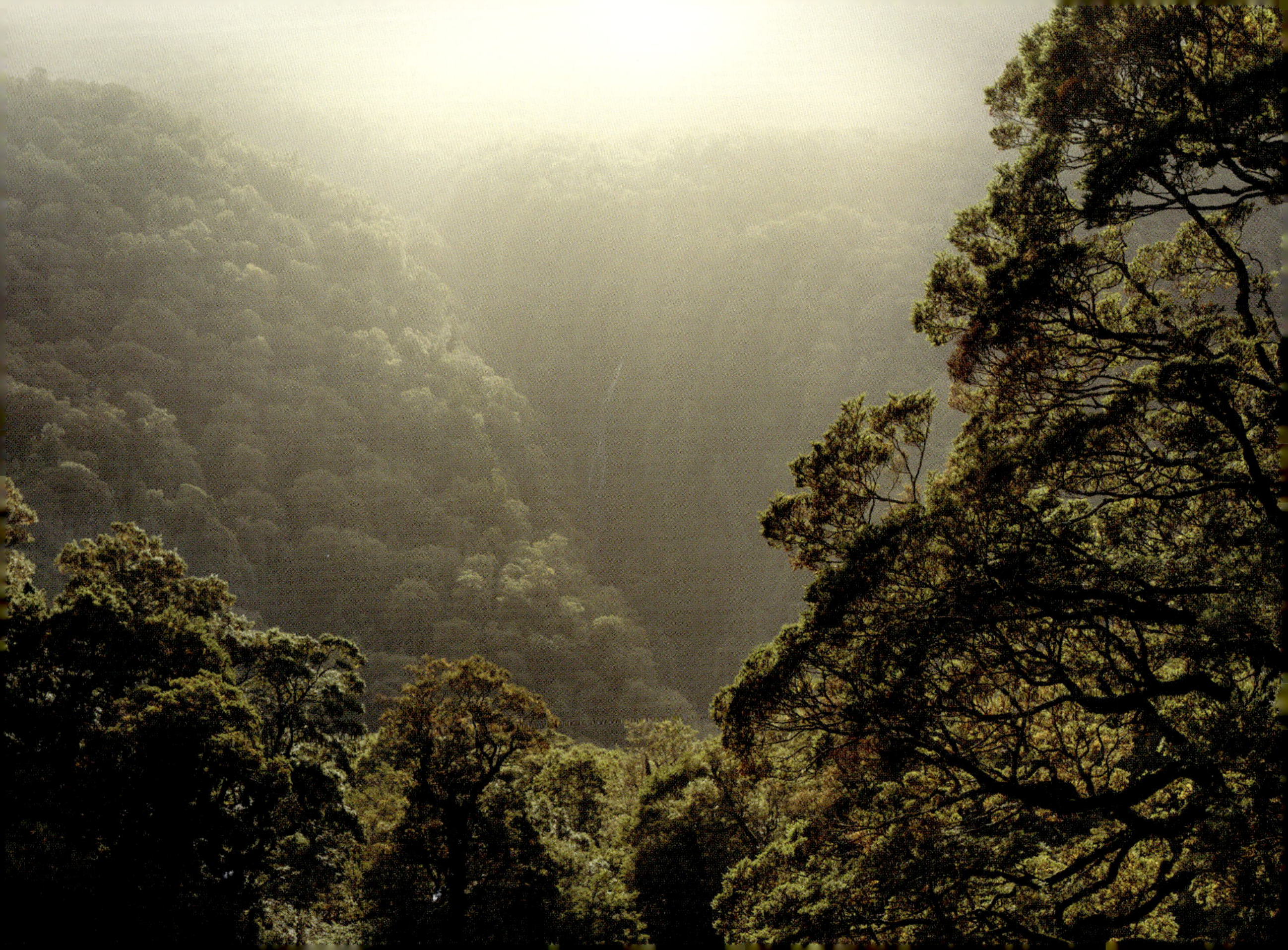

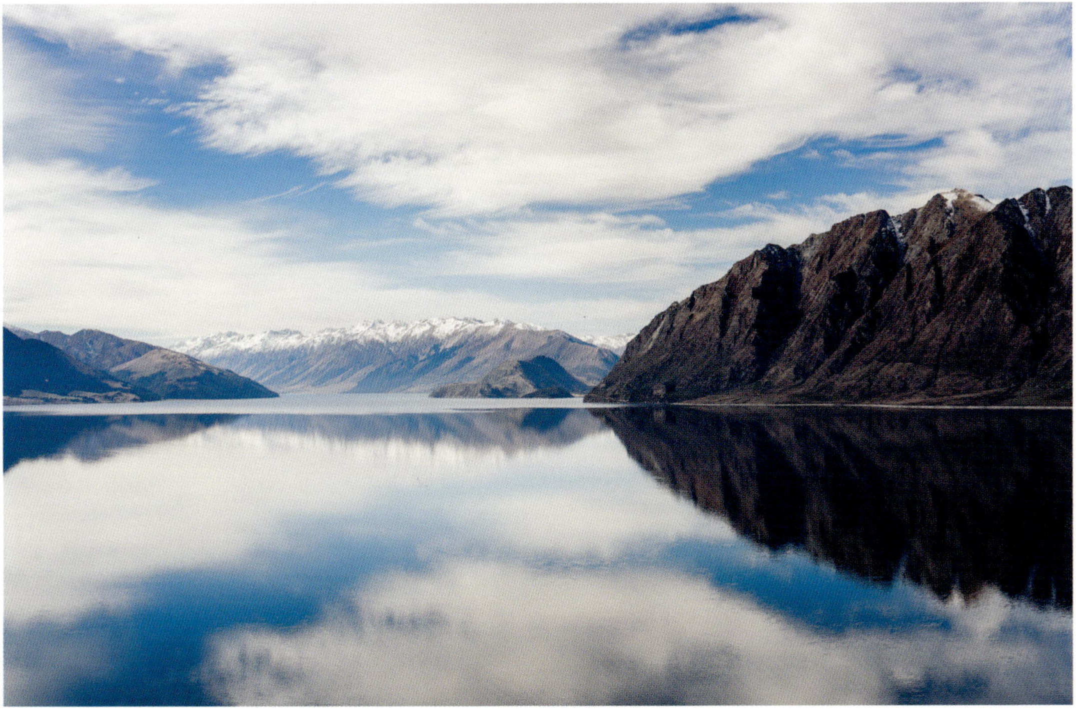

Reflections at Lake Hawea, Central Otago.

opposite: Afternoon light on the beech forest, near Haast, West Coast.

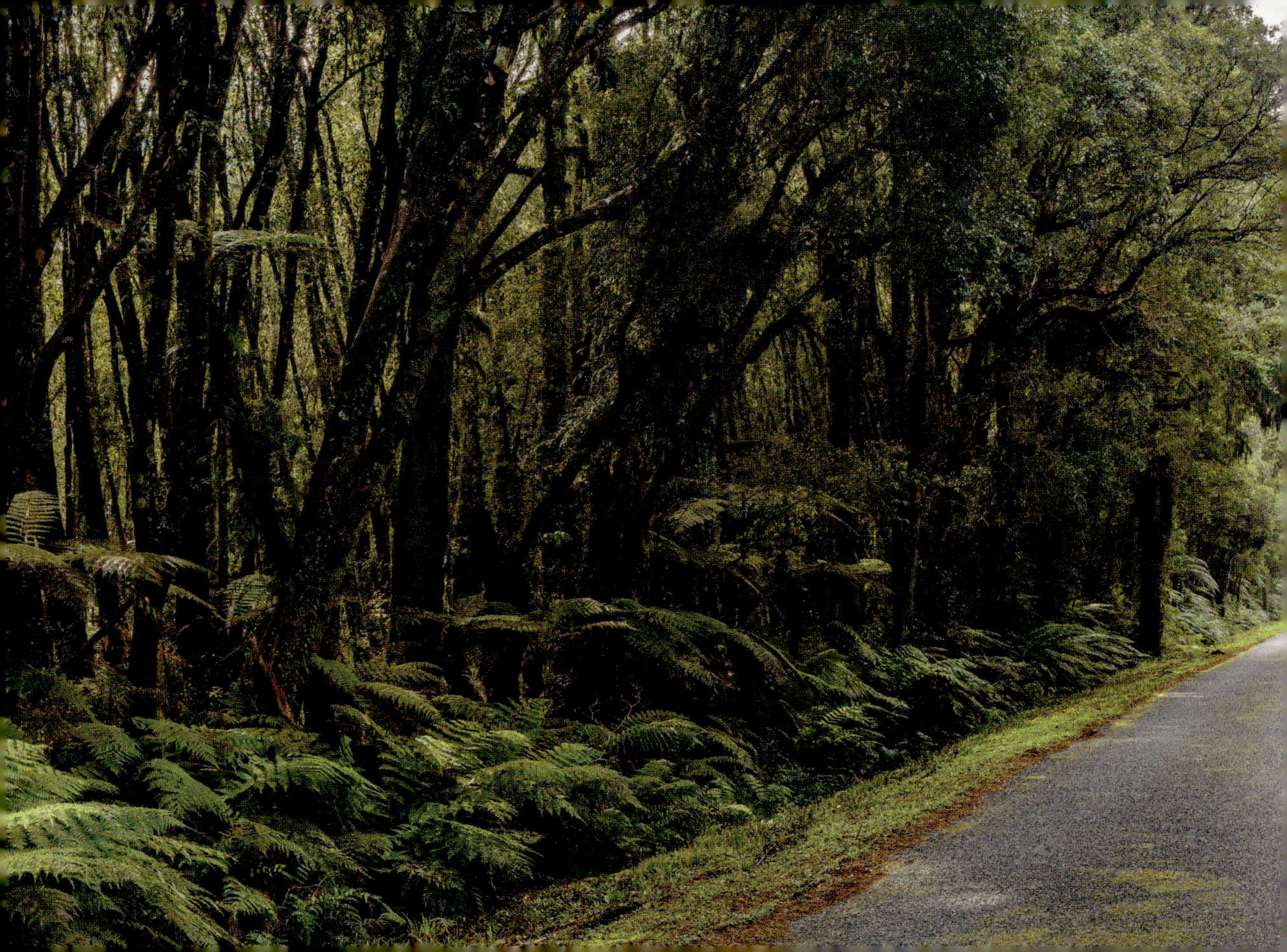

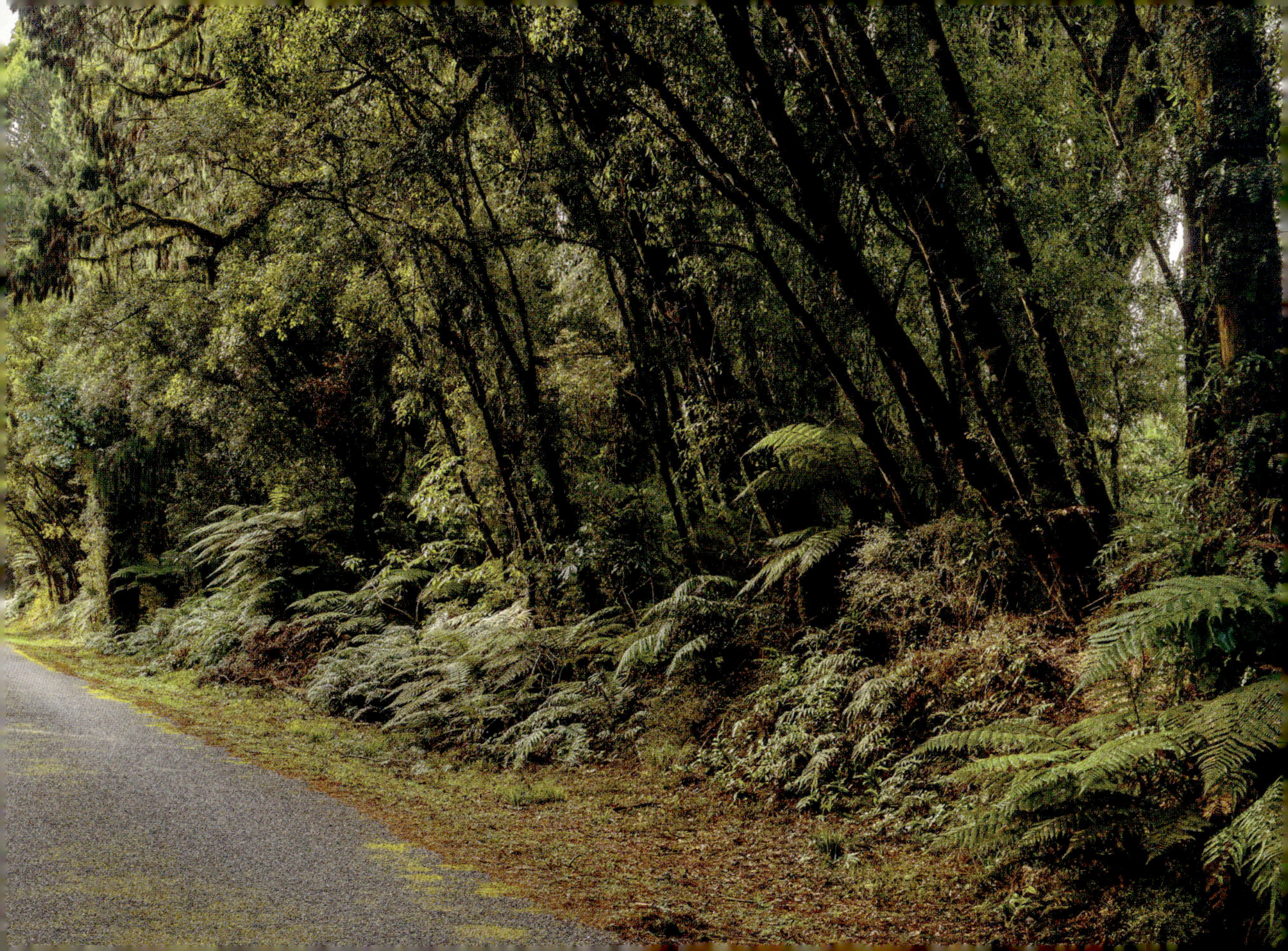

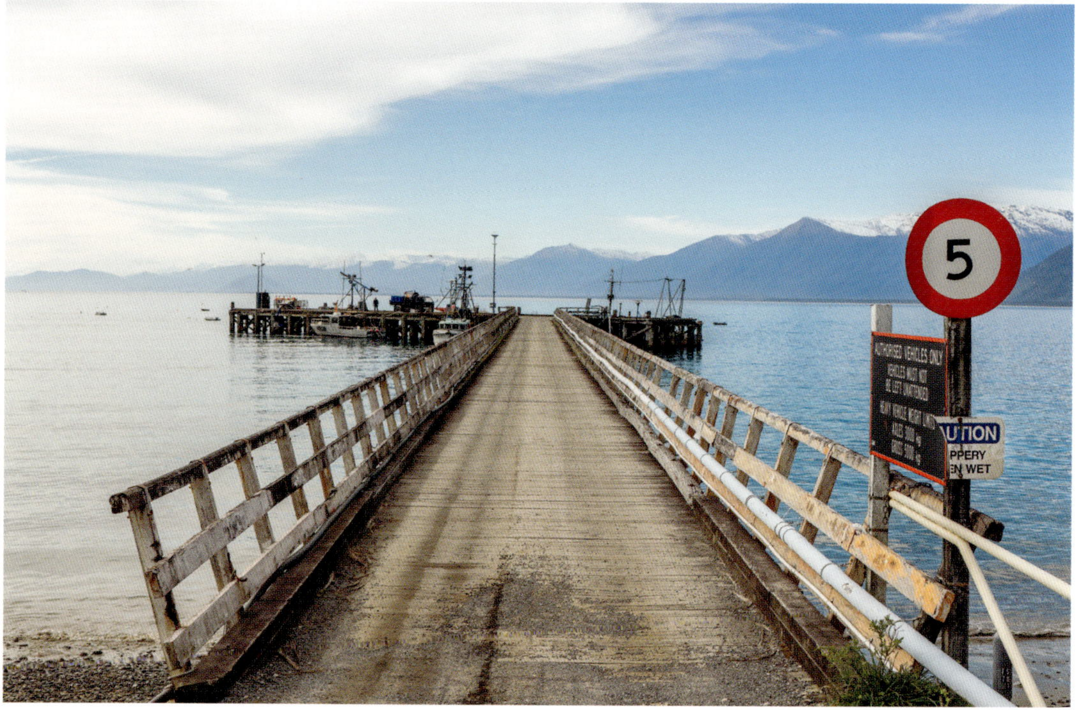

Afternoon at Jacksons Bay, West Coast.

previous: The road through Hannah's Clearing, West Coast.

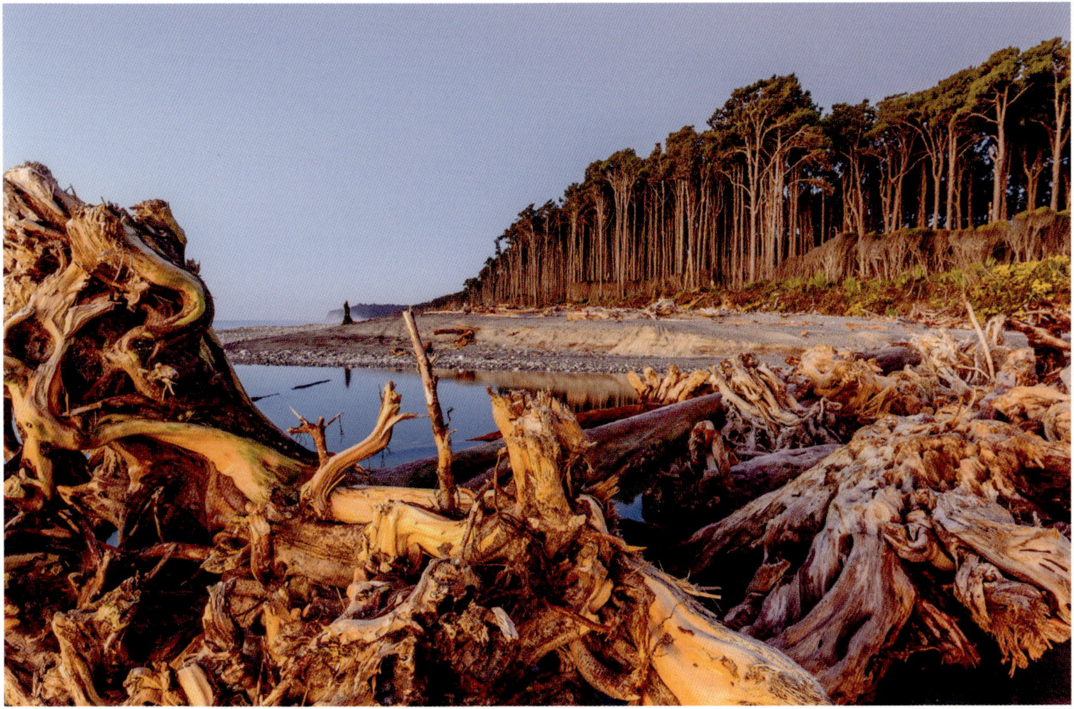

Amongst the driftwood at Dusk, Bruce Bay, West Coast.
overleaf: The dawn of a new day at Lake Paringa, West Coast.

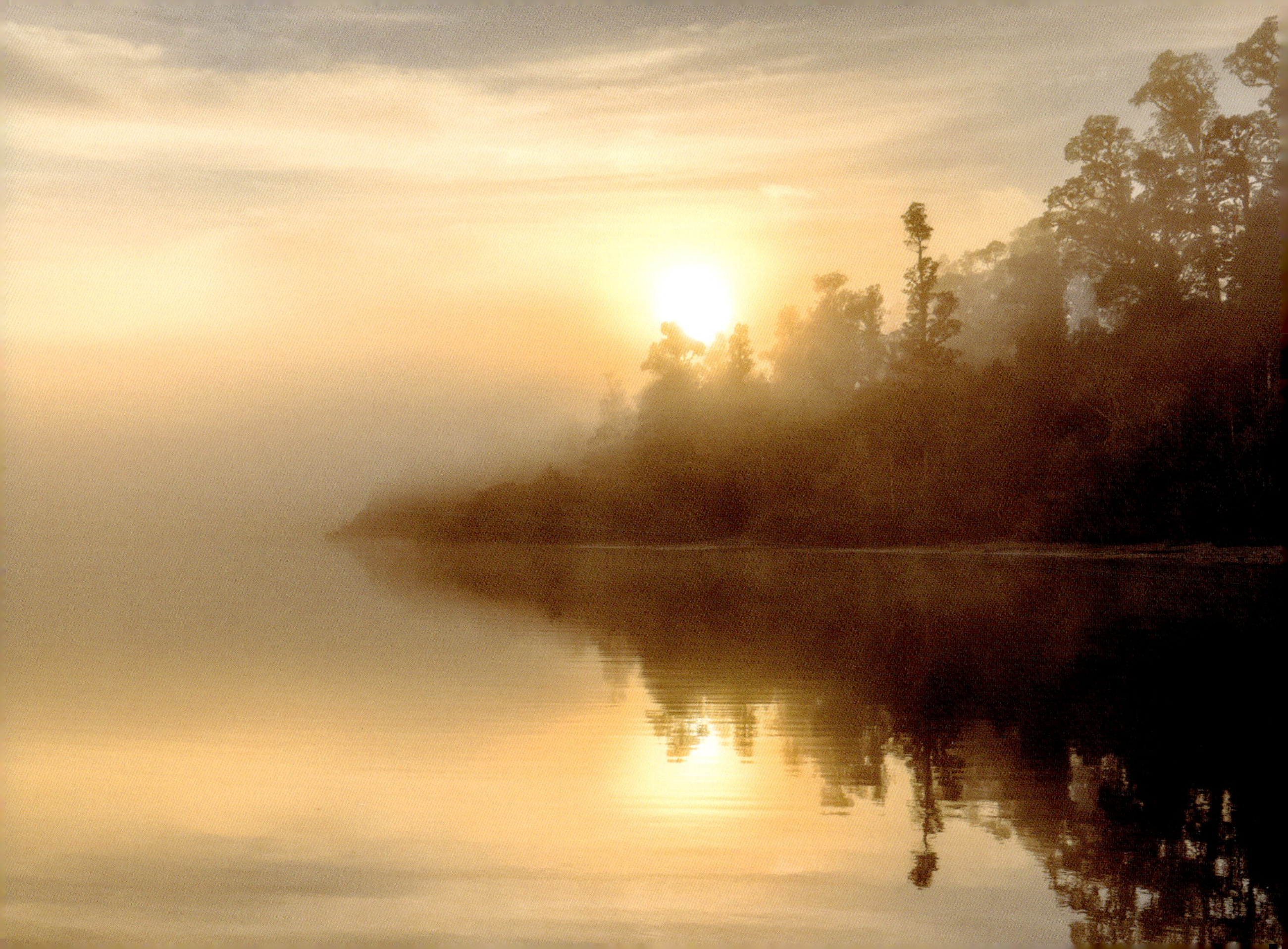

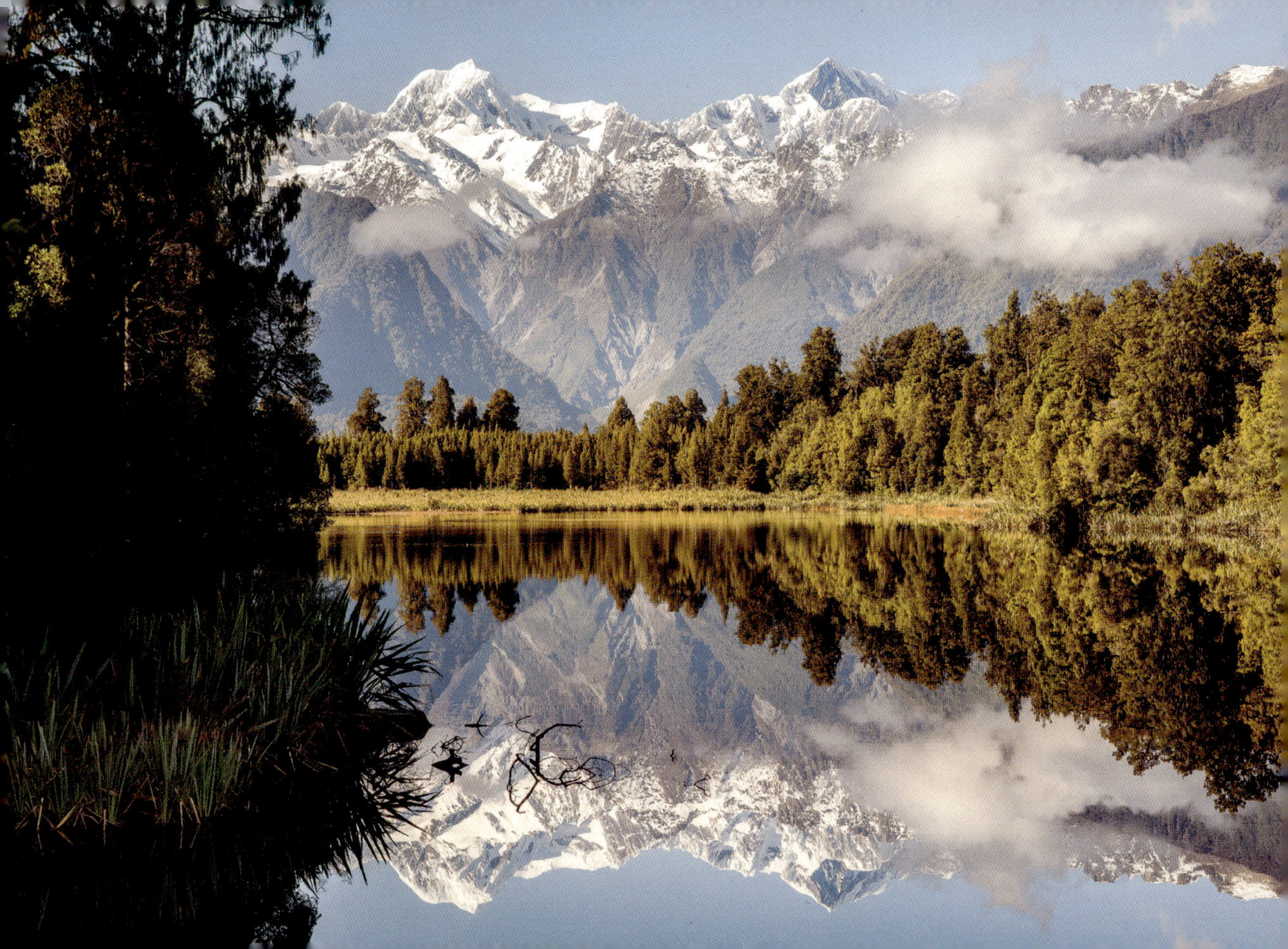

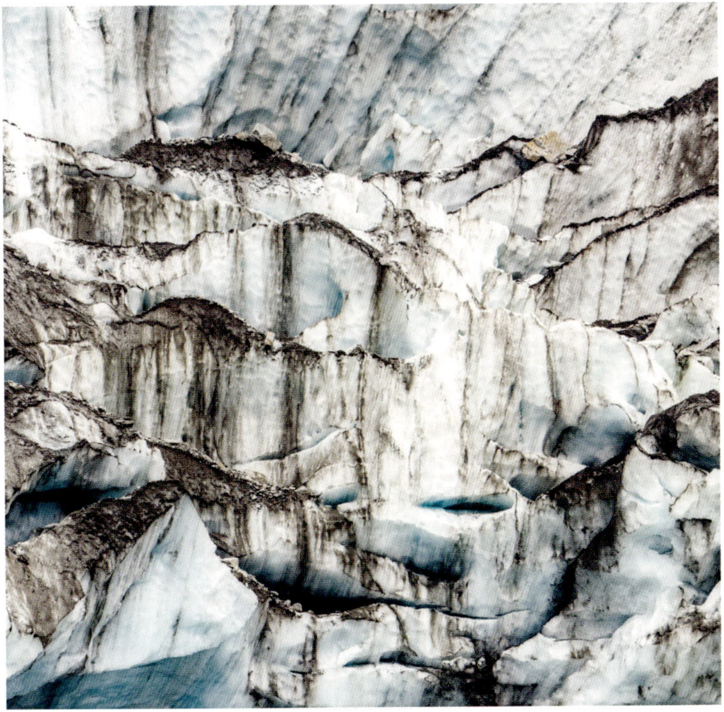

Patterns in the ice, Fox Glacier, West Coast.

opposite: Morning reflections of Mt Tasman and Mt Cook, Lake Matheson.

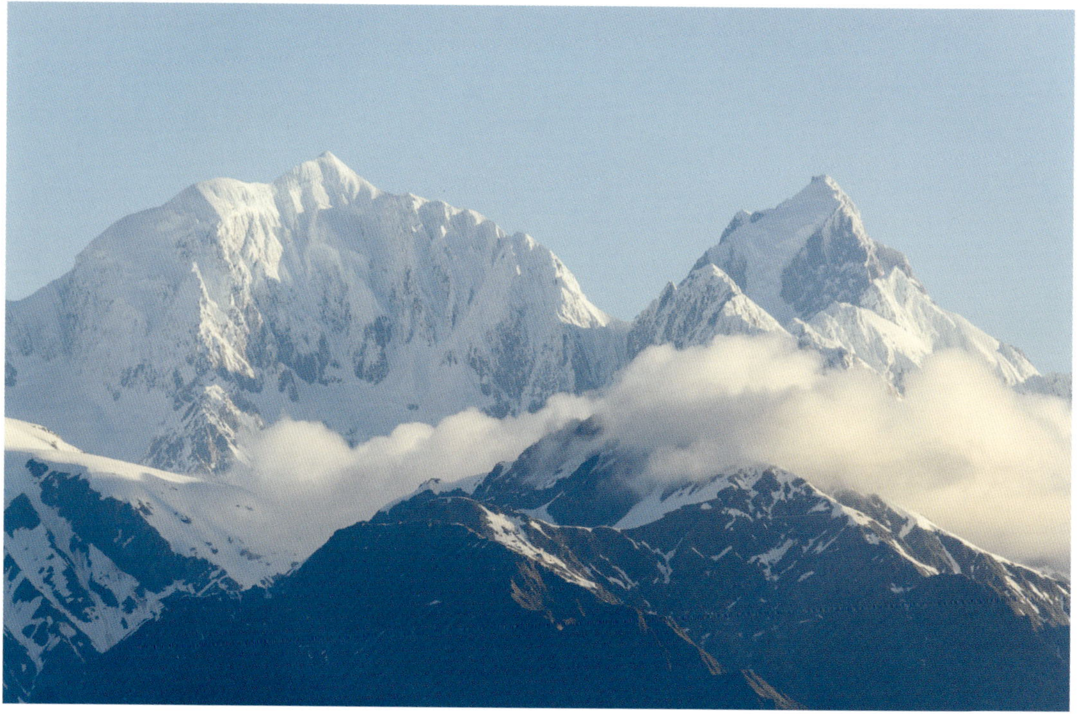

Mt Cook and Mt Tasman from Okarito Trig Lookout, West Coast.
opposite: Light over Three Mile Lagoon and The Southern Alps, Okarito.

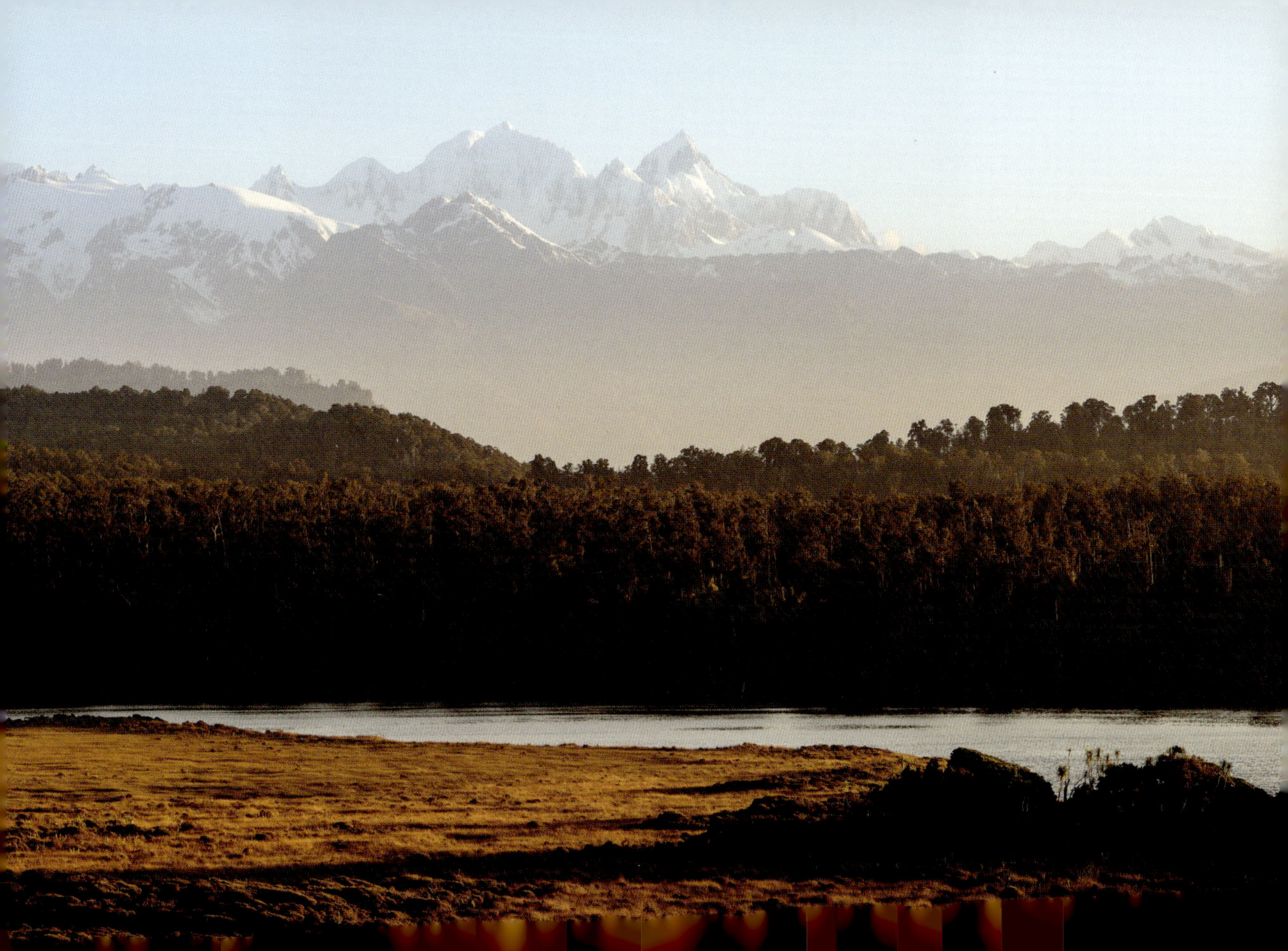

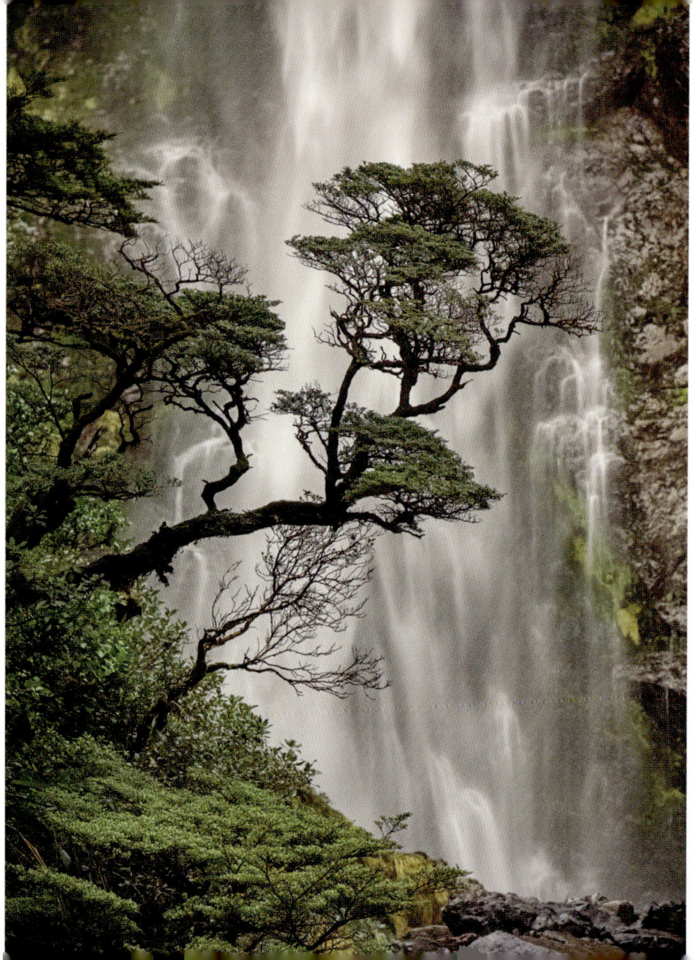

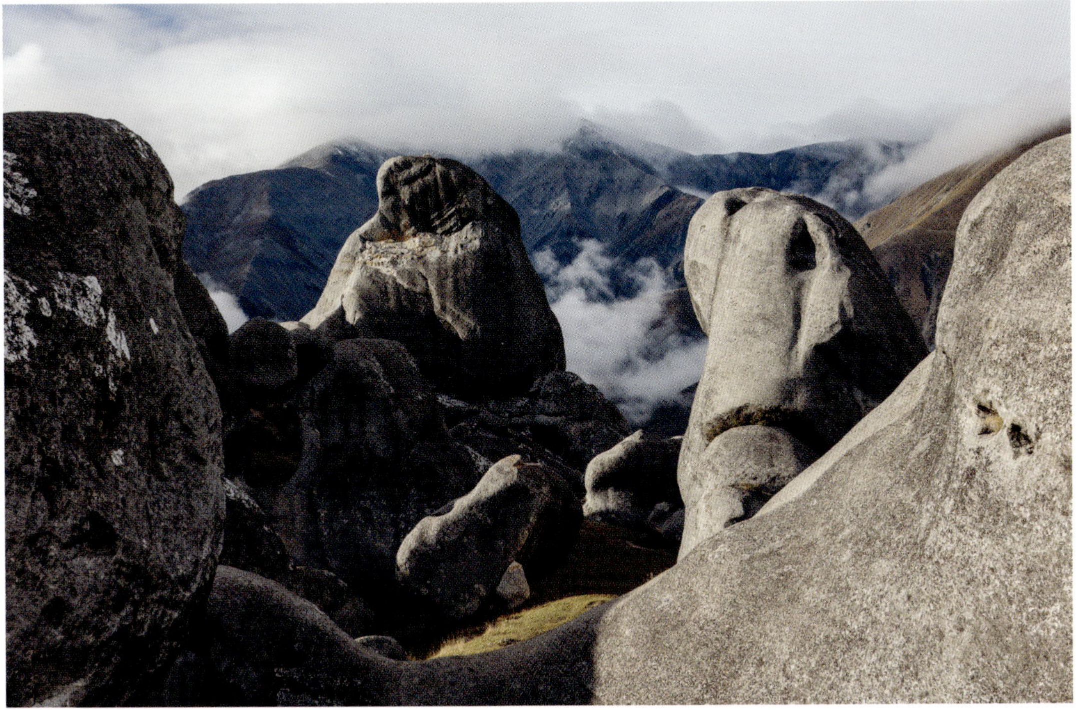

Rock formations at Castle Hill, Kura Tawhiti Conservation Area, Canterbury High Country.
opposite: The Devil's Punchbowl, Arthur's Pass National Park.

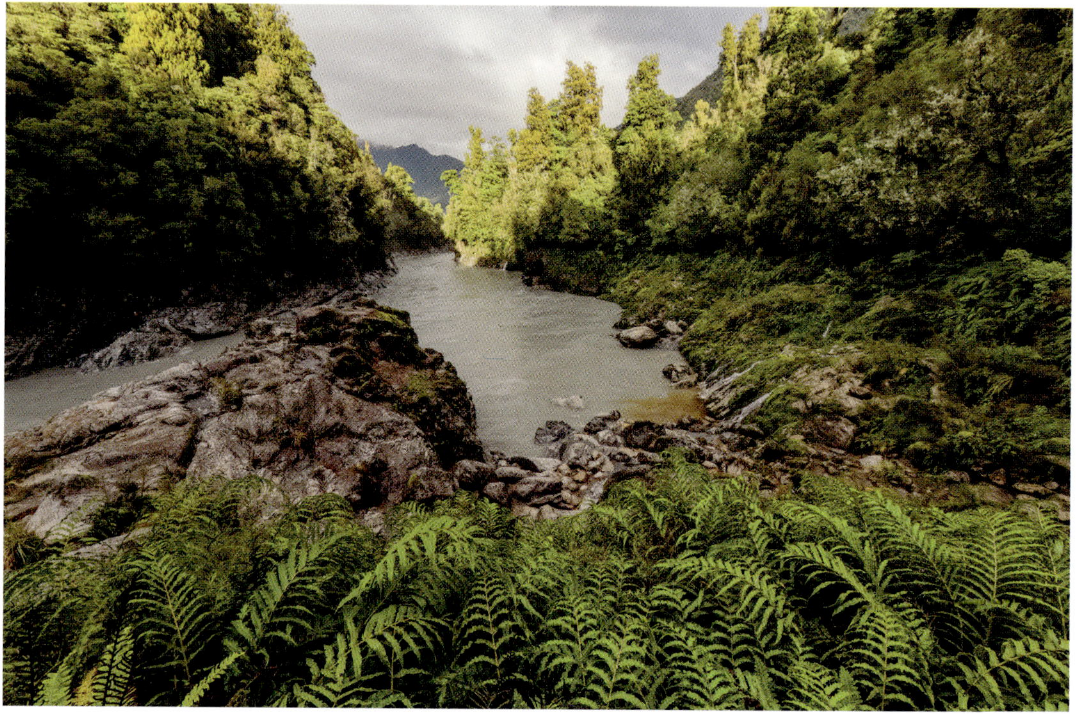

The Hokitika Gorge, Hokitika, West Coast.
opposite: Double rainbow at the Pancake Rocks blowhole, Dolomite Point, Paparoa National Park.

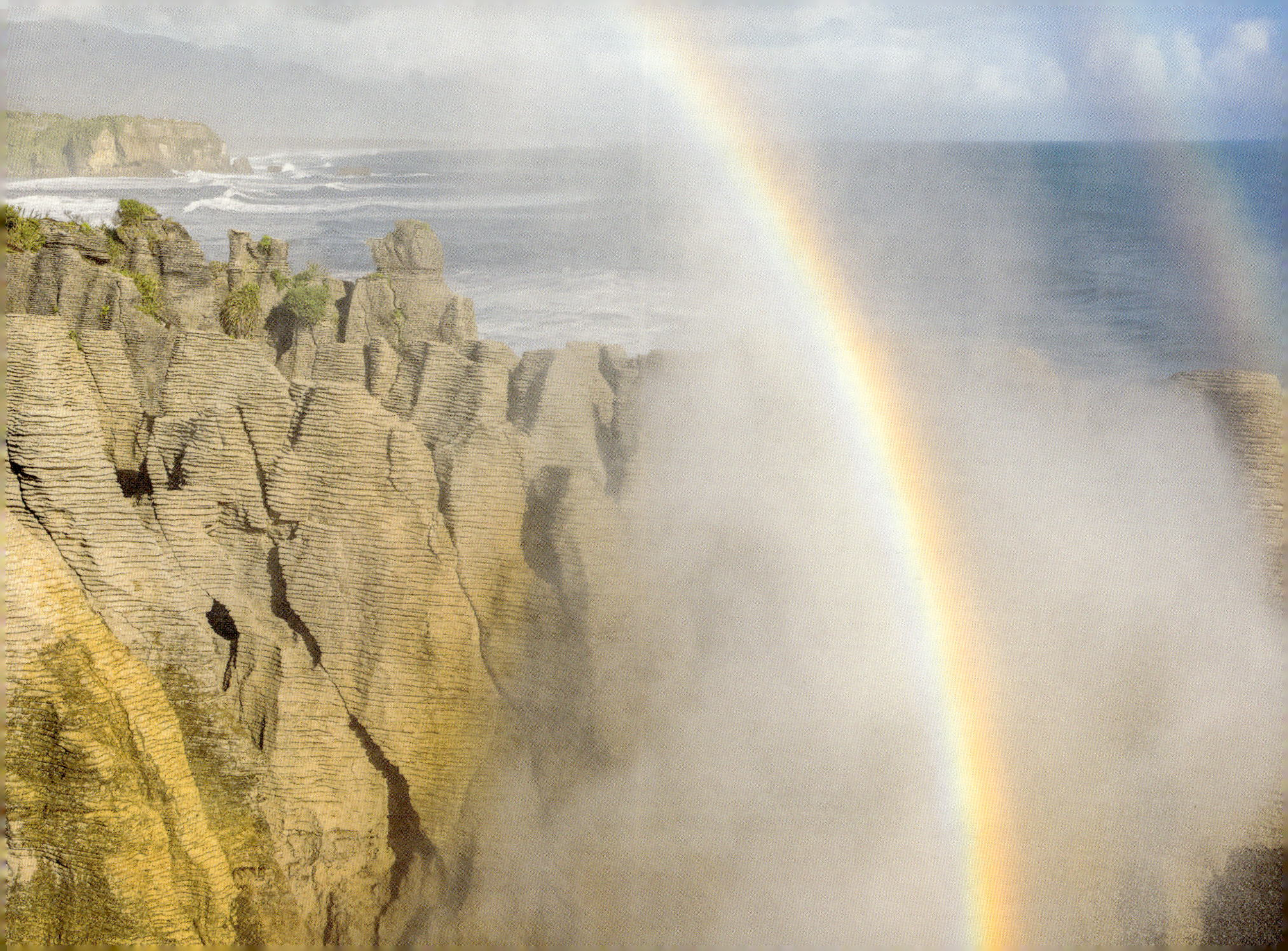

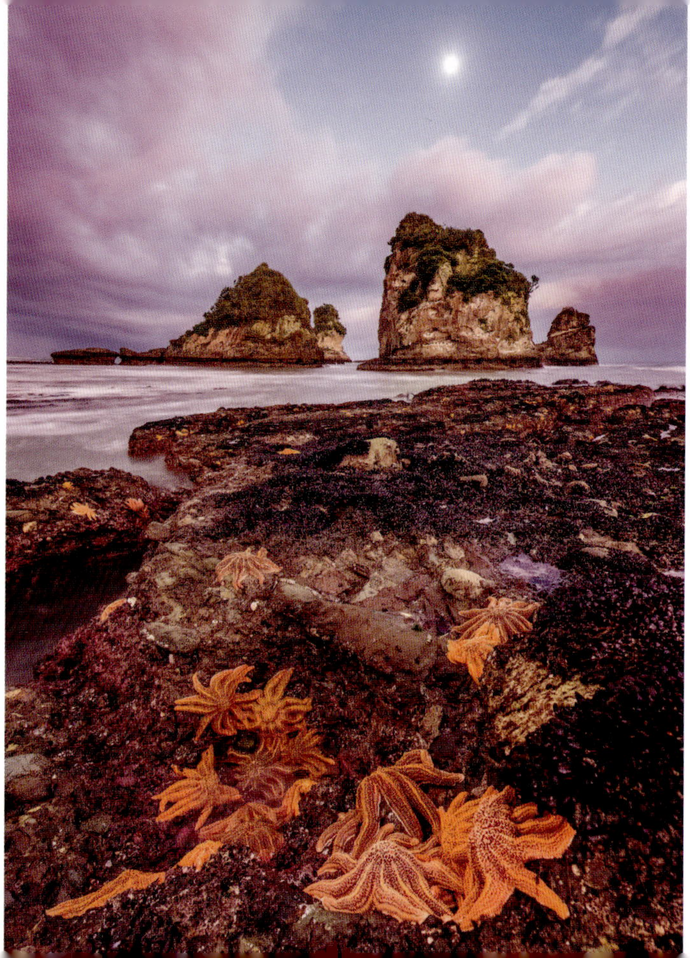

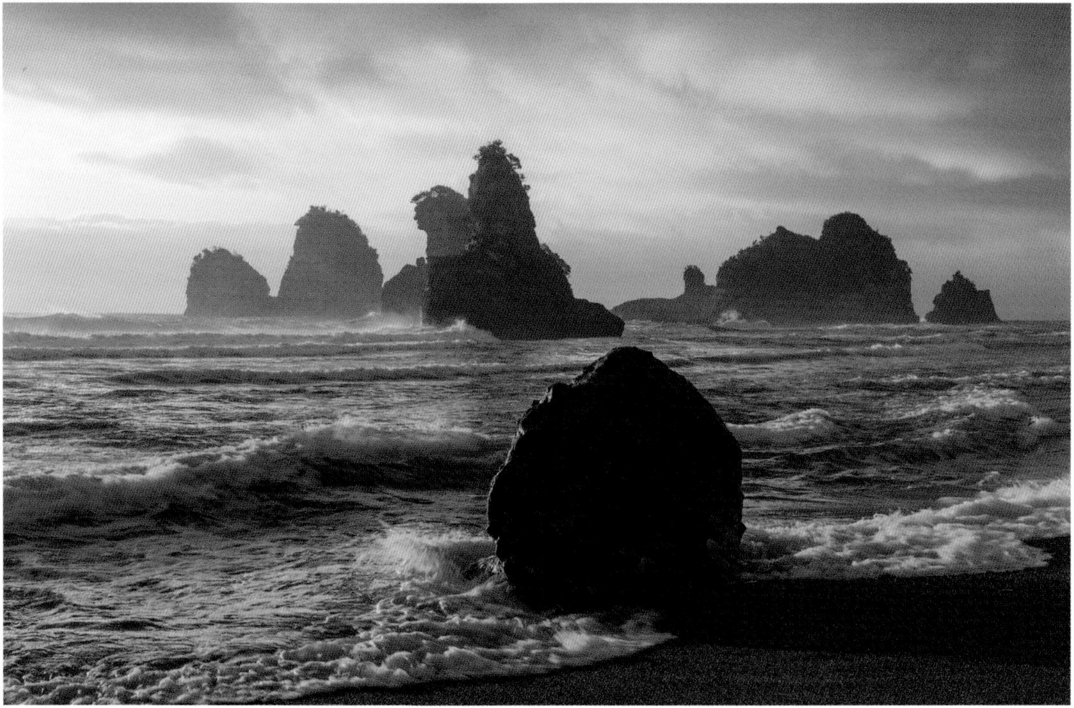

Storm at sunset, Motukiekie Beach, West Coast.
opposite: Dawn on the shore at Motukiekie Beach, West Coast.

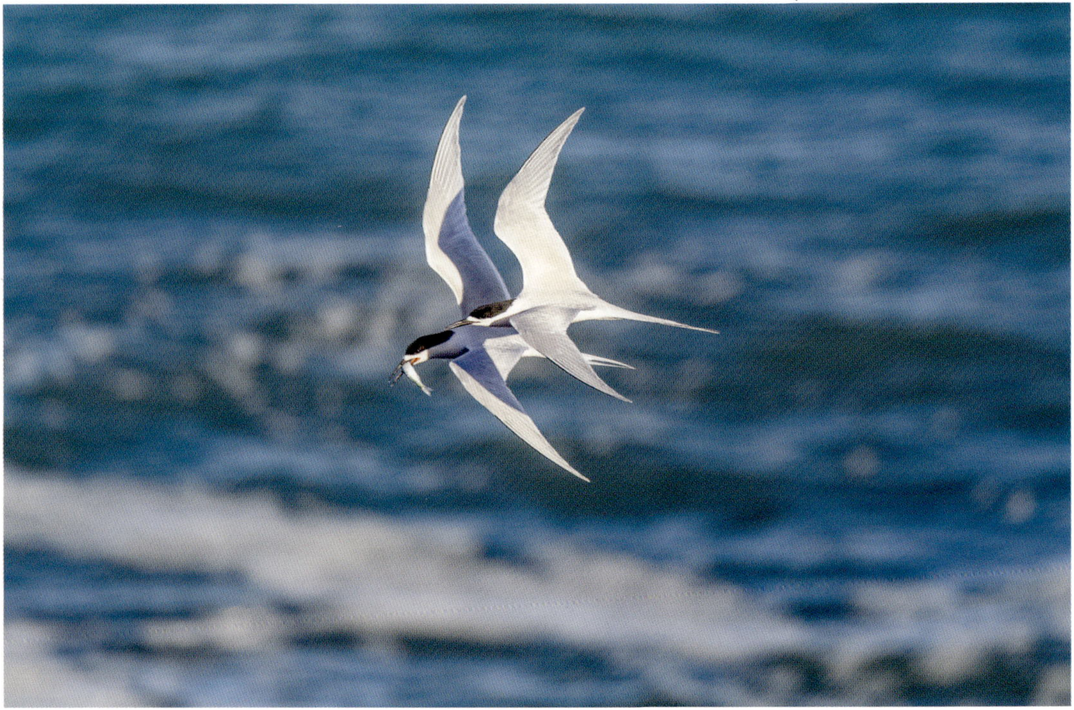

Synchronised Terns flying in the morning light at Punakaiki, West Coast.
opposite: Sunrays in the sea mist, Meybille Bay, Buller.

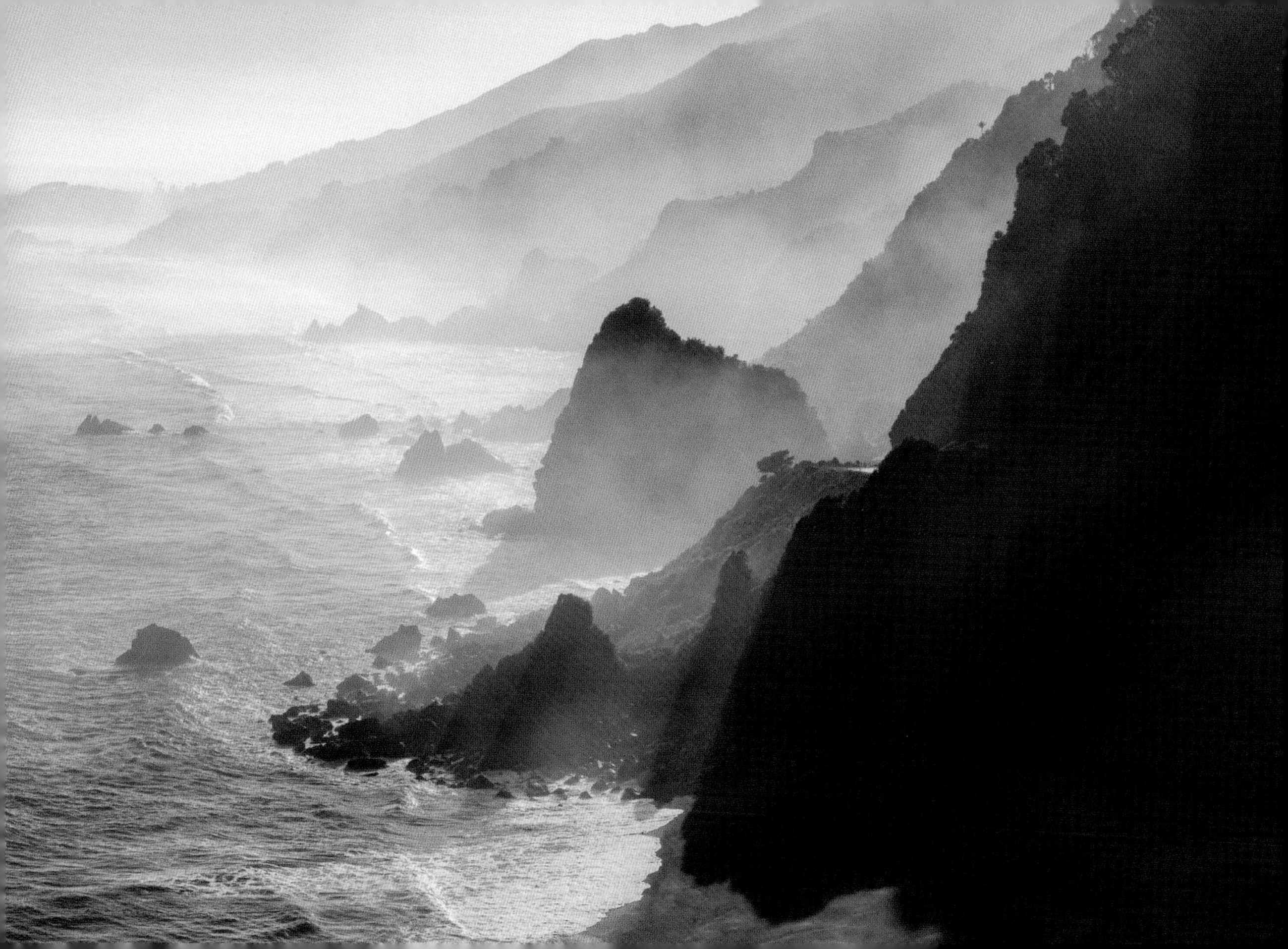

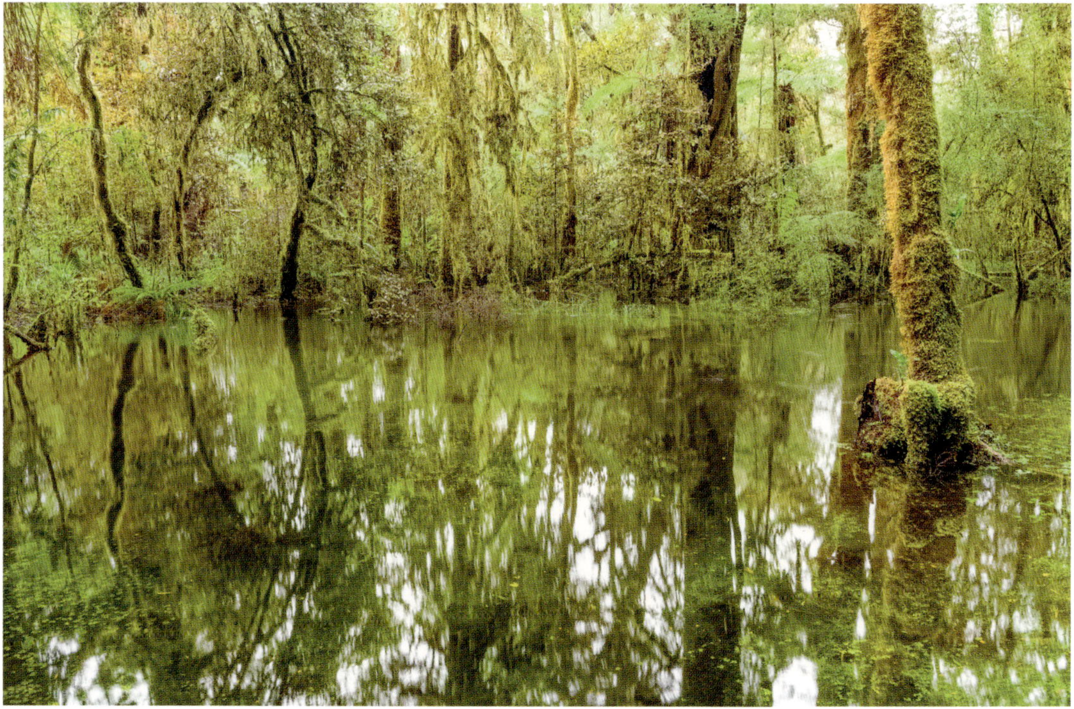

Flooded forest floor, Kahurangi National Park.

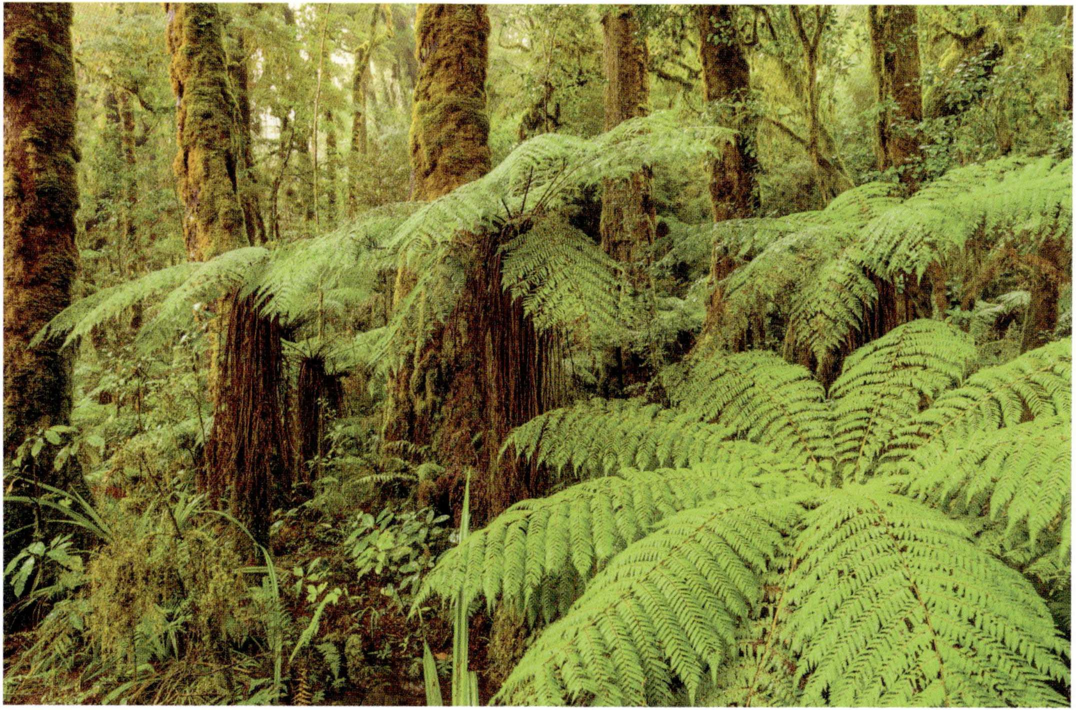

Native forest in Oparara Basin, Kahurangi National Park.

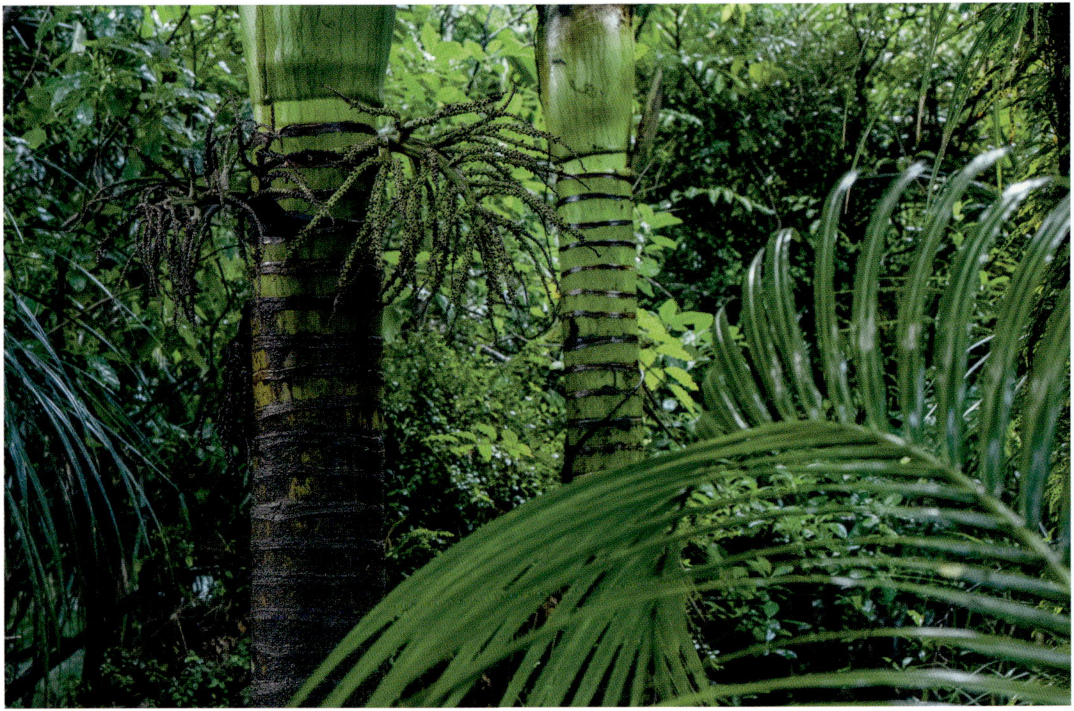

Nikau palms on the Heaphy Track, Karamea.
opposite: Moria Gate Arch and the Oparara River, Oparara Basin, Karamea.
overleaf: Split Apple Rock at dusk, Abel Tasman National Park.

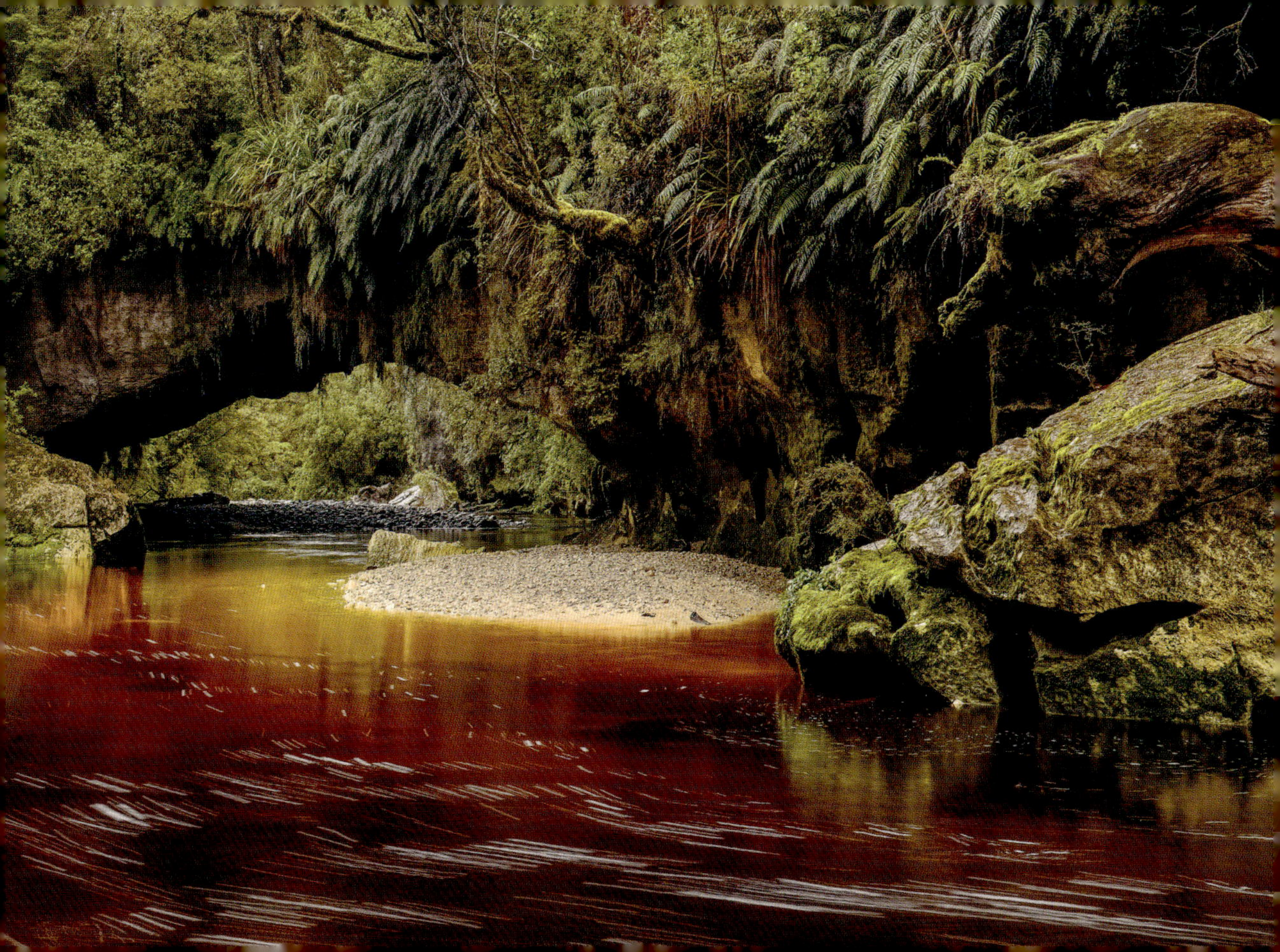

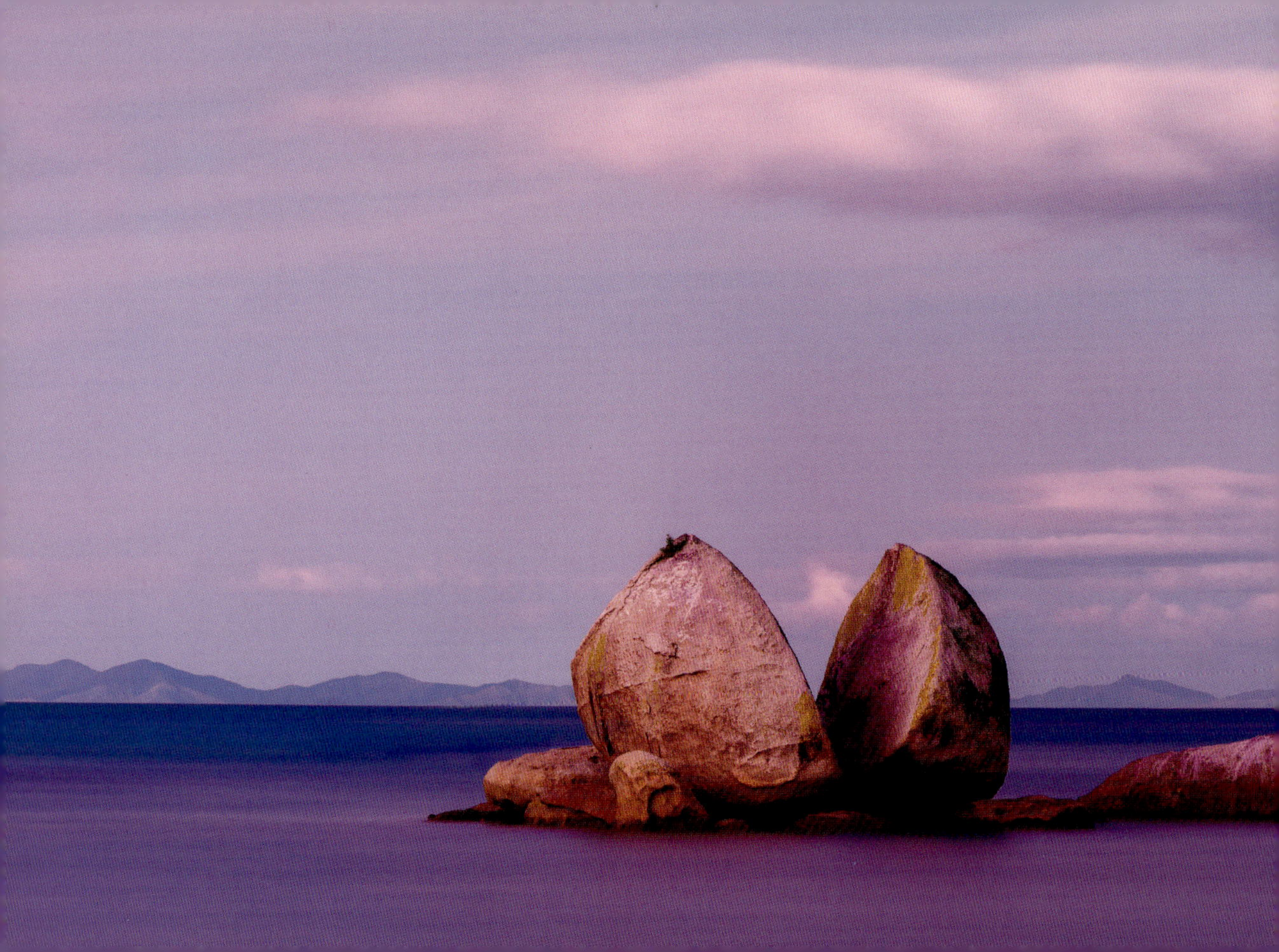

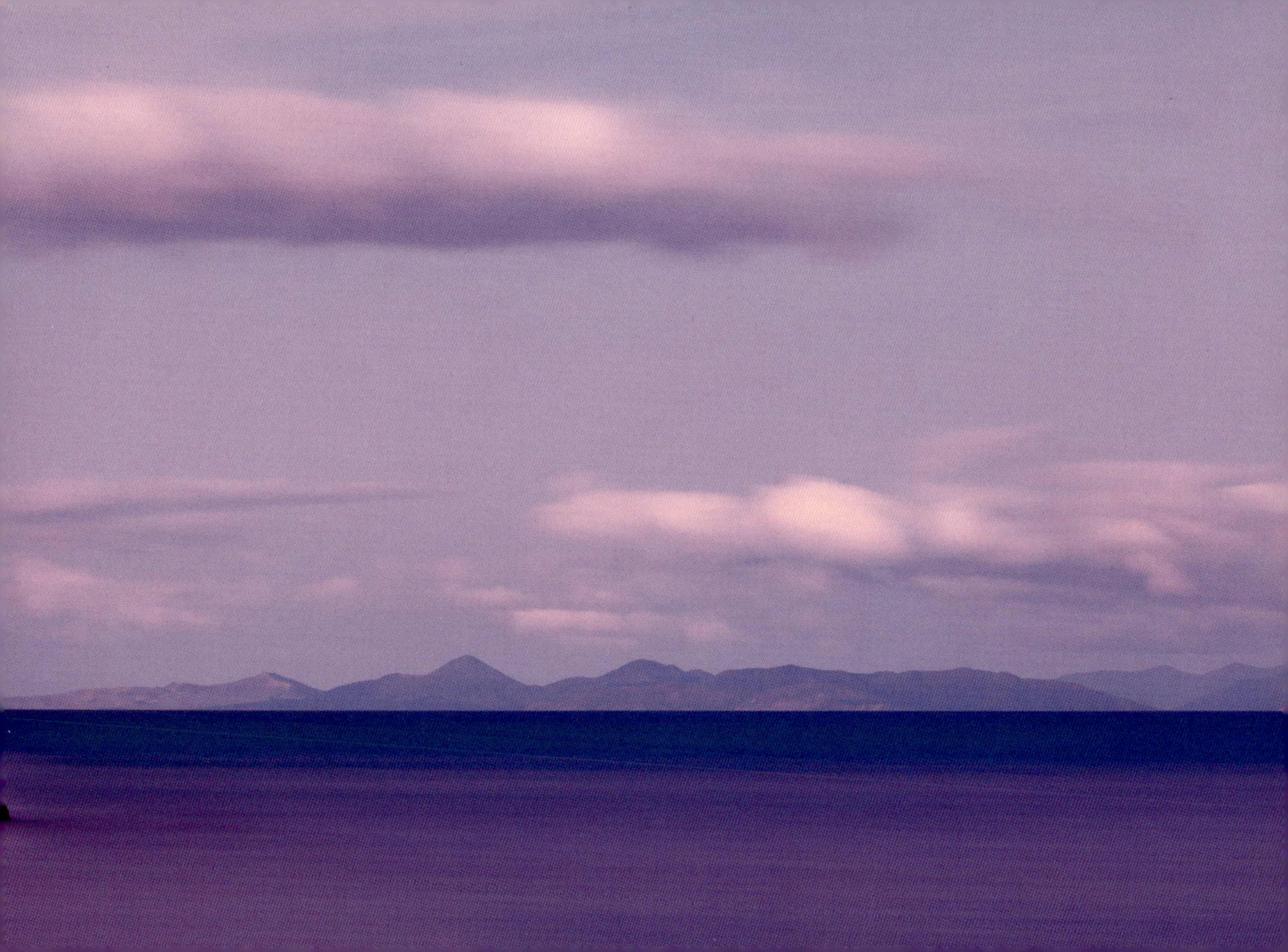

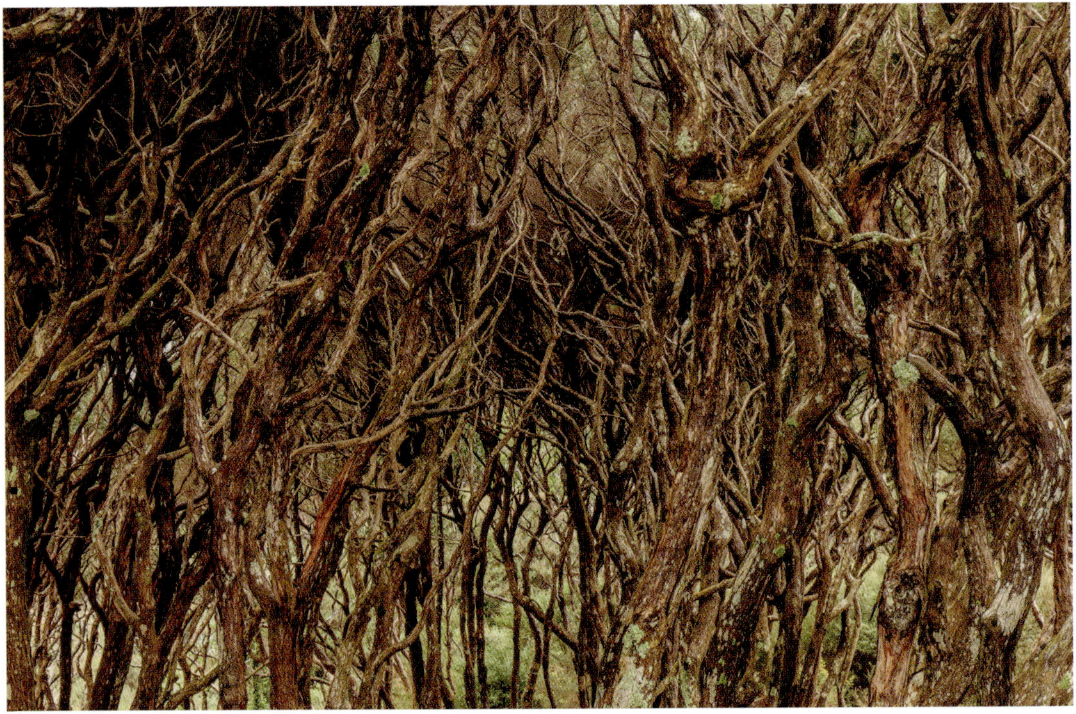

Twisted Manuka trees, Golden Bay.

opposite: The Archway Islands, Wharariki Beach, Golden Bay.

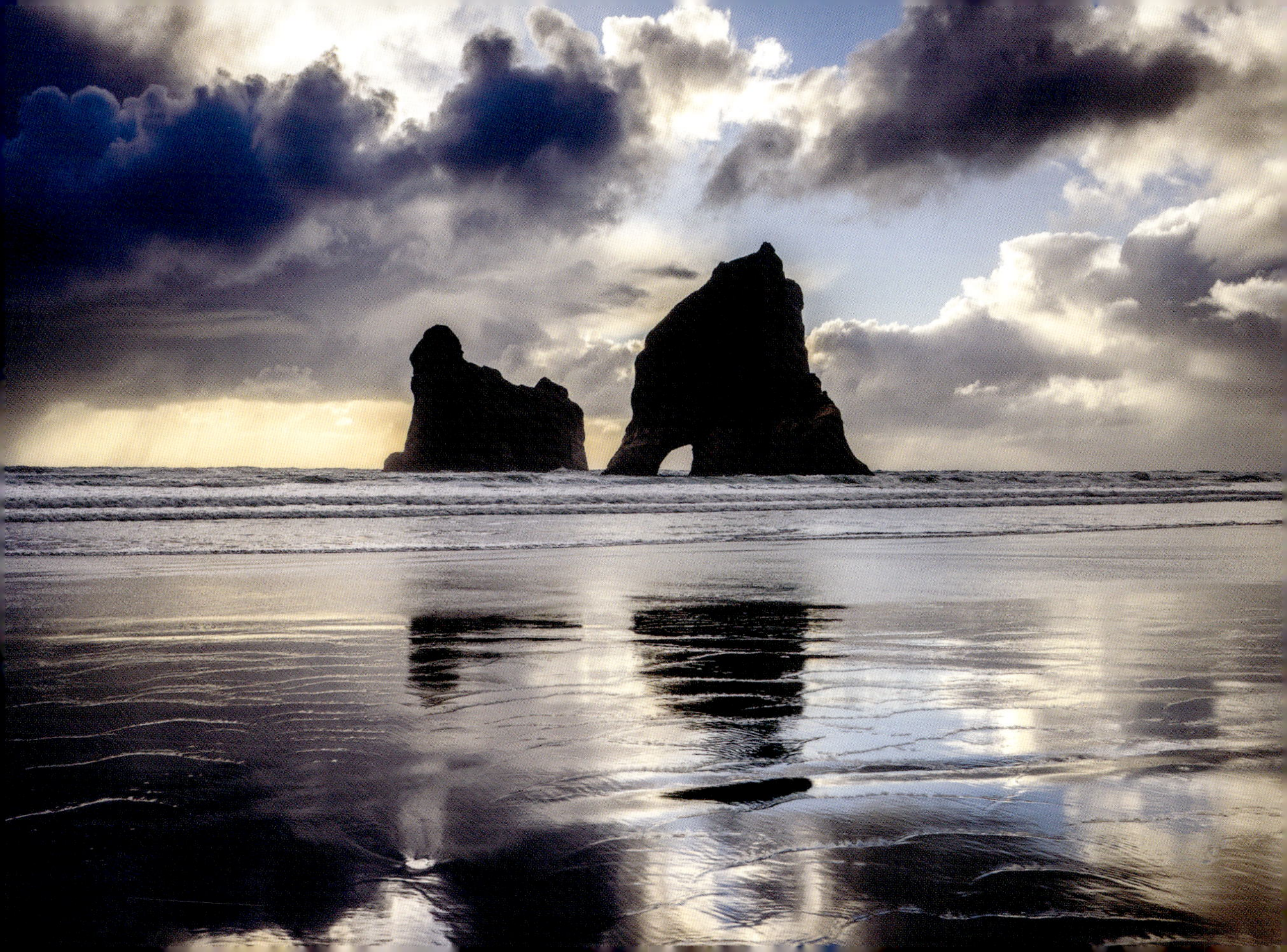

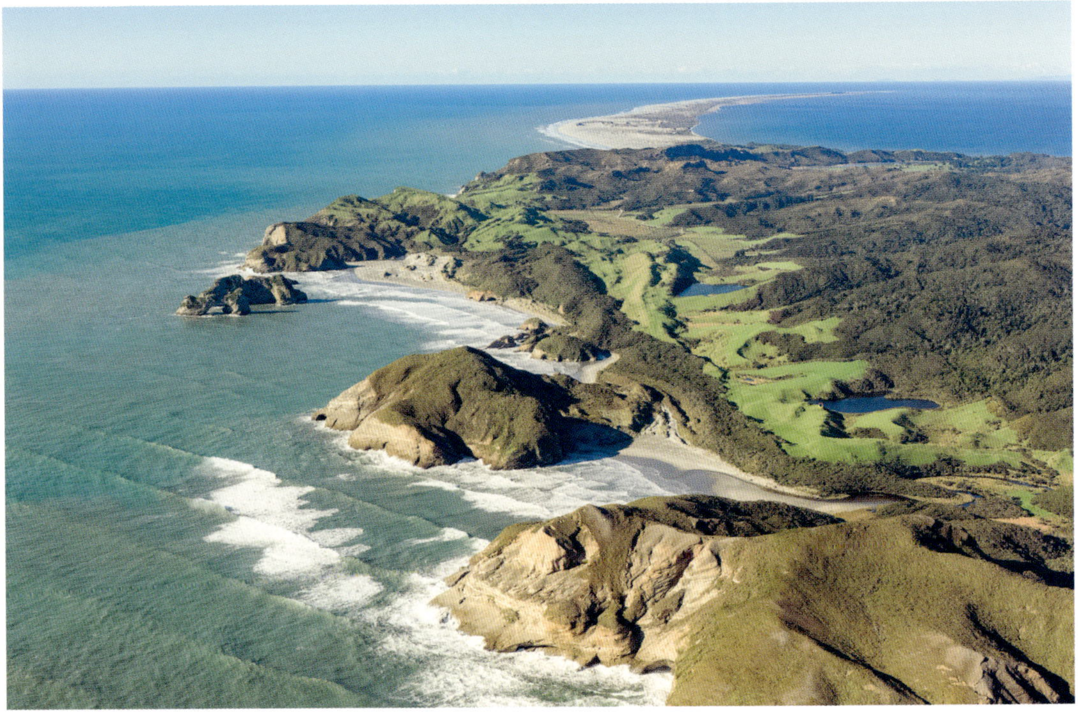

Aerial over Wharariki Beach and Farewell Spit, Golden Bay, Tasman.

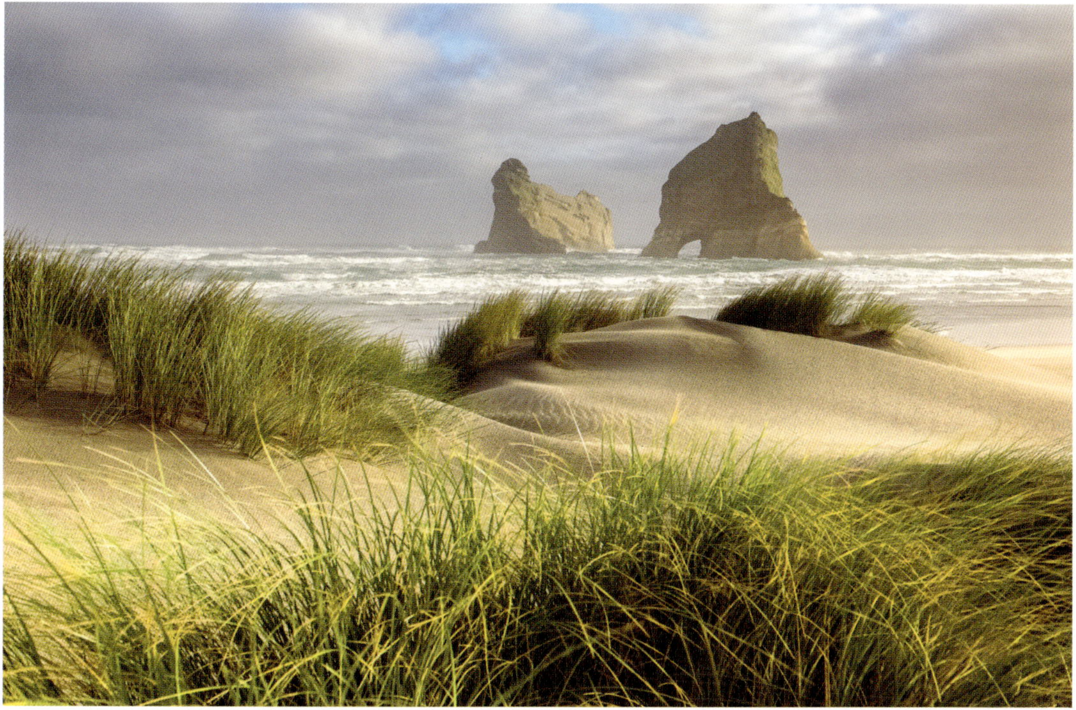

Light breaks through the clouds, The Archway Islands, Wharariki Beach, Tasman.
overleaf: The sandy shores of Golden Bay, Tasman.

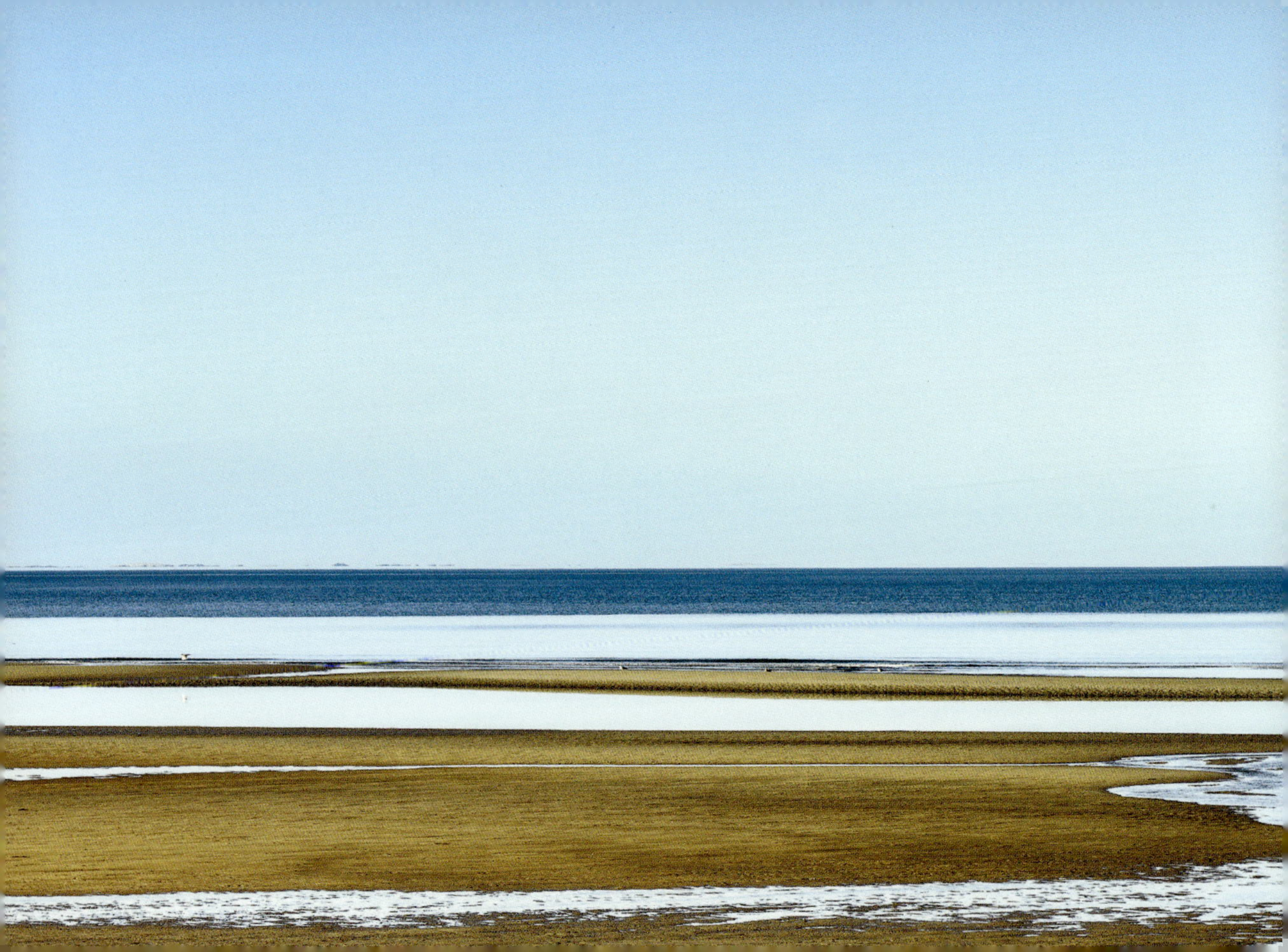

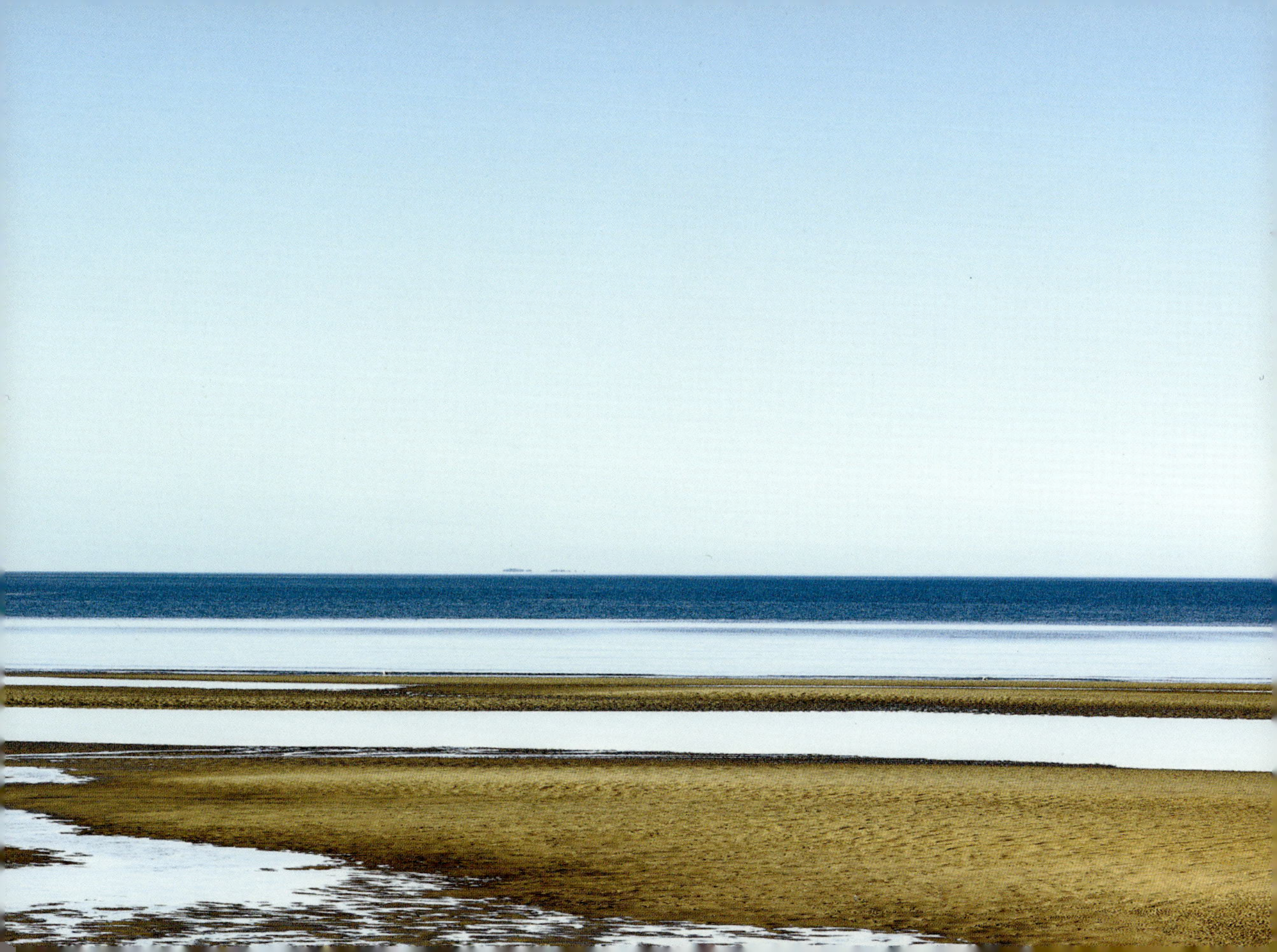

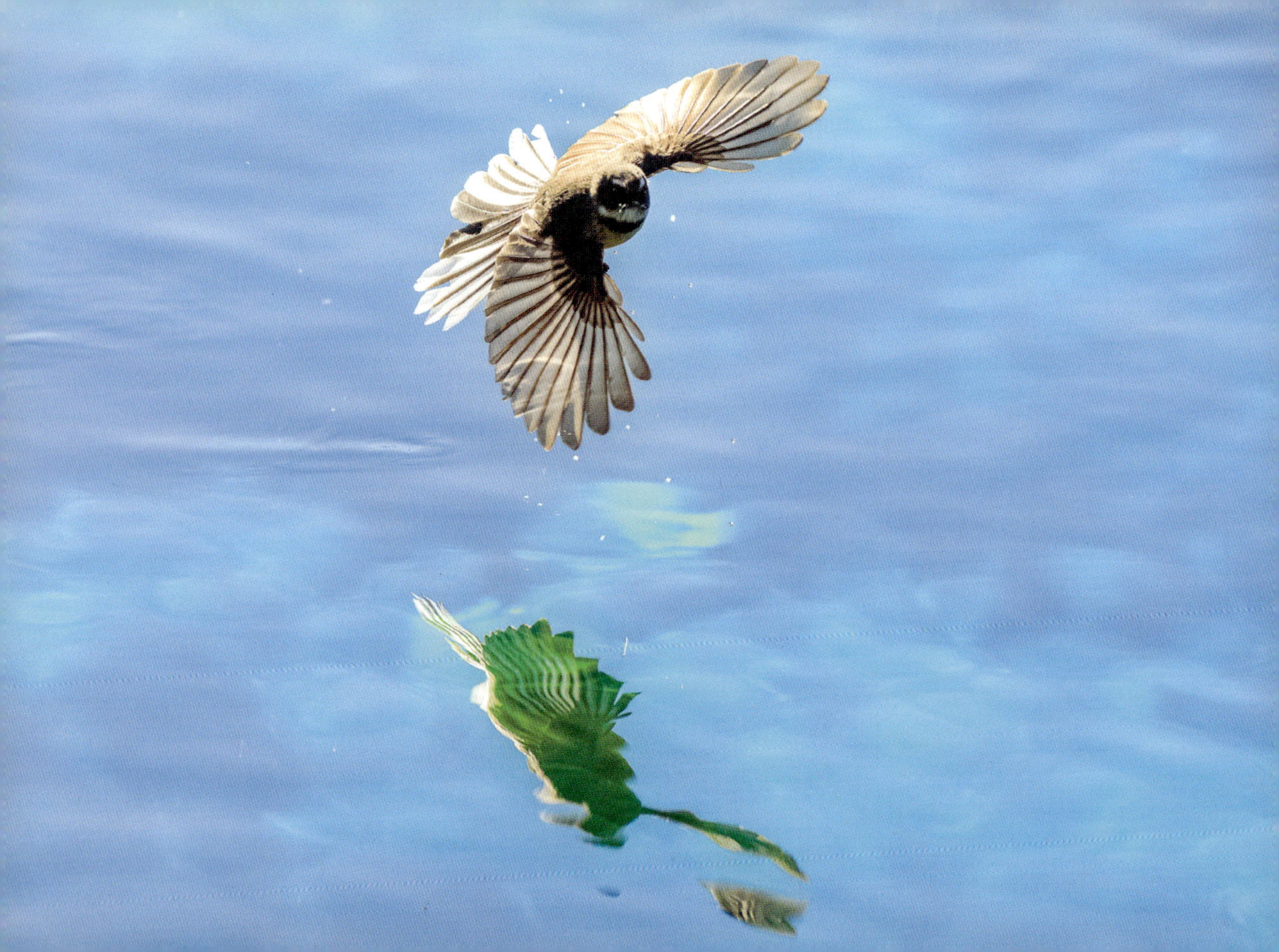

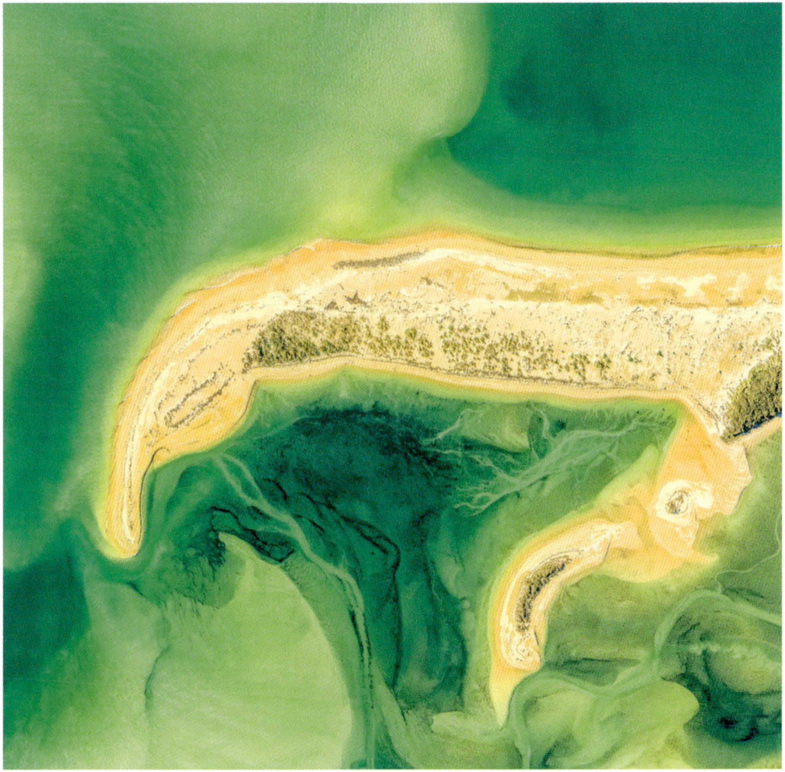

AERIAL OVER AWAROA INLET, ABEL TASMAN NATIONAL PARK.
OPPOSITE: A FANTAIL IN FULL FLIGHT, TE WAIKOROPUPŪ SPRINGS, GOLDEN BAY.

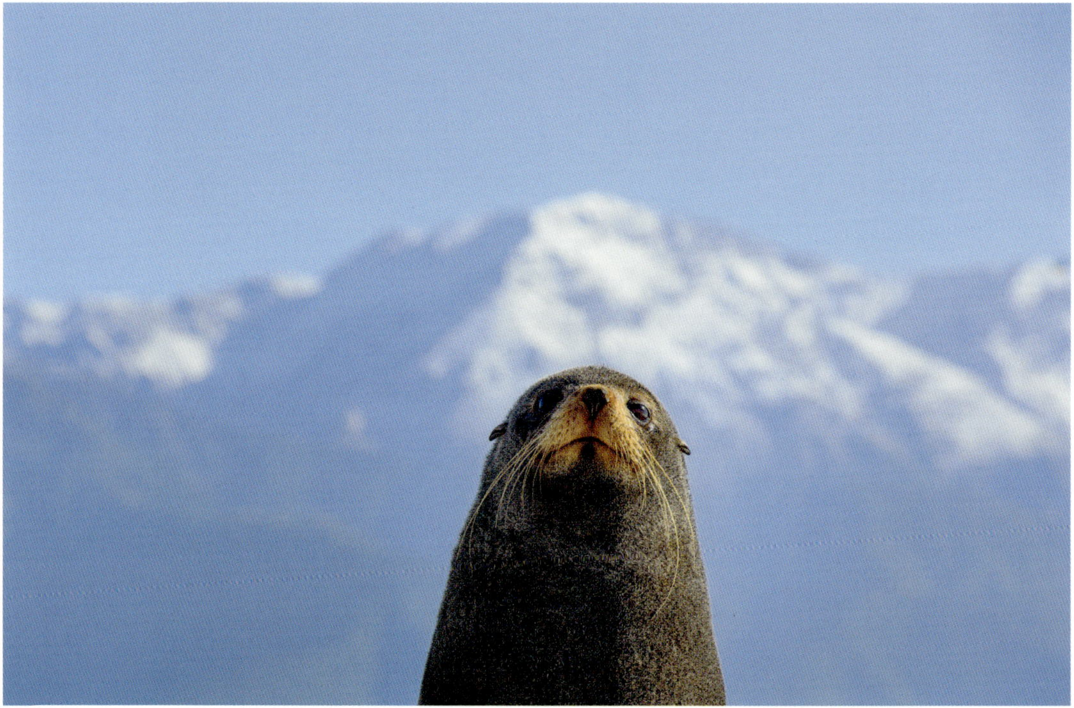

A curious fur seal, Kaikoura Coast.
opposite: The wintery Kaikoura Ranges meet the Pacific Ocean.

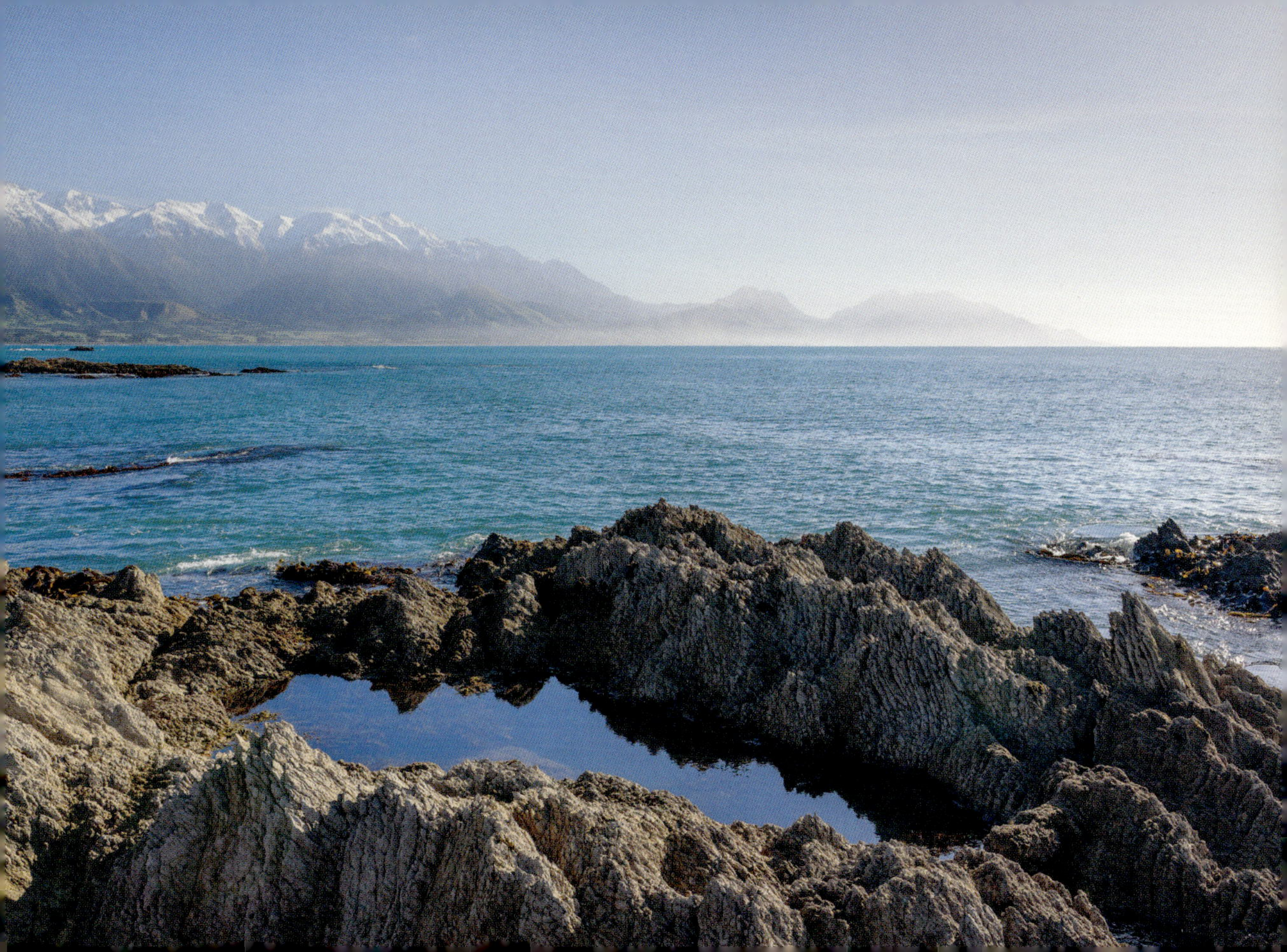

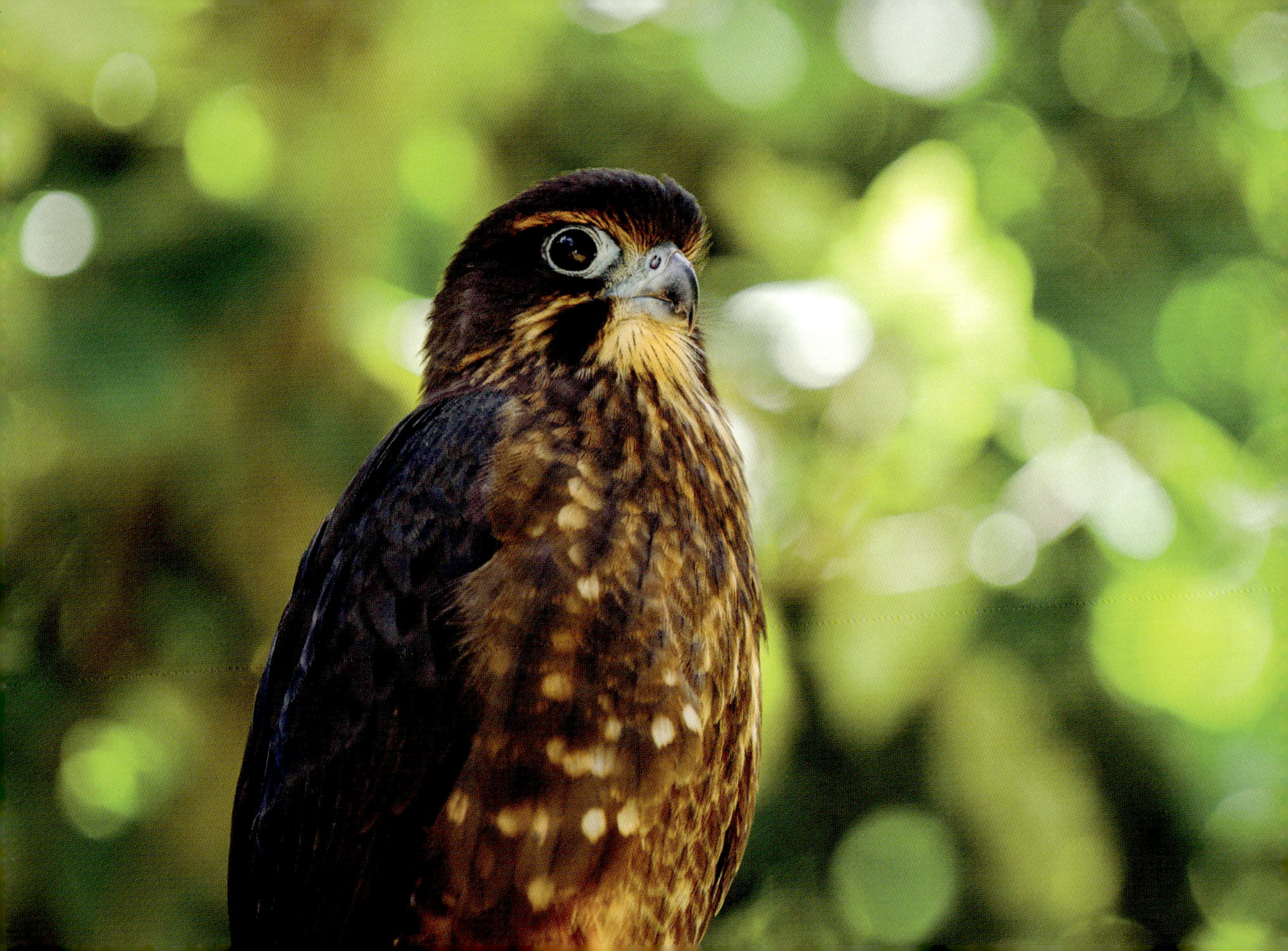

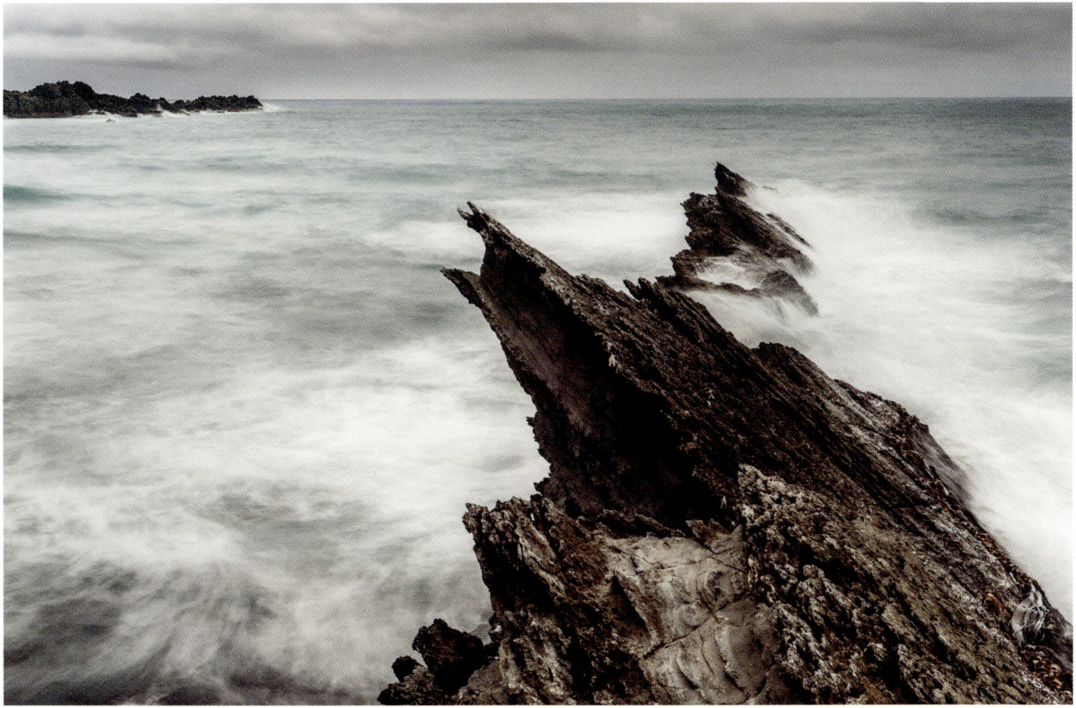

Rock formations on the coast, Cape Palliser, Wairarapa.
opposite: A close encounter with a native New Zealand Falcon
Zealandia Sanctuary, Wellington.

"Crossing the Tongariro"

Overlooking the Southern Crater and Mt Ngauruhoe.

The Central Plateau is a wild, untouched wilderness that is frequented by many every year. The Tongariro Crossing makes this land highly accessible. Whilst proving to be one of the greatest day walks in the world, it is also one of the most dangerous.

The day hike takes you through the centre of the North Island's volcanic geography. The steep, arduous walk up the Devil's Staircase to the Southern Crater is thigh burning, but once there you stand at the foot of one of New Zealand's most recognisable volcanic cones, Mt Ngauruhoe.

Whilst many choose to attempt to scale Mt Ngauruhoe before continuing on to complete the rest of the crossing, this makes for an even more challenging day. Its scree clad steep slopes make for hard work, but the view is rewarding for those who persist - but don't let time pass you by, you are not yet half way on your adventure.

This land is dangerous, and many incidents occur here every year. If you choose to cross the Tongariro, be prepared, listen to the locals, respect the land and the weather. It is a magical experience, but not at the expense of one's safety.

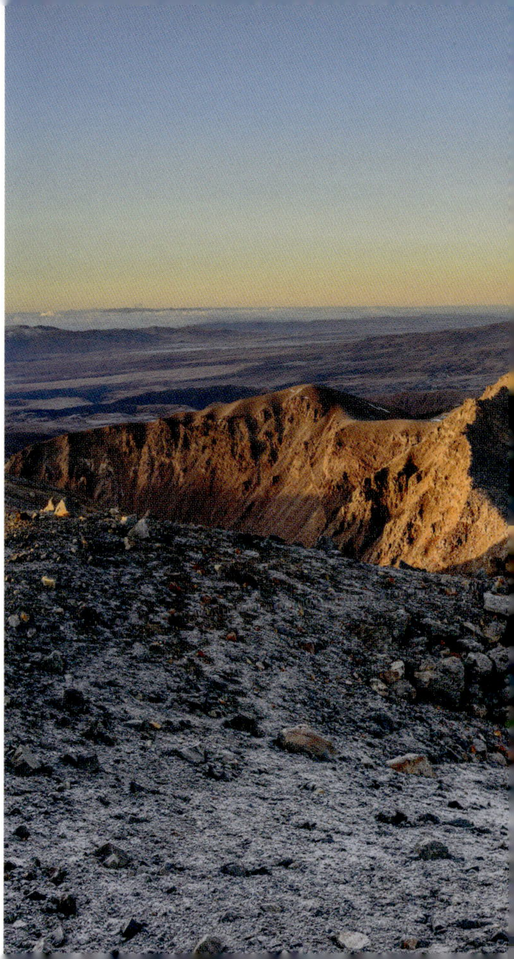

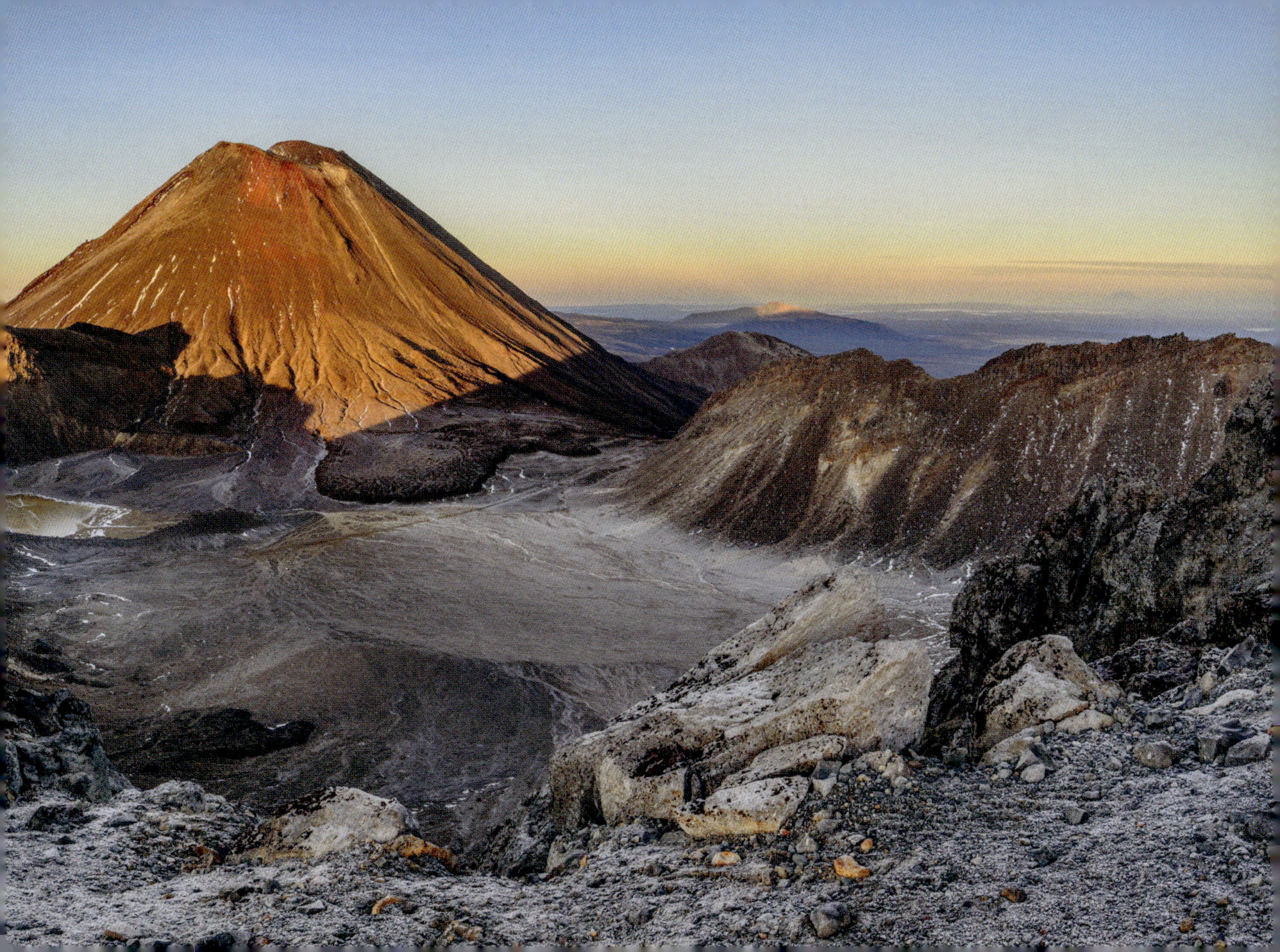

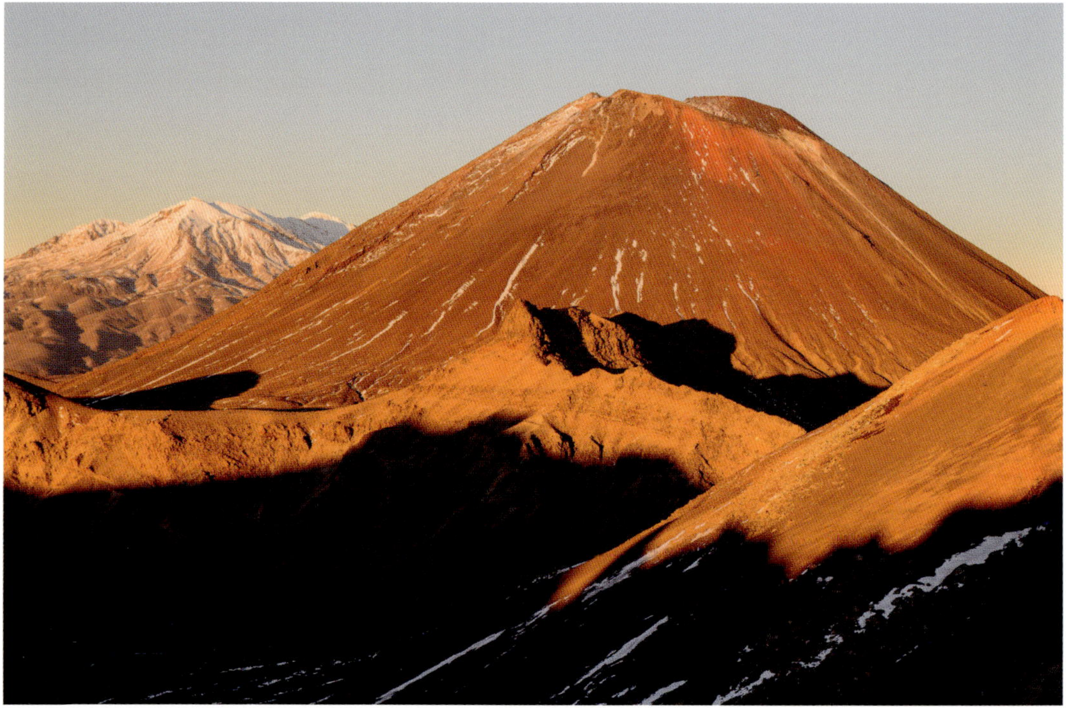

Mt Ngauruhoe and the snow capped Mt Ruapehu at first light, Tongariro National Park.
opposite: The Red Crater, Tongariro Crossing, Tongariro National Park.

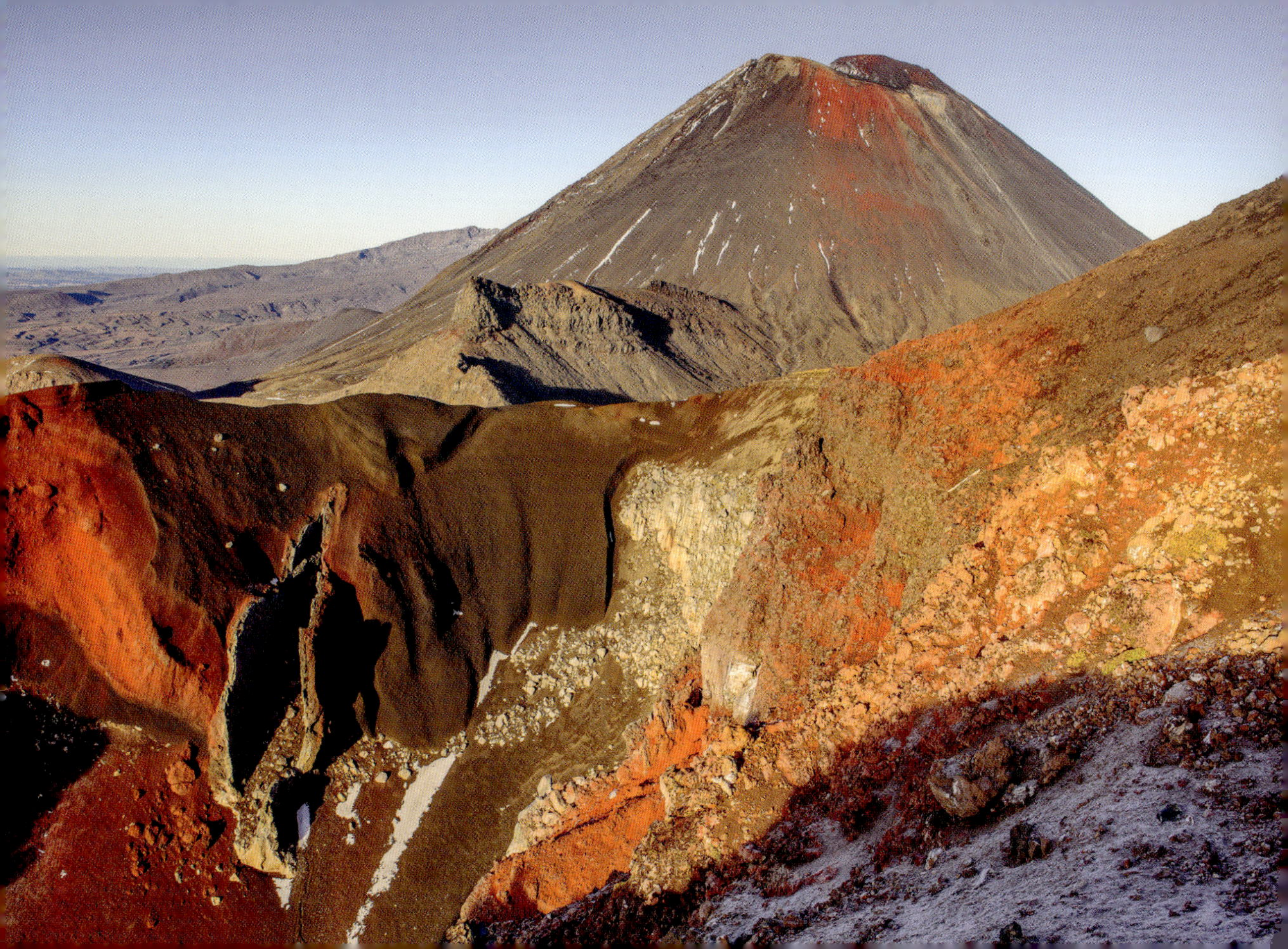

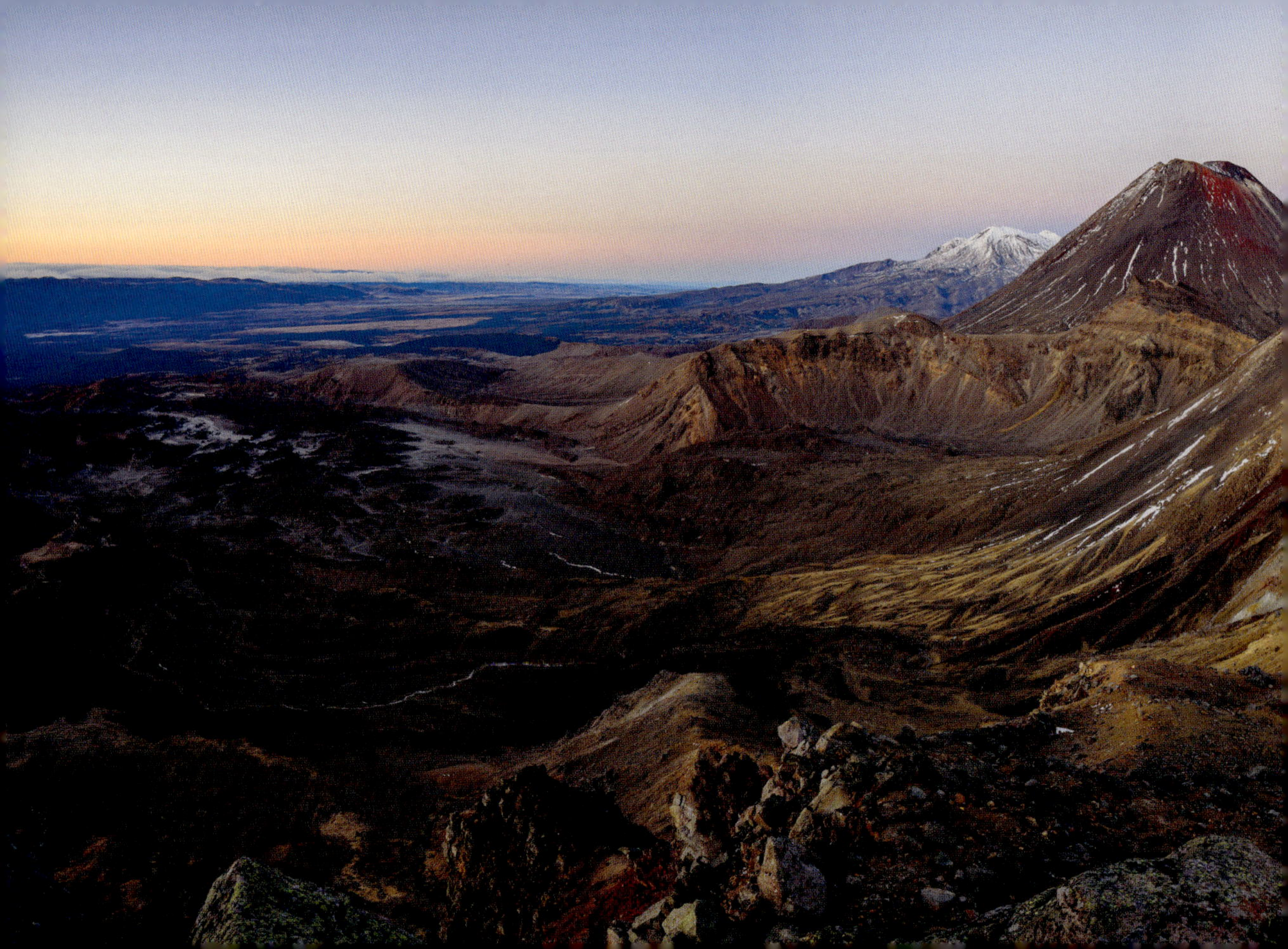

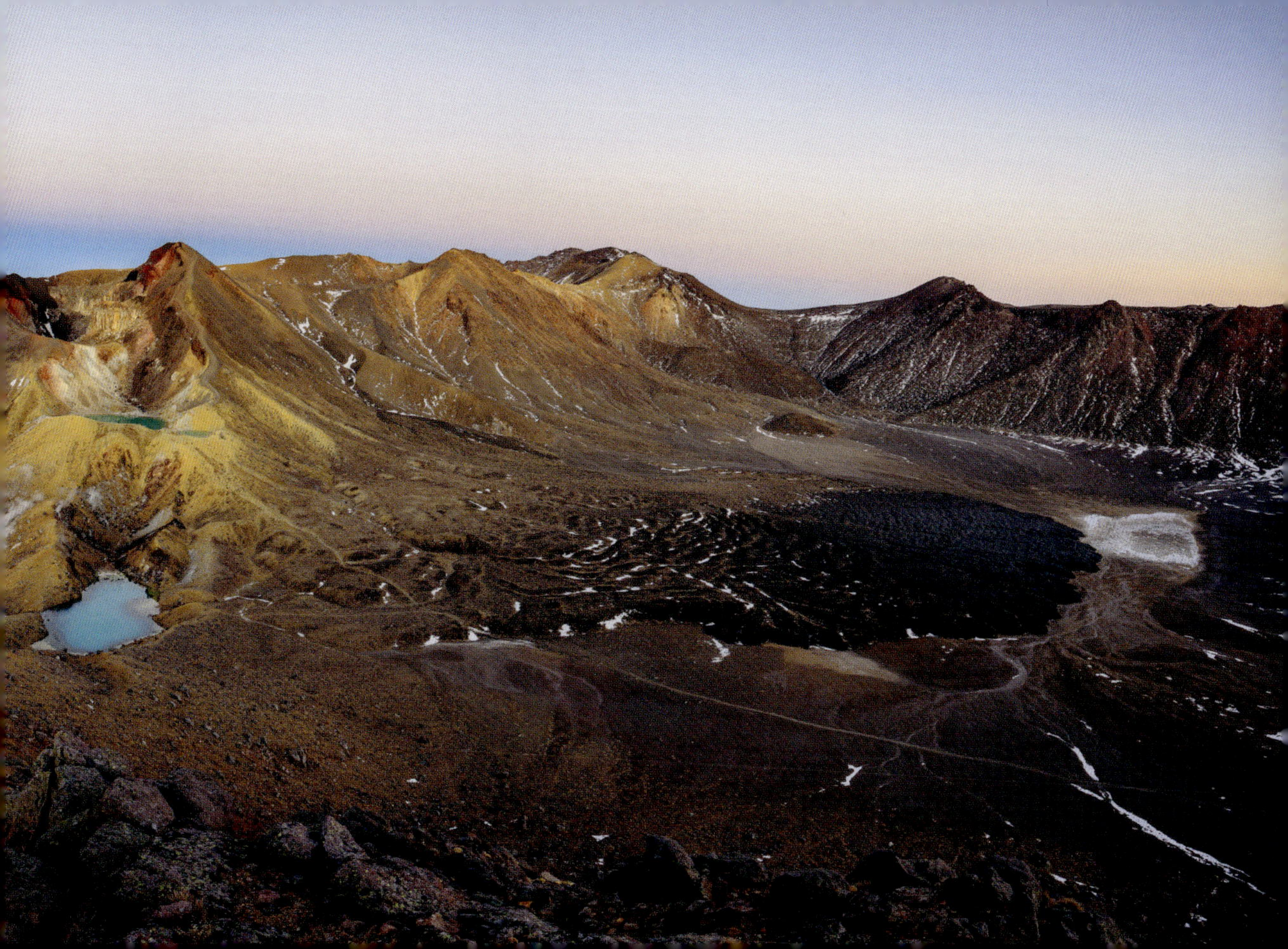

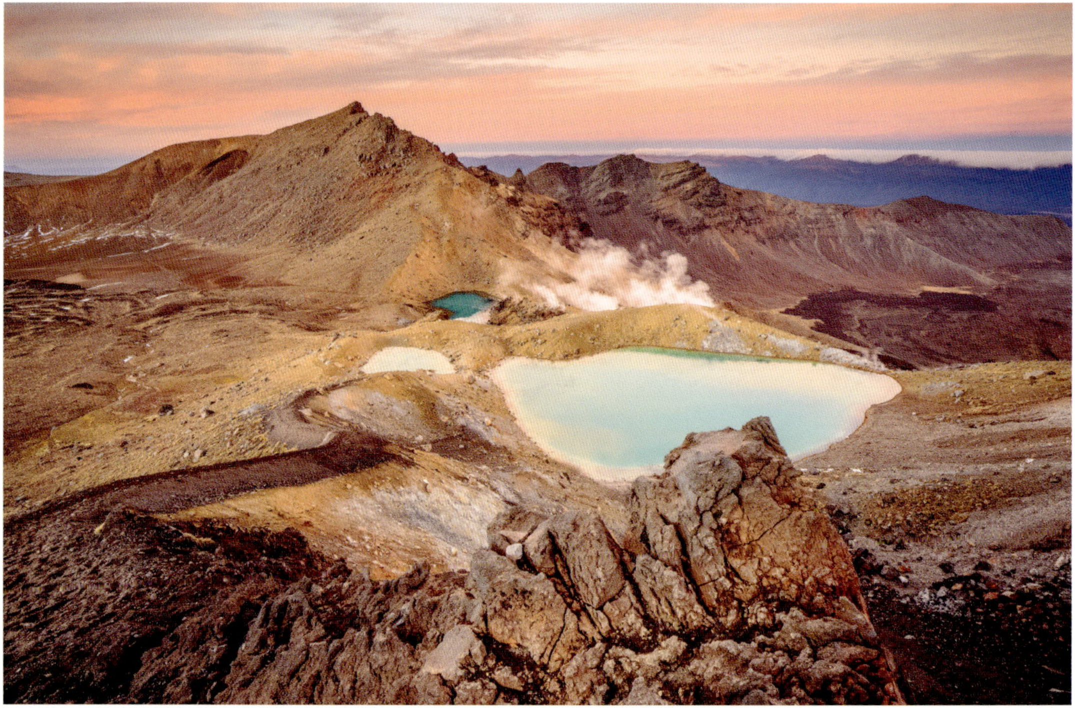

The Emerald Lakes at sunset, Tongariro Crossing, Tongariro National Park.
Previous: The Volcanic Plateau - Mt Ruapehu, Mt Ngauruhoe, the Red Crater, Mt Tongariro, The Oturere valley (left) and the Central Crater (right).

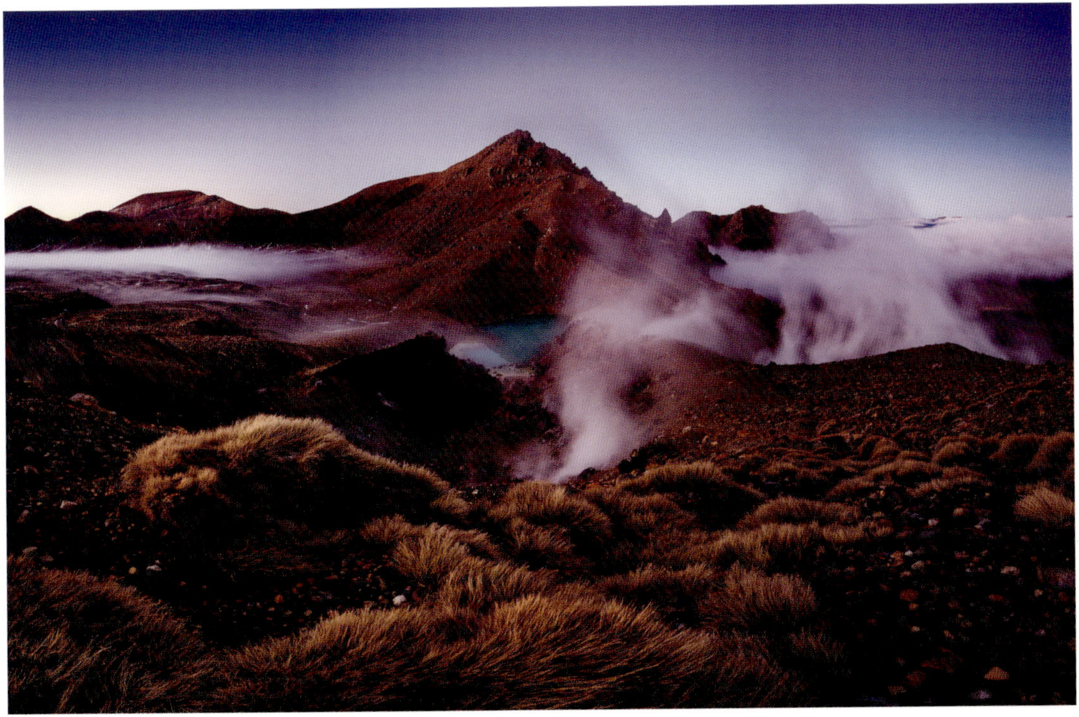

Night falls over the geothermal vents surrounding the Emerald Lakes,
as mist begins to fill the Central Crater, Tongariro Crossing.
overleaf: Overlooking the Blue Lake, Tongariro Crossing.

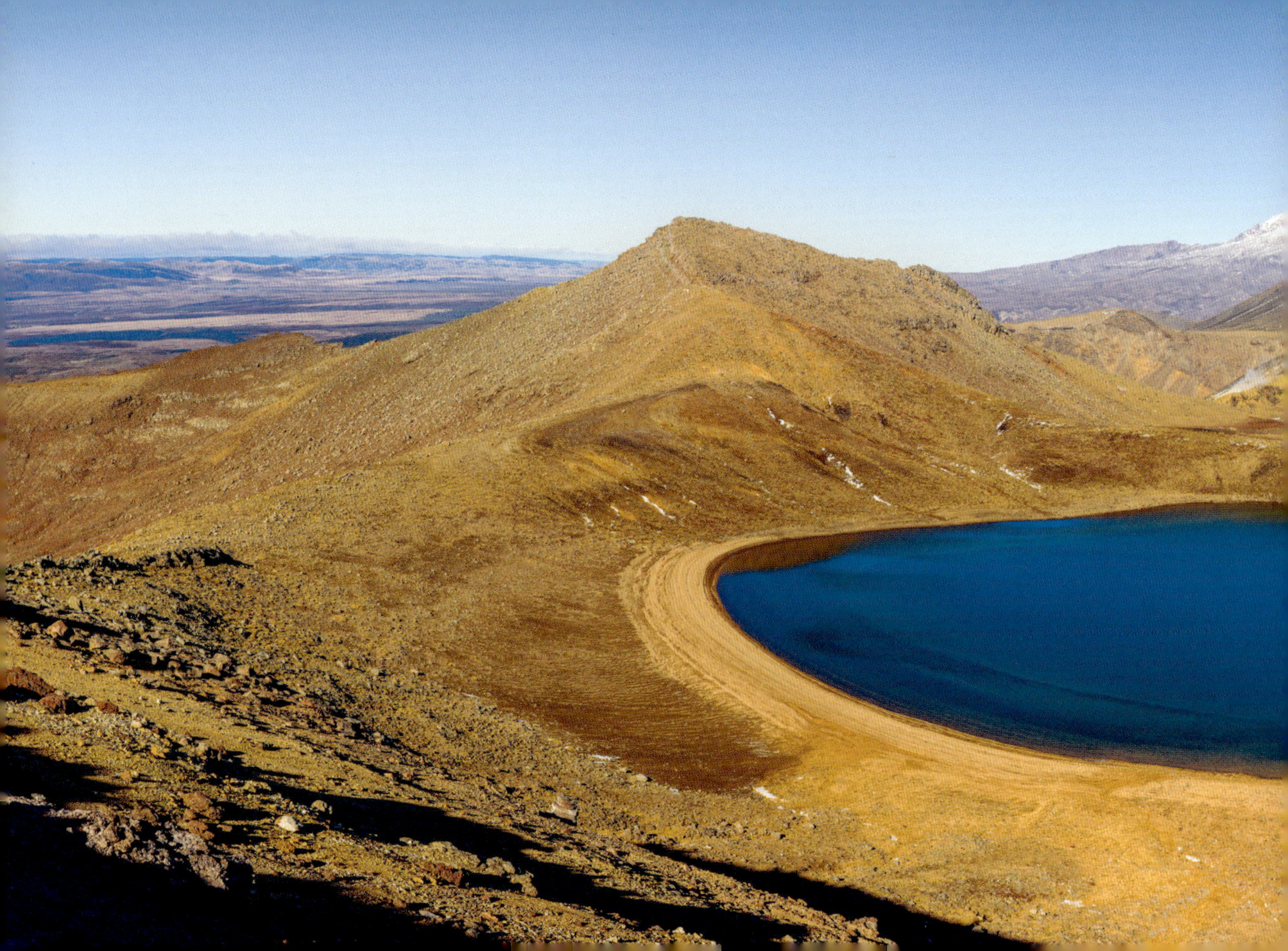

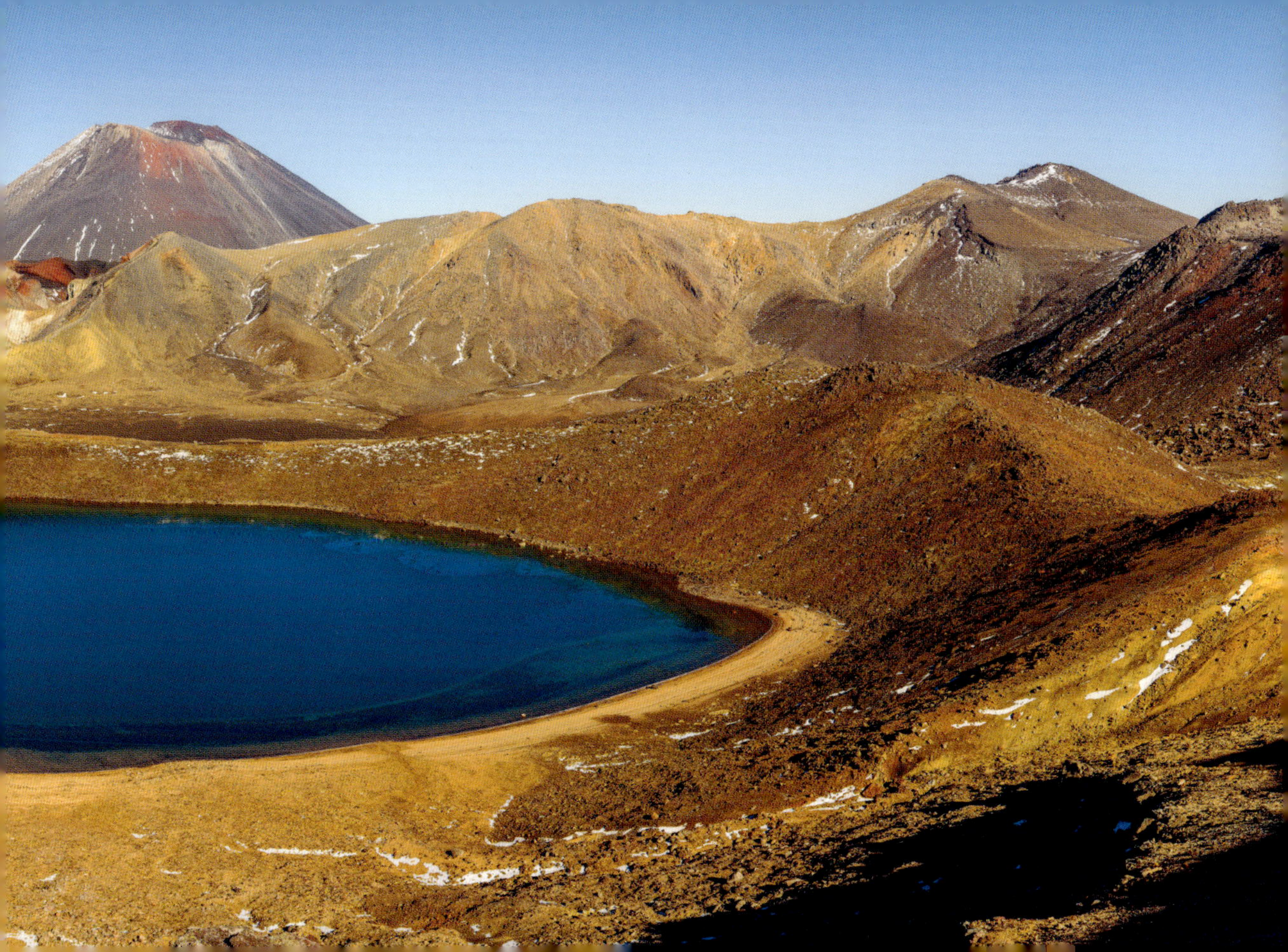

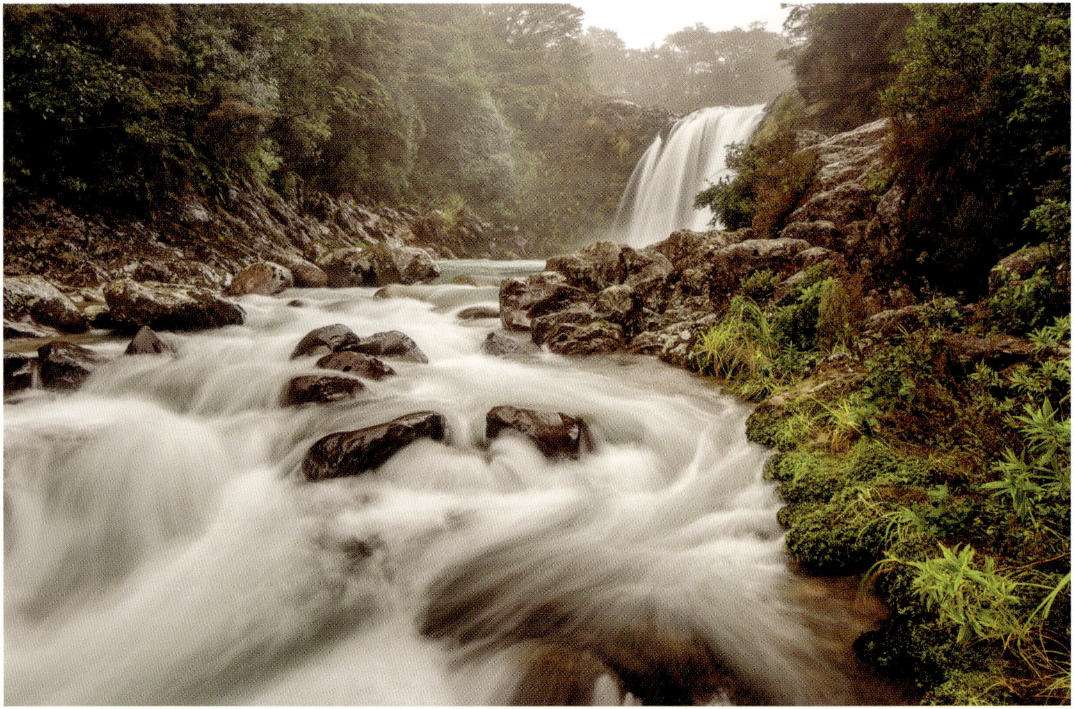

Pouring rain at Tawhai Falls, Tongariro National Park.
opposite: The sunkissed Te Whaiti-Nui-A-Toi canyon, Whirinaki Te Pua-a-Tāne Conservation Park, Bay of Plenty.

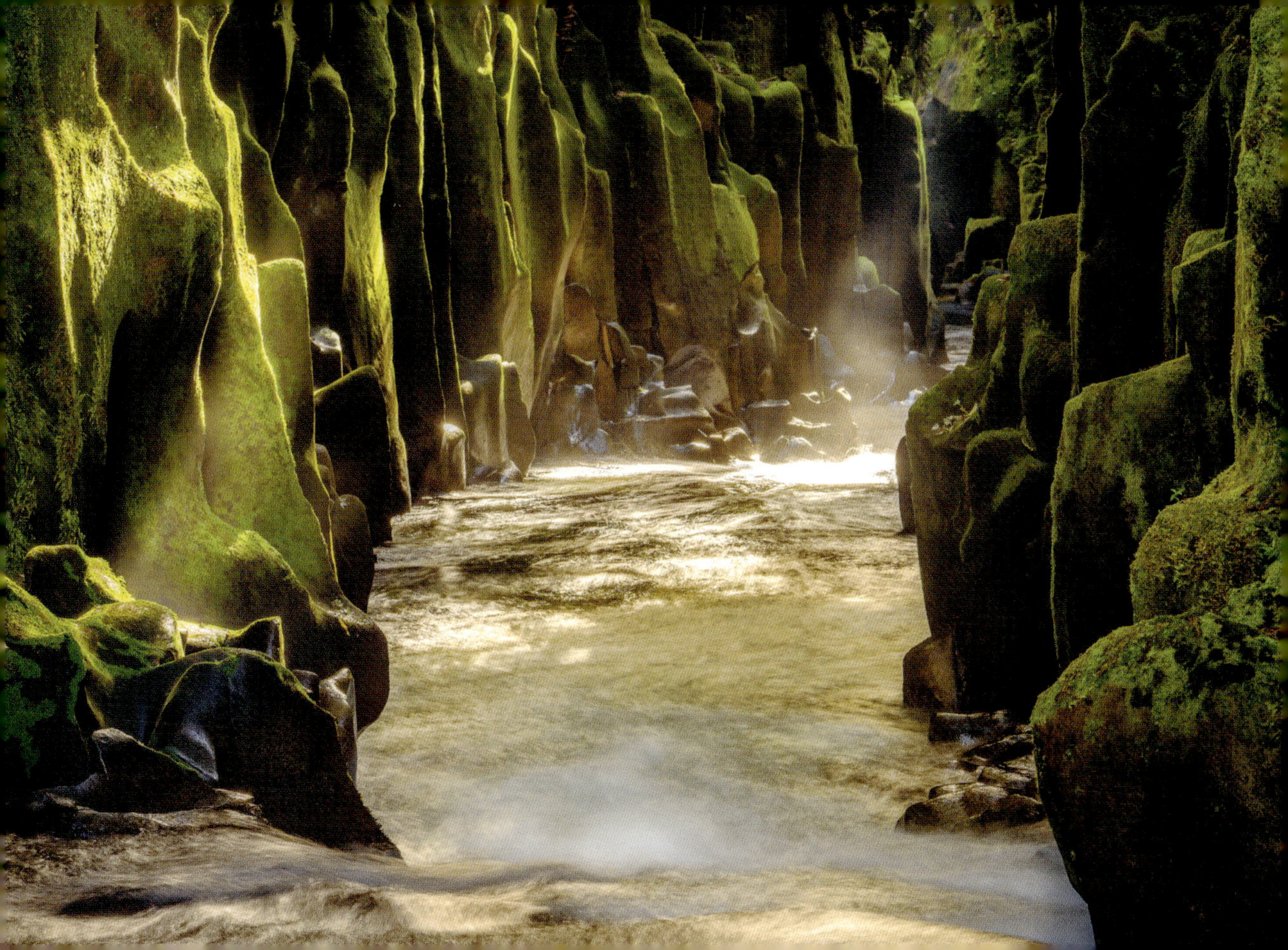

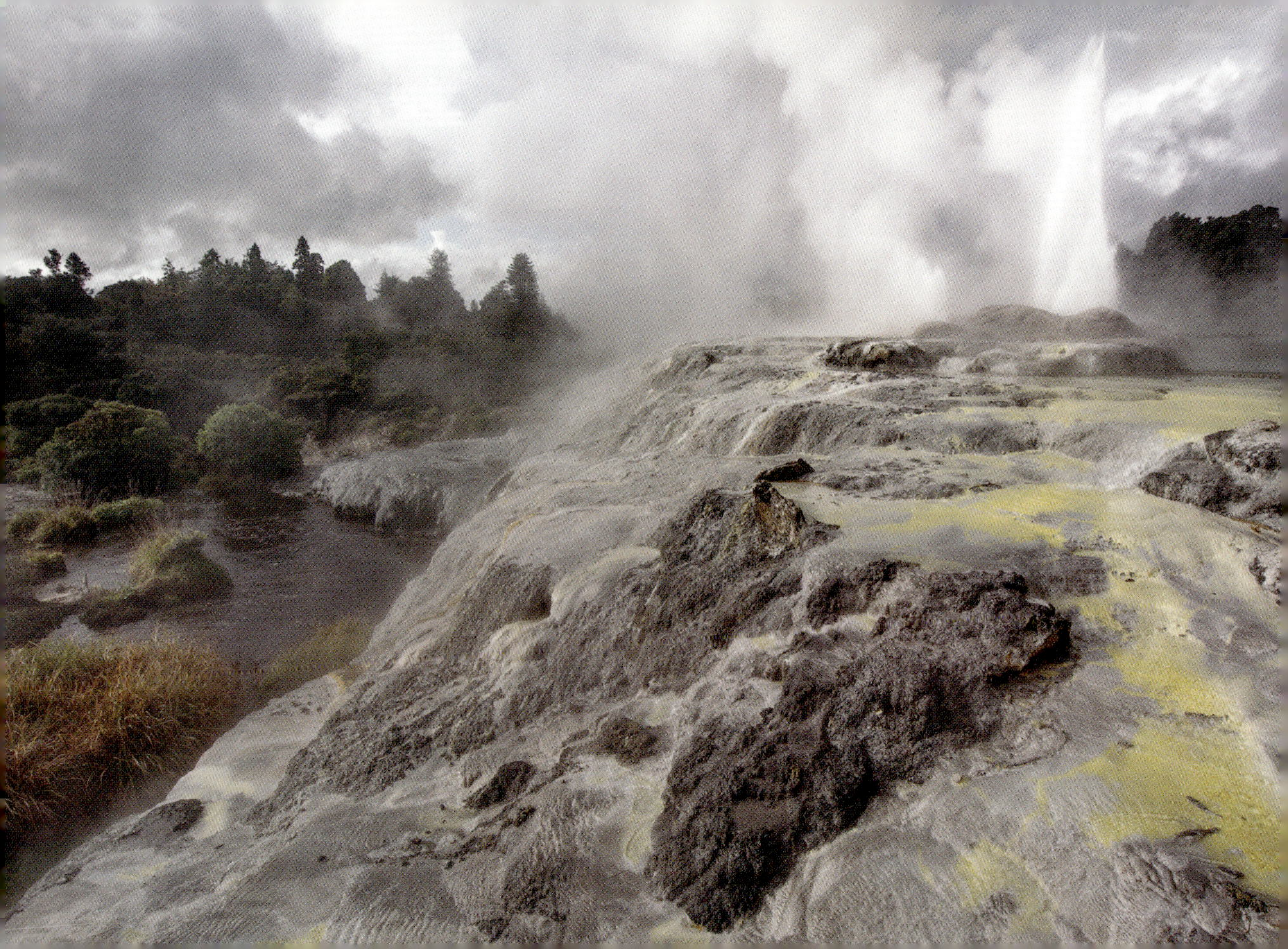

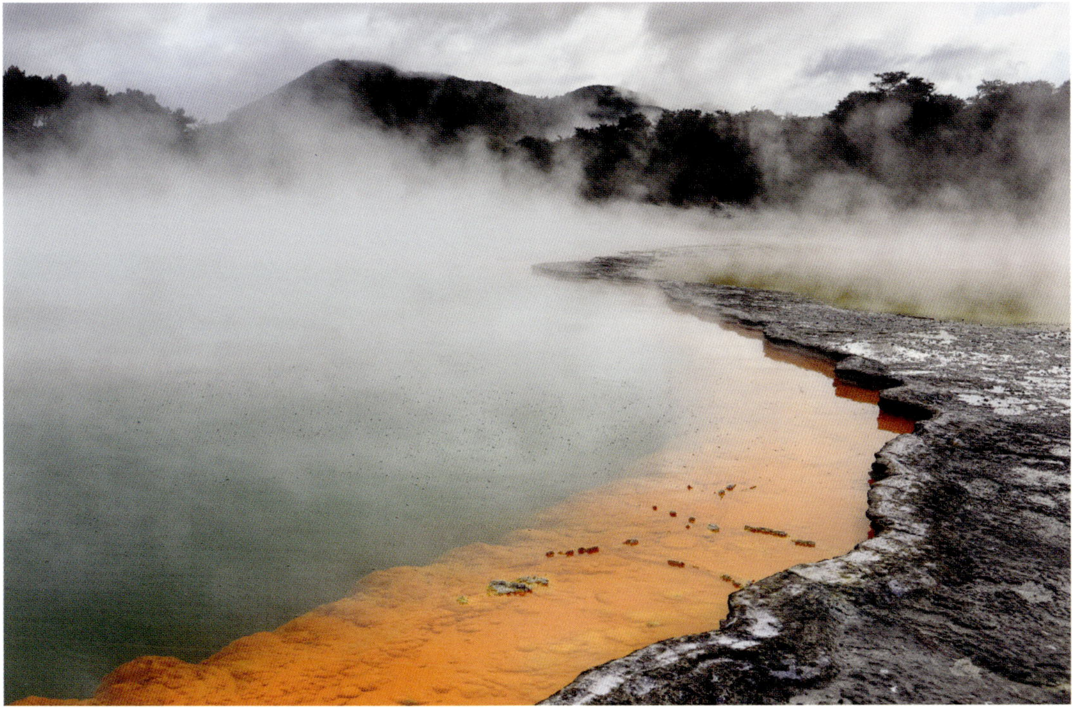

THE CHAMPAGNE POOL, WAI-O-TAPU GEOTHERMAL AREA, ROTORUA.
OPPOSITE: POHUTU GEYSER ERUPTING, TE WHAKAREWAREWA THERMAL VALLEY, ROTORUA.

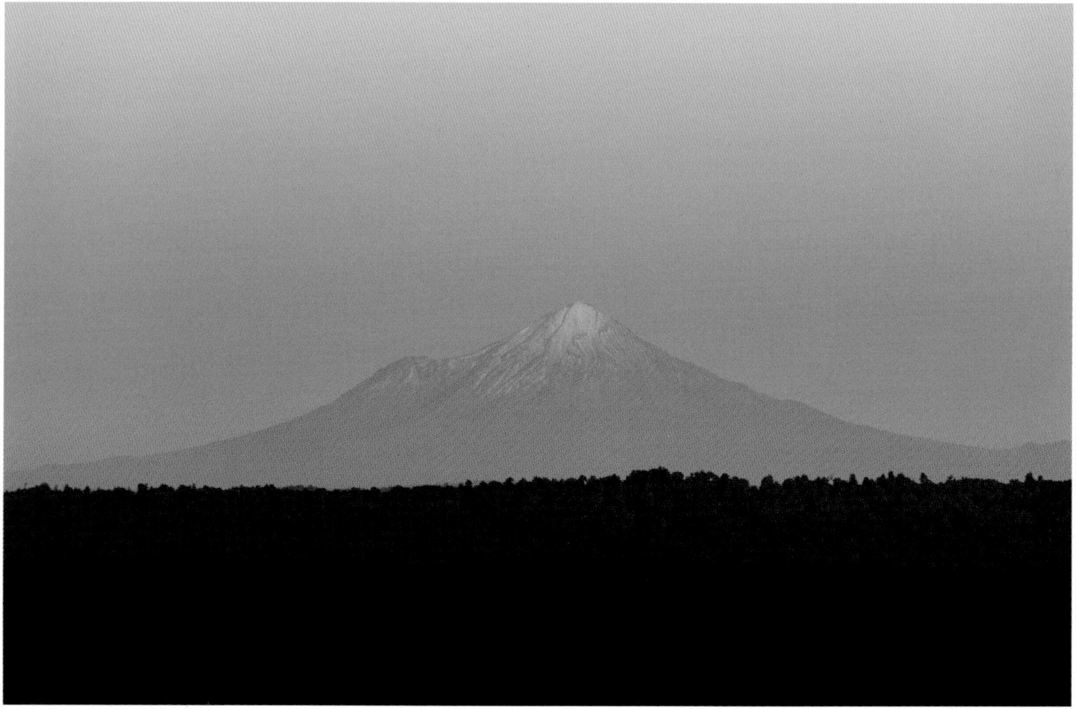

Mt Taranaki at dawn viewed from Tongariro National Park.
opposite: Afternoon light in the lush green Hikumutu Hills near Taumaranui.
overleaf: Morning mist in the hills near the Whanganui River.

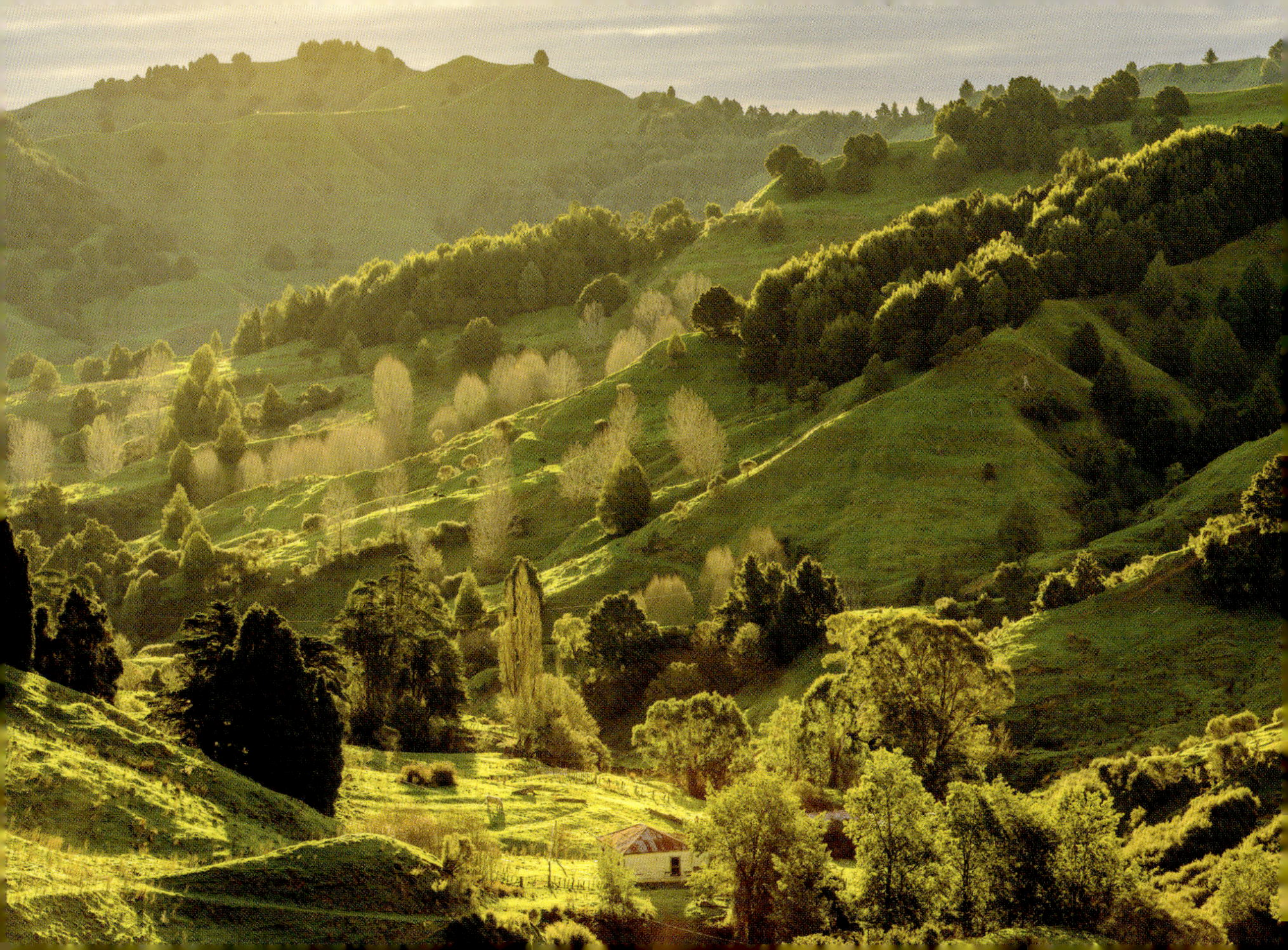

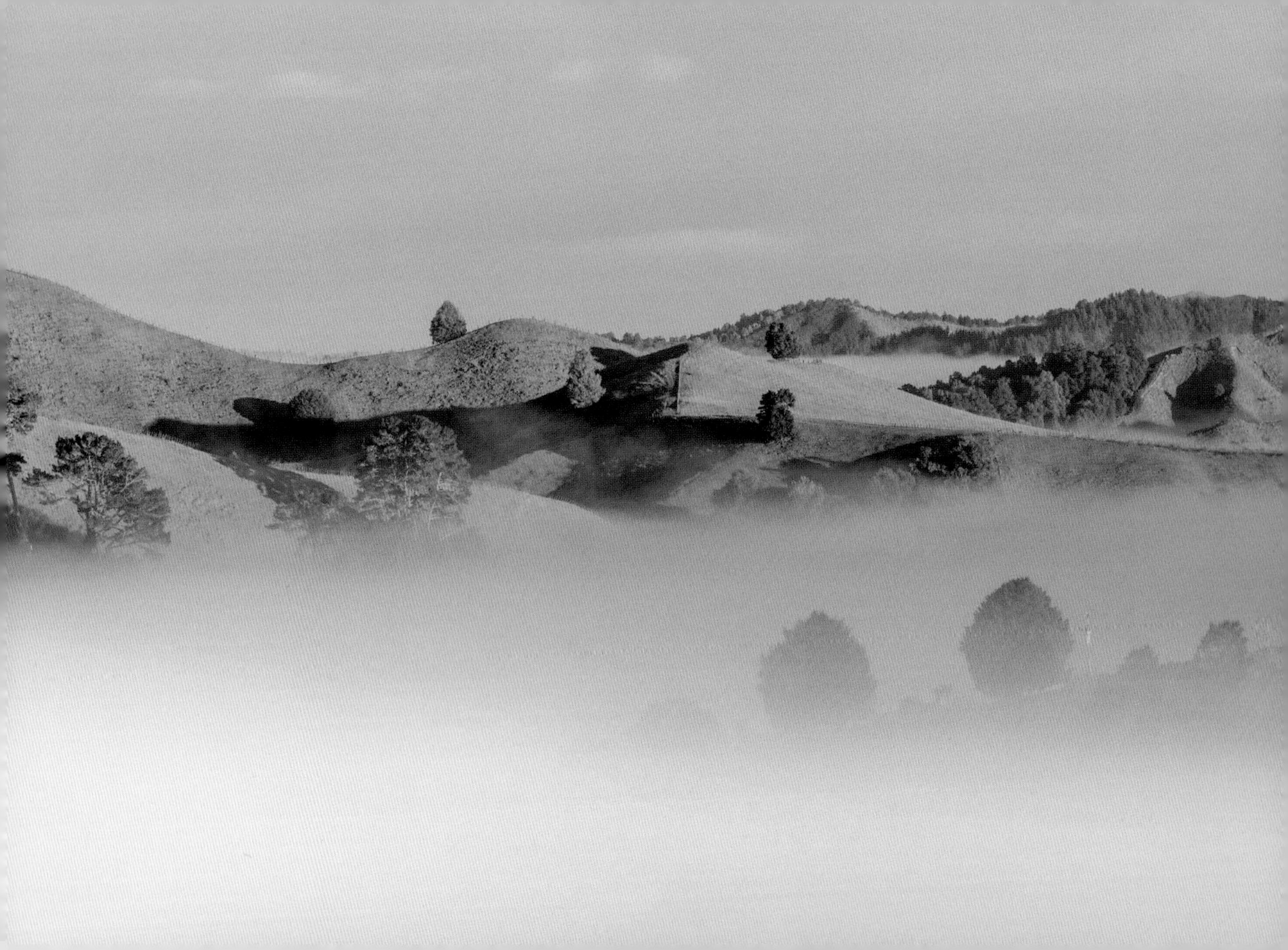

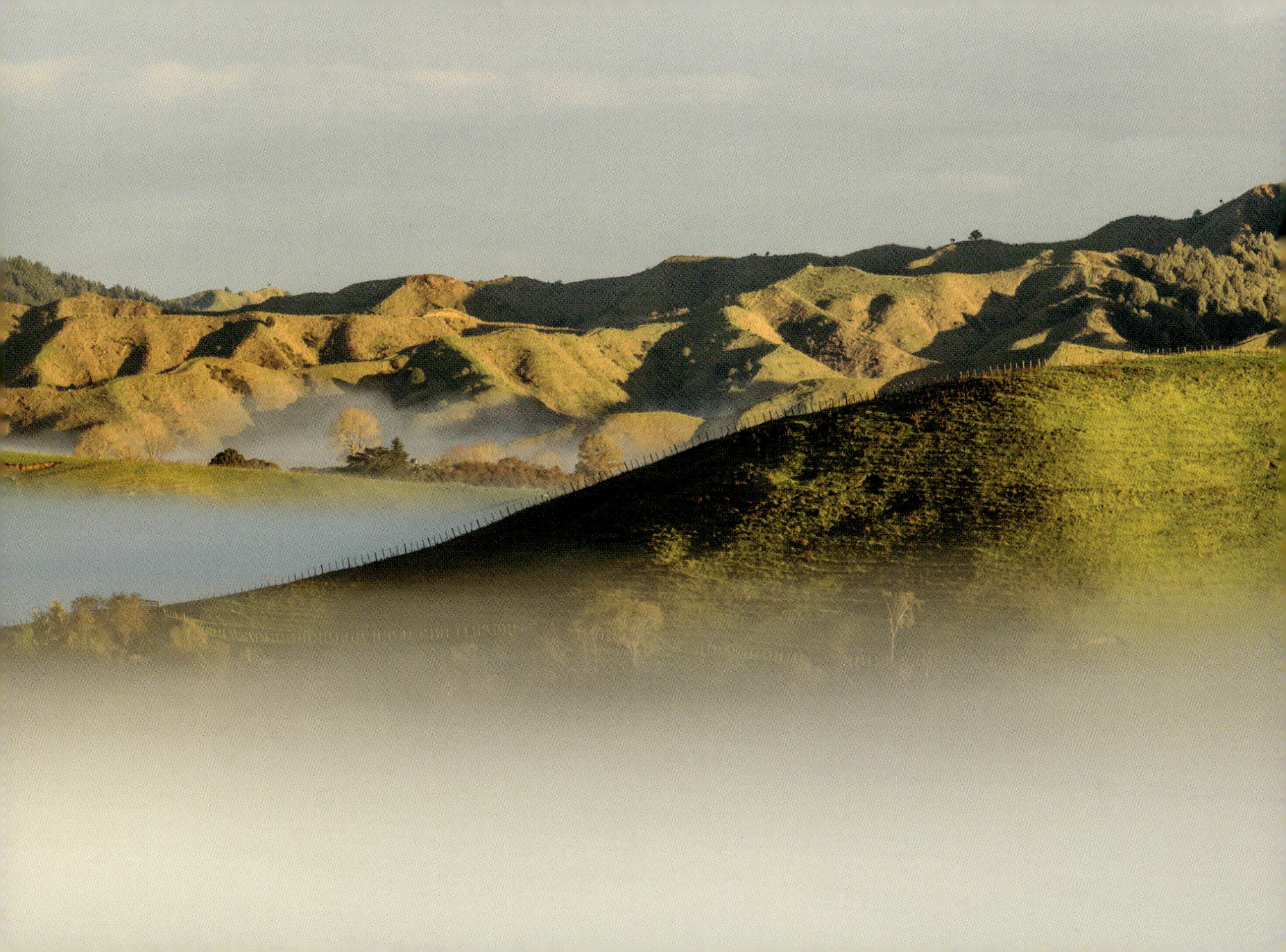

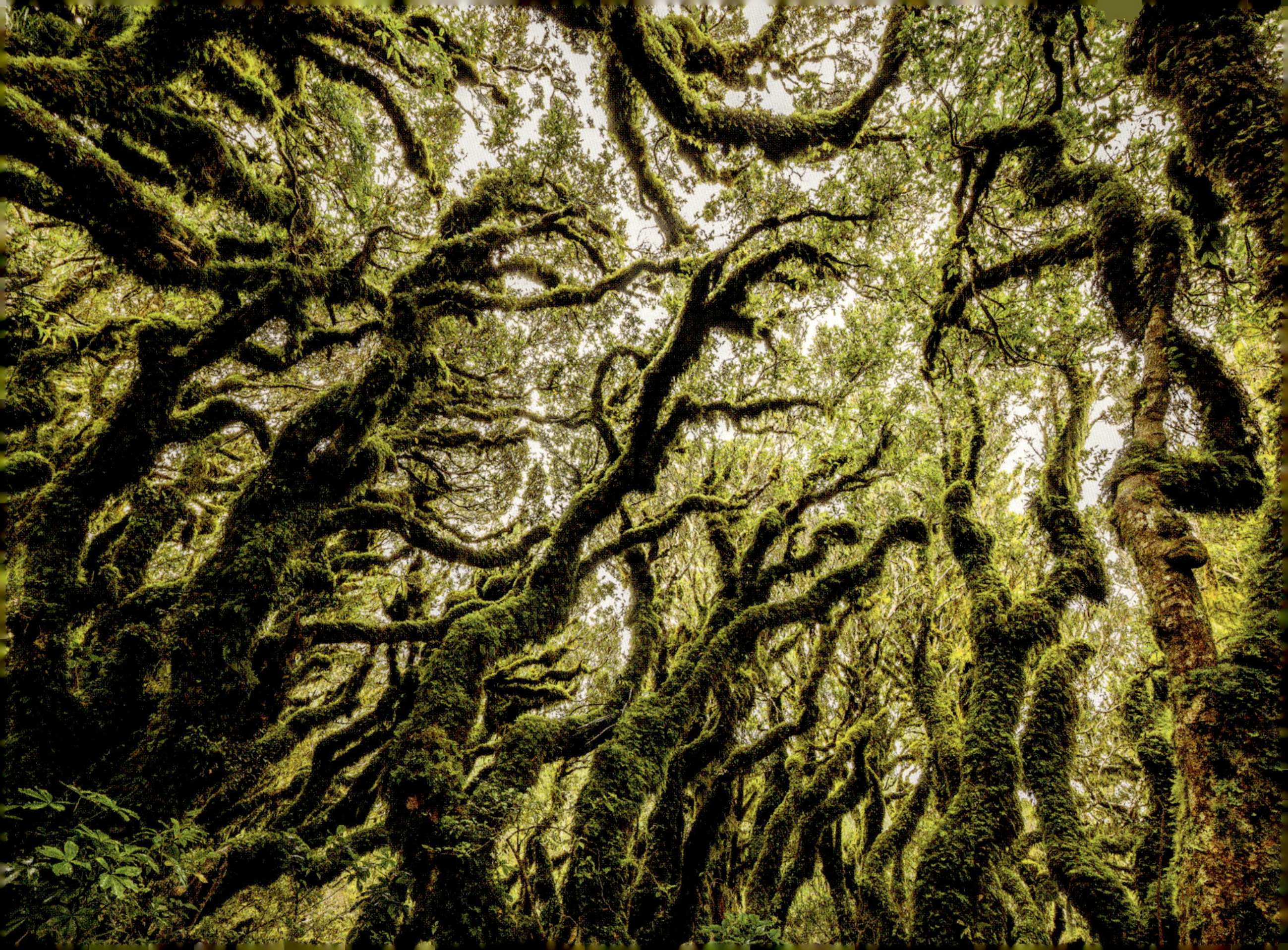

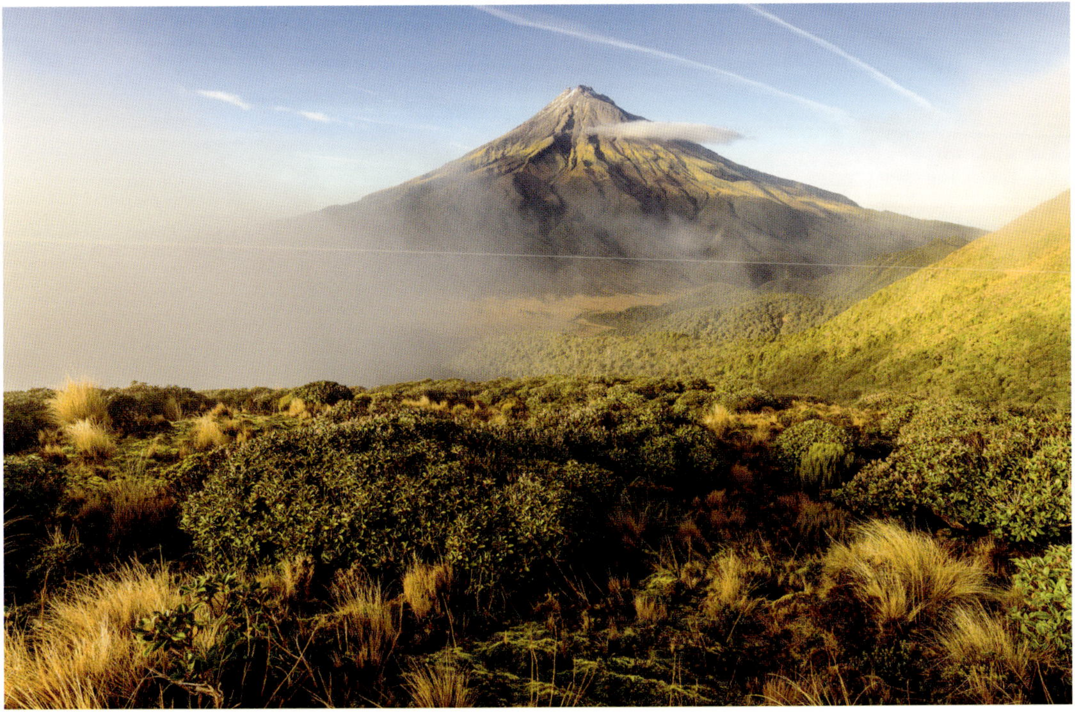

Mt Taranaki with the mist rolling in, Pouakai Circuit Track, Egmont National Park.
opposite: The Goblin Forest, Egmont National Park, Taranaki.
overleaf: Sunrise at the Pouakai Tarns, Egmont National Park.

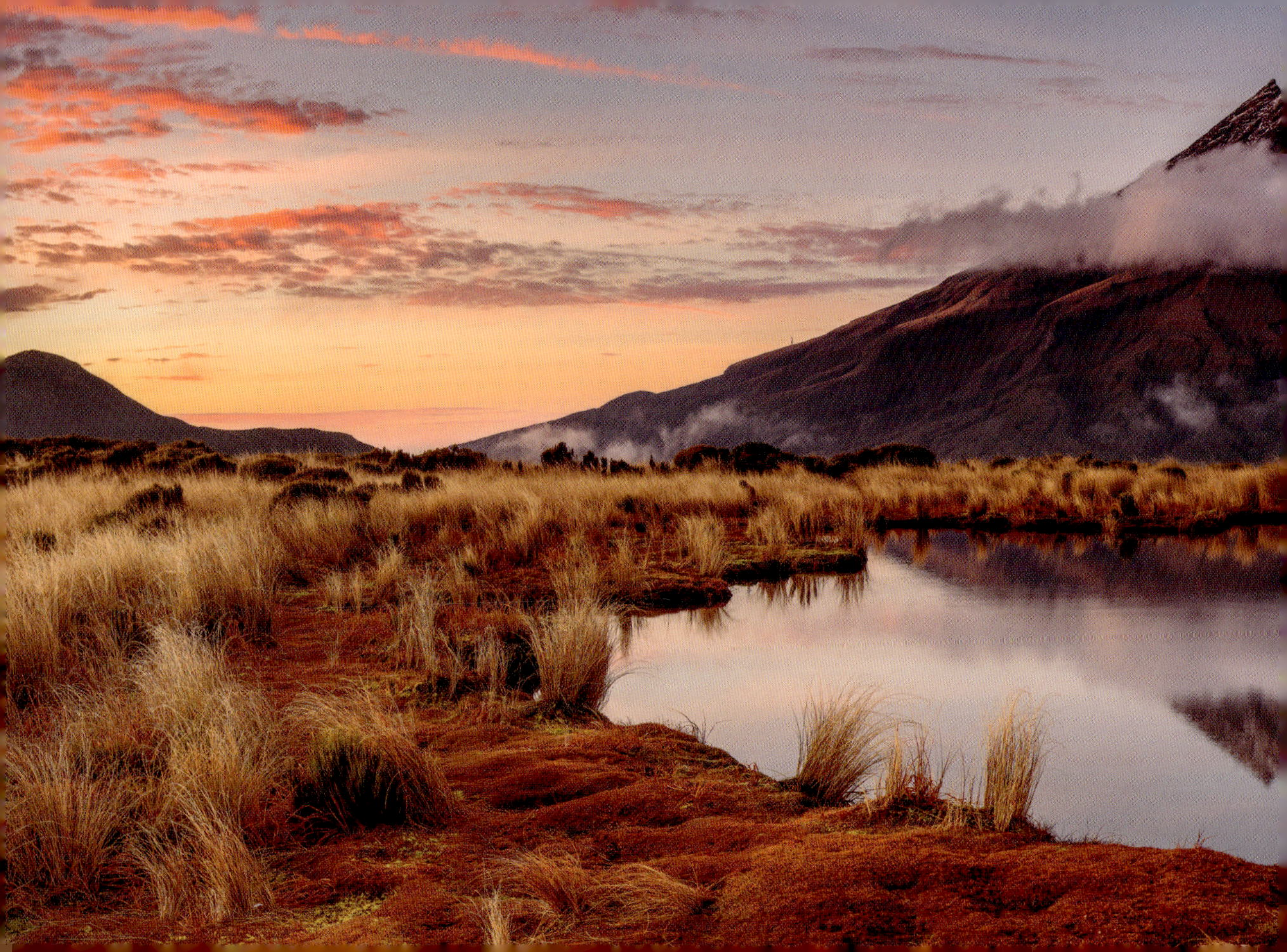

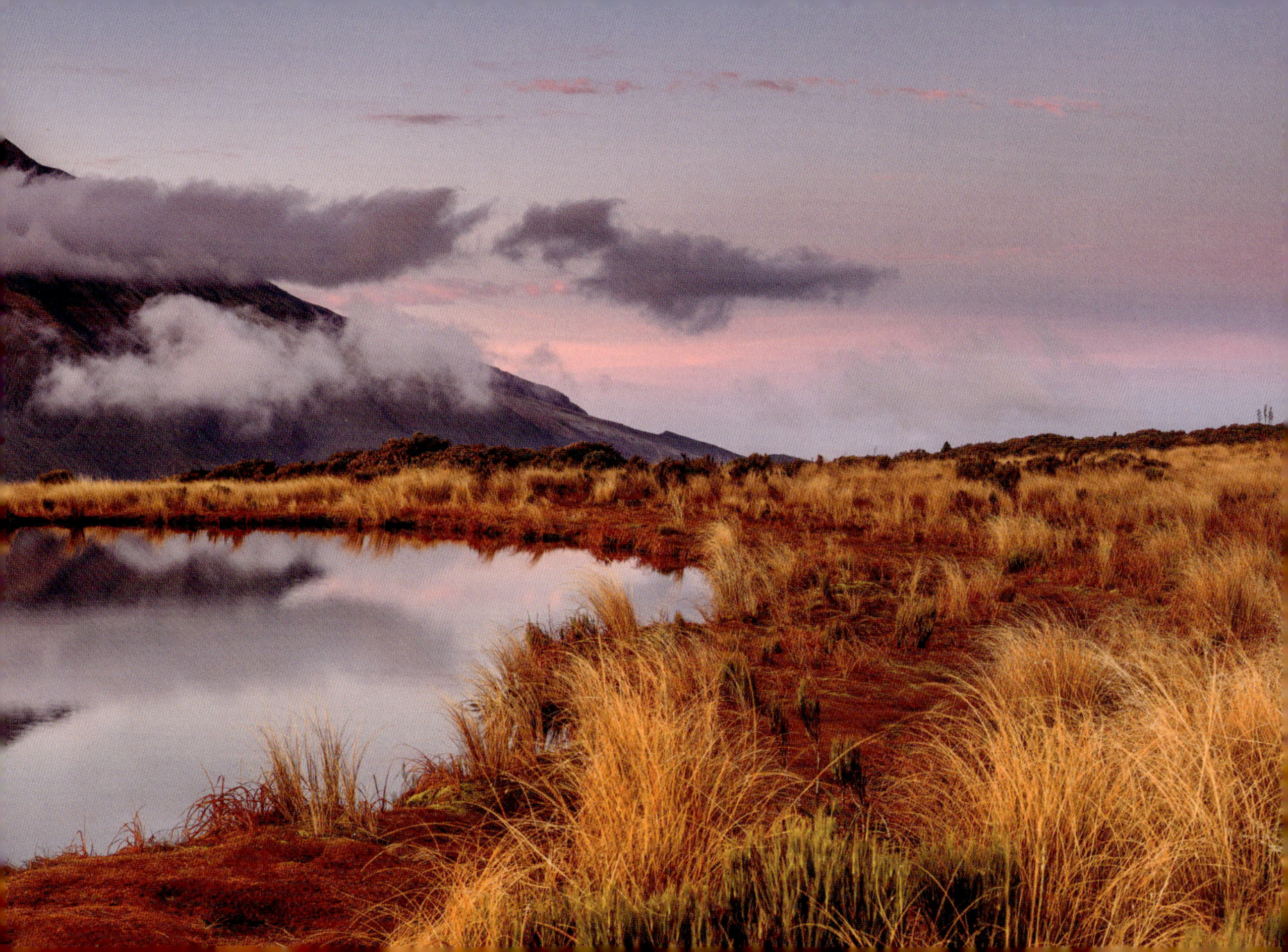

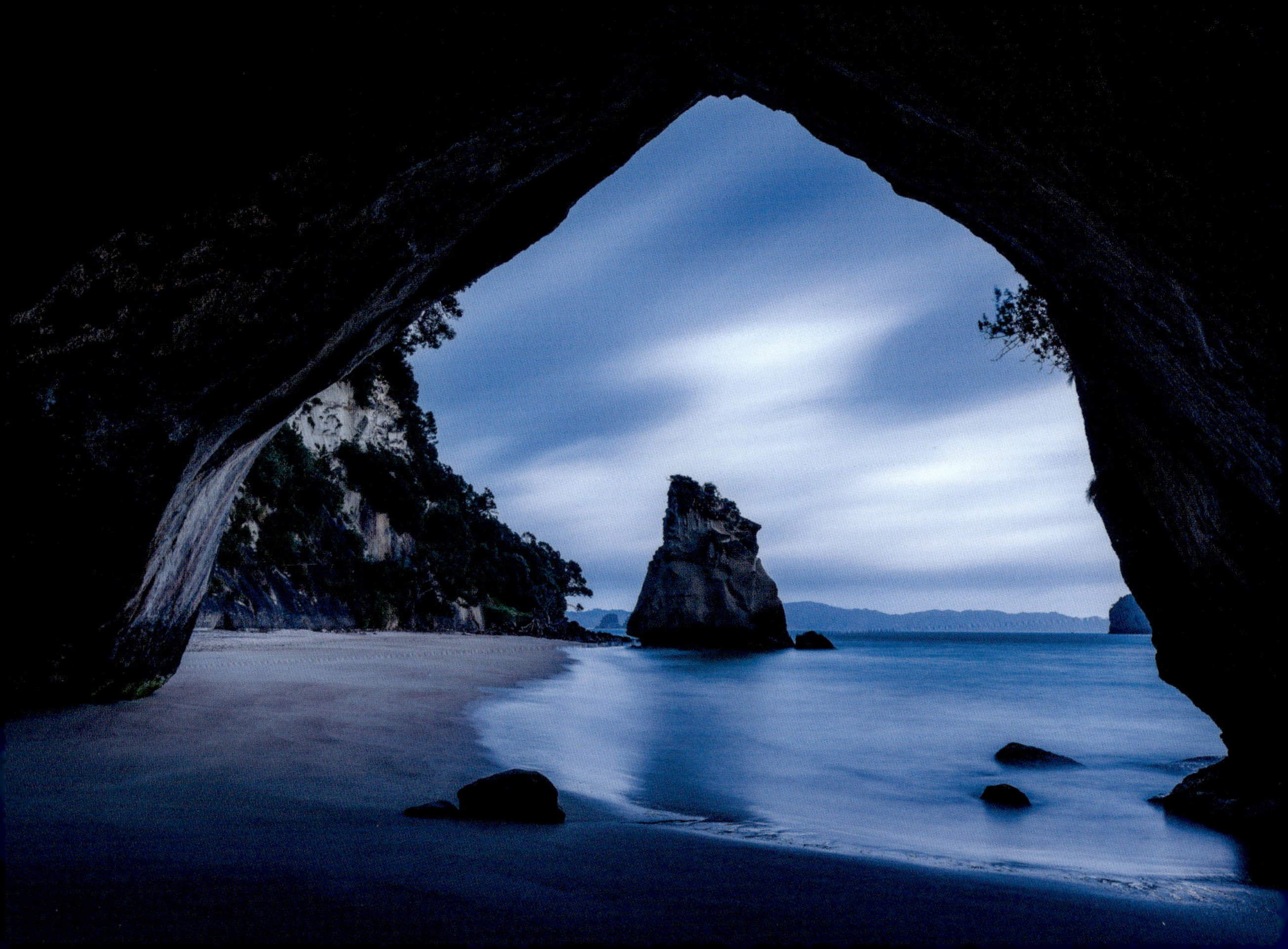

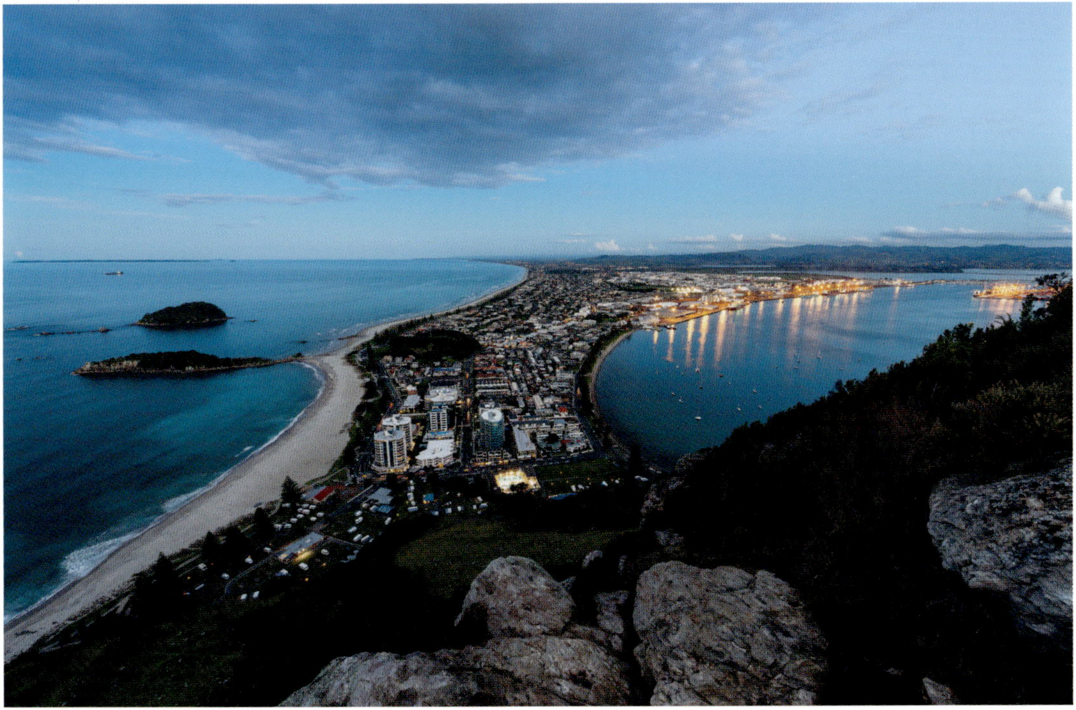

View from the summit of Mount Maunganui at dusk, Tauranga.
opposite: Dawn at Cathedral Cove, Coromandel Peninsula.

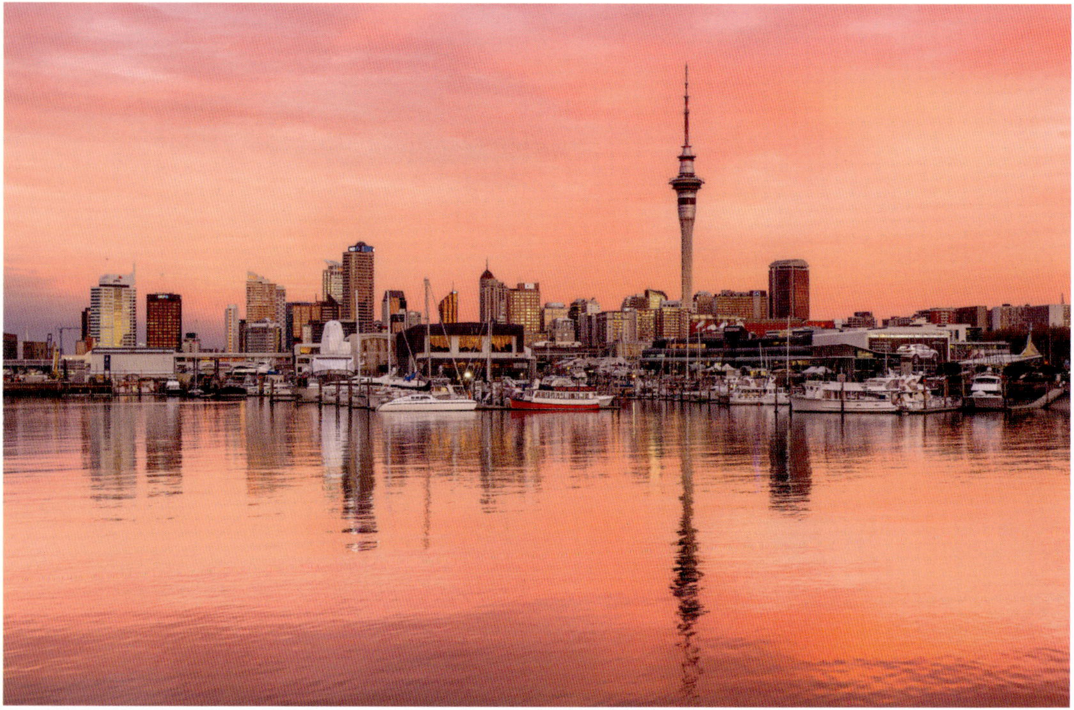

Sunset over the city skyline, St Marys Bay, Auckland.
opposite: Dusk over the Waitemata Harbour and downtown
Auckland as viewed from the Sky Tower.

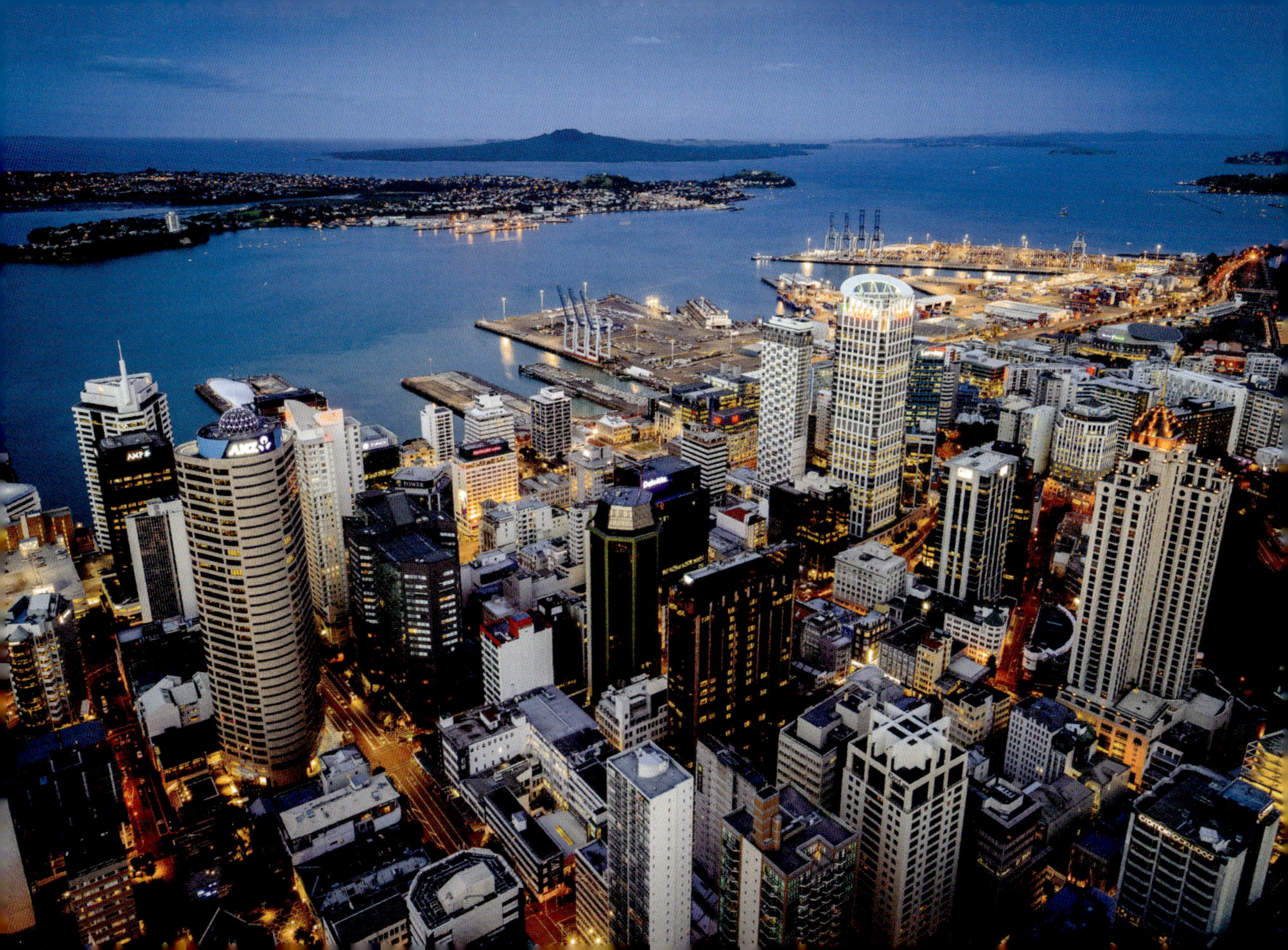
ANZ

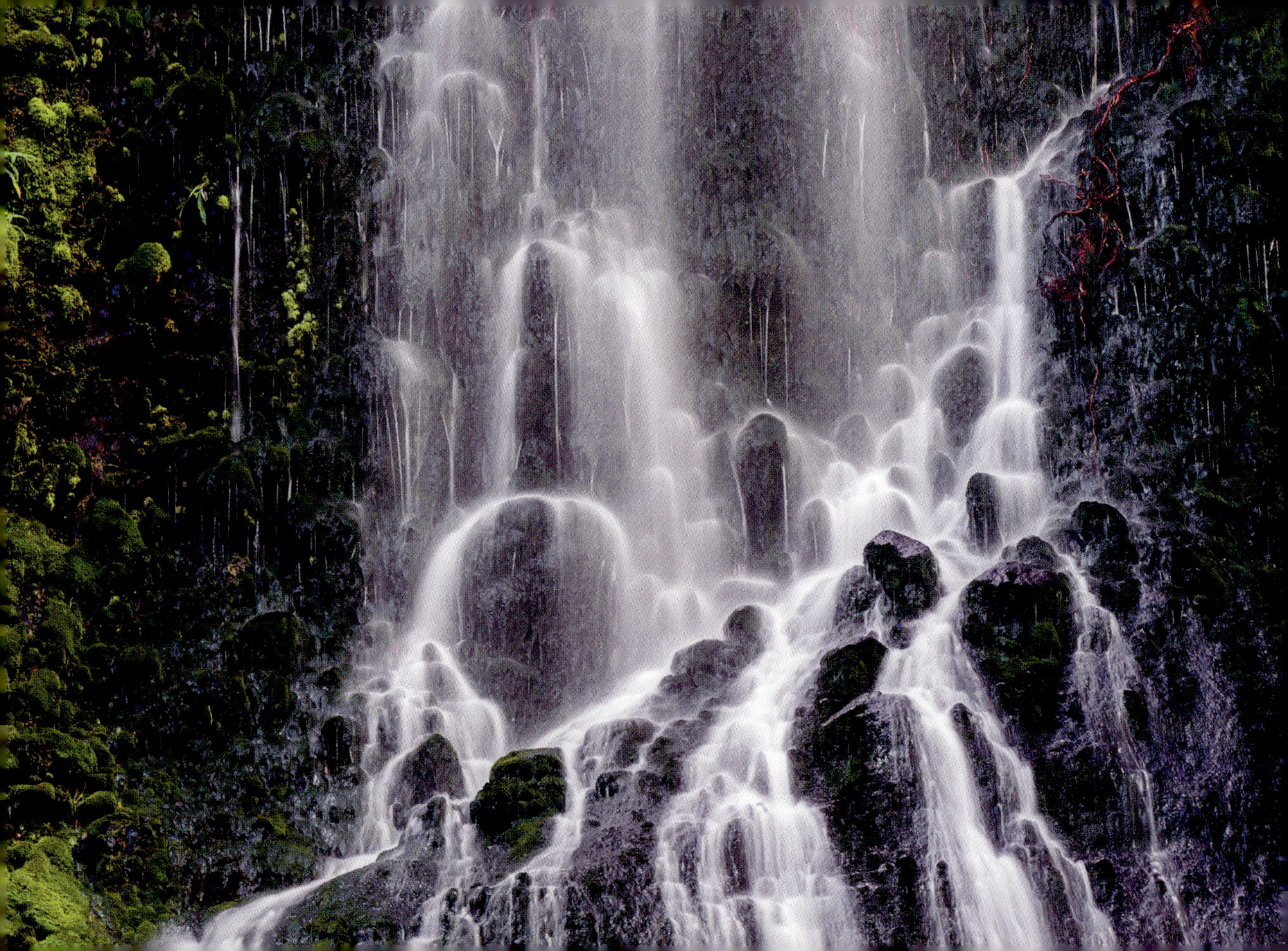

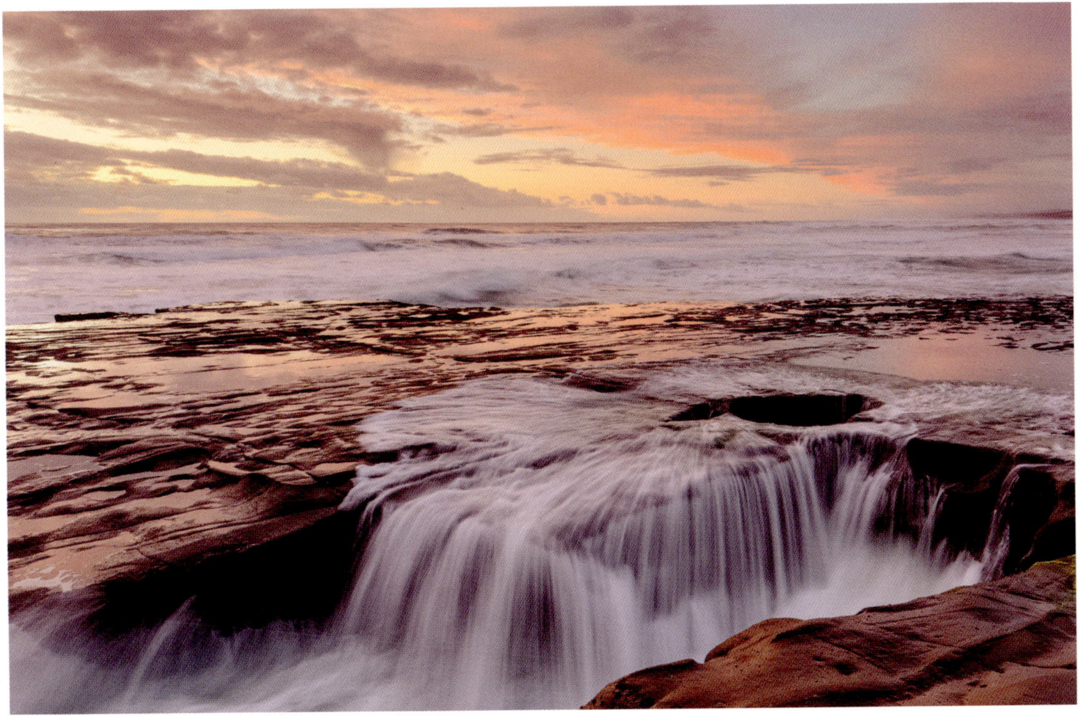

Sunset over the blowhole at Fisherman's Rock, Muriwai Beach, Auckland.
opposite: Kitekite Falls, Karekare, Waitakere Ranges, Auckland.

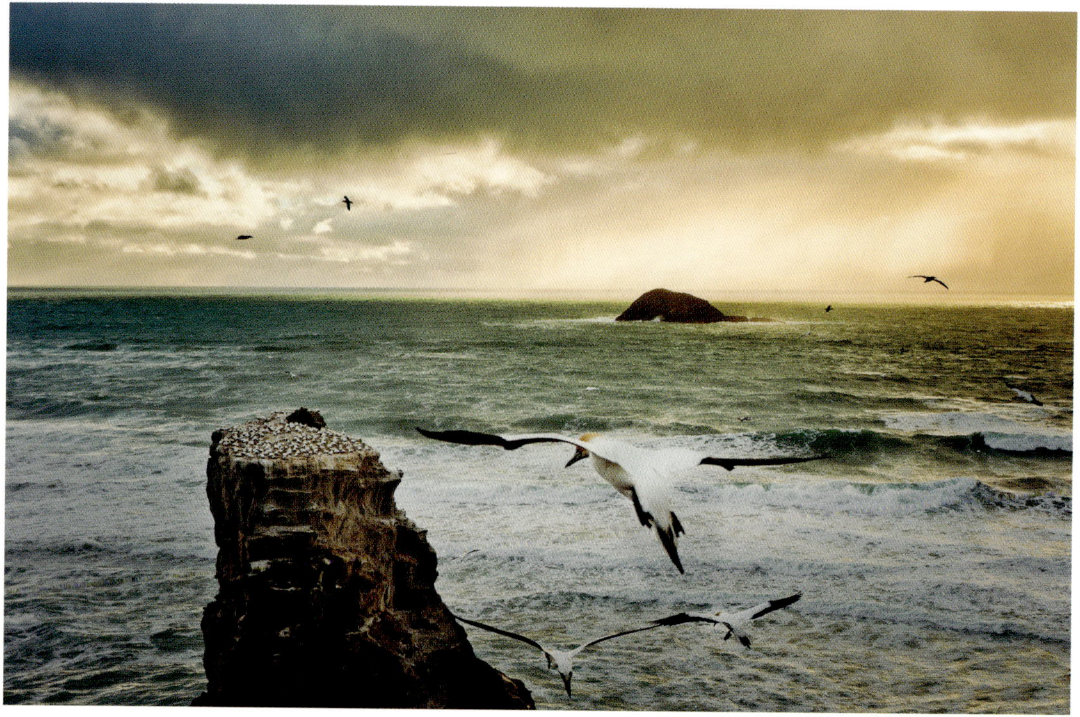

Gannets in flight over Motutara and Oaia Islands, Muriwai Beach, Auckland.
opposite: An Australasian Gannet takes flight from the cliff tops whilst others nurse their young, Muriwai Beach.

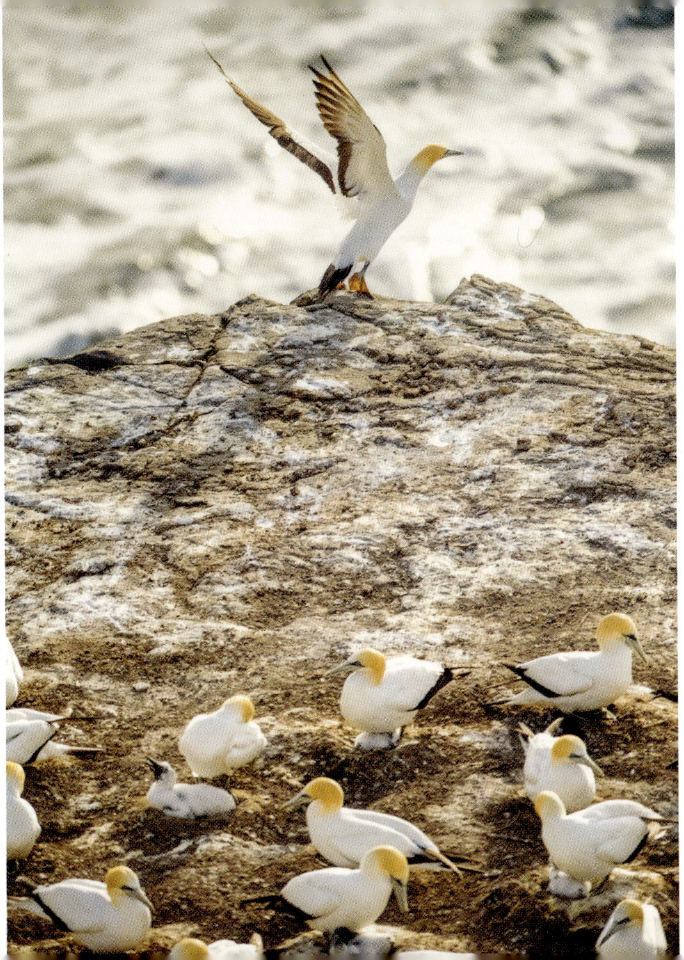

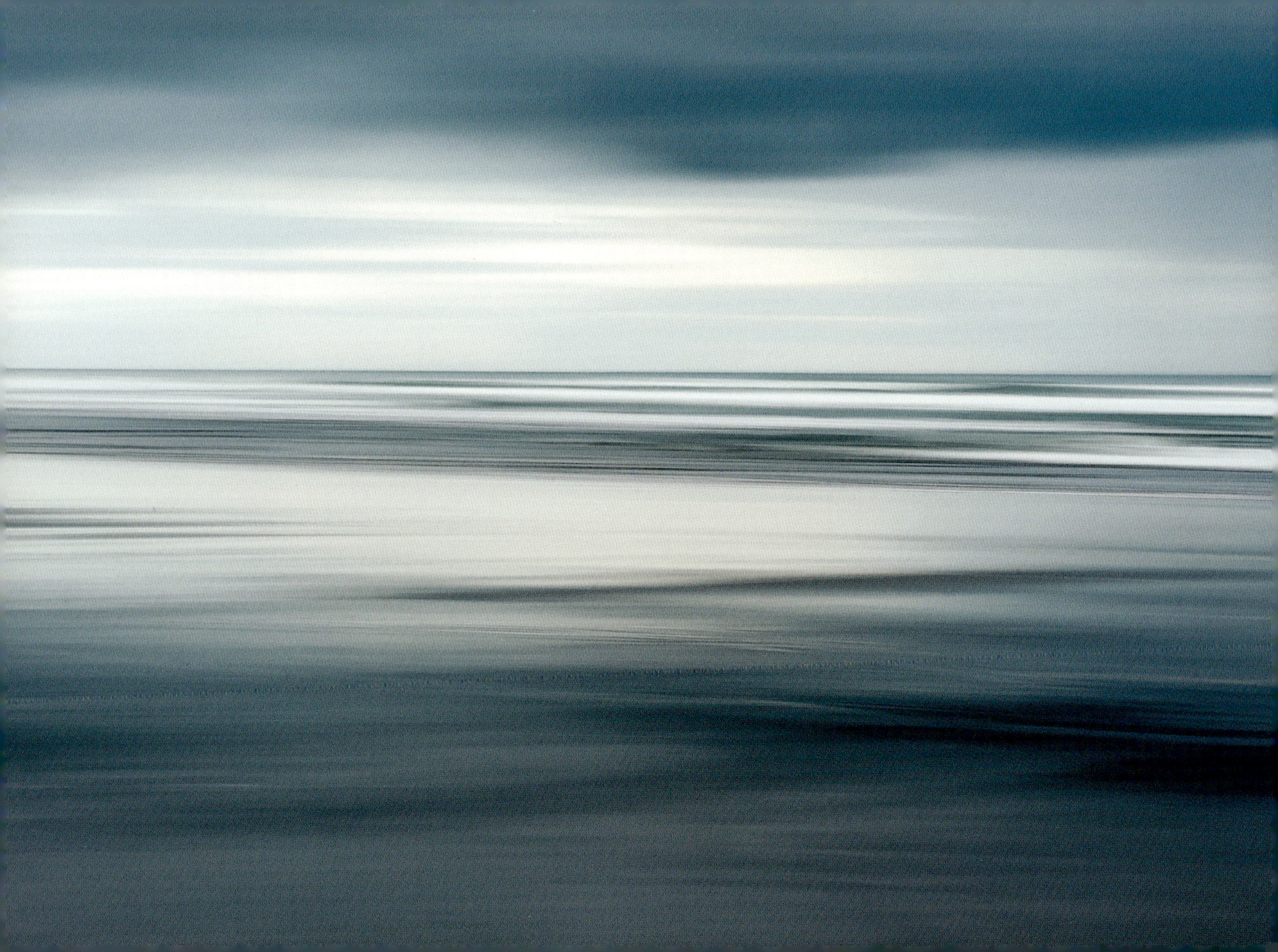

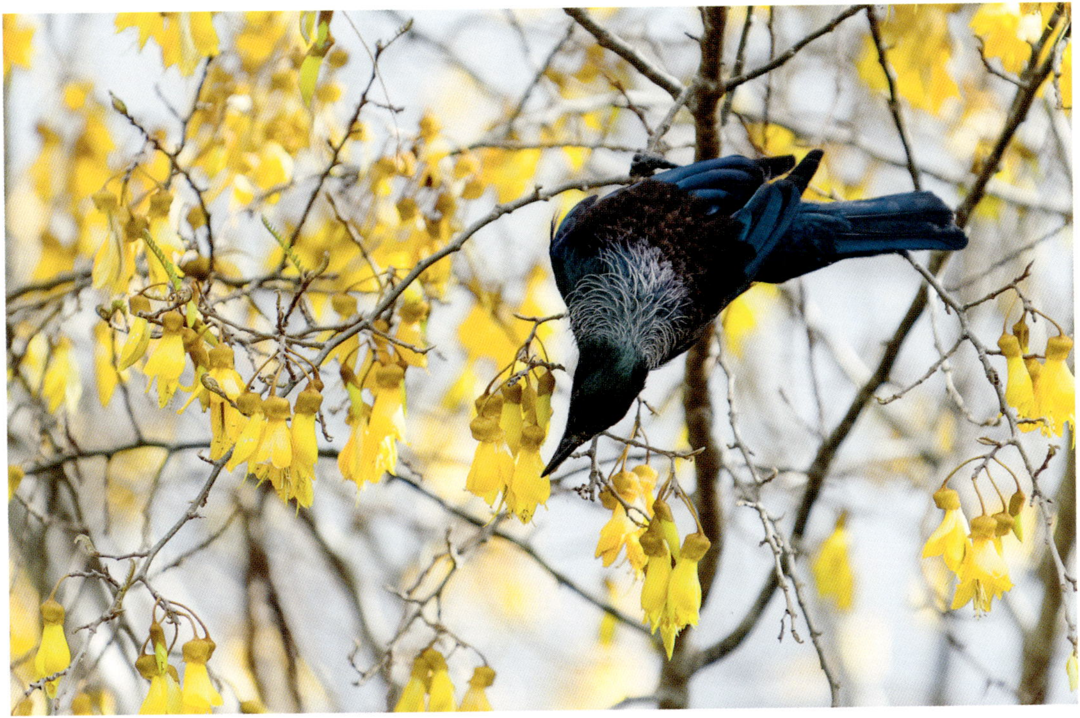

A native Tui in a Kowhai Tree, Birdwood Valley, Auckland.
opposite: Bethells Beach blues, Auckland.

ACKNOWLEDGEMENTS

To pursue one's passion is no easy task, and it is only achievable with the support of those close to you. Firstly, and most importantly, I would love to thank my parents, Ron and Jude. Without their constant love and support, their guidance, and their listening ears my path would have been much harder to follow, perhaps impossible. You are my best friends, and the best parents I could ever have wished for. Thank you for believing in my journey, and for helping me get back up when I am down.

My two sisters, Kerryn and Tracy, and my brother-in-law Craig. Thank you for continual support and encouragement, and for believing in me. To my two nephews Luke and Isaac, you both are beautiful souls, believe that you can do anything with your lives, dream big, work hard, and don't be afraid to do something special with your lives, anything and everything is possible.

To Shelly, Graeme, Chris Thompson, Chris Dickson, Sarah and Rose, thank you for being sounding boards, for your listening ears and continual inspiration over the past few years on this challenging path of entrepreneurial creative endevour.

Also thank you to all of you who have purchased this book. Without that support I wouldn't be able to share my photography with the world. New Zealand will always be my true love, and I am blessed to be on this path of passion and photography. Thank you all, and may you take time to see the natural beauty that surrounds you wherever you call home.

New Zealand | The Southern Realm

by *Jason Law*

Print Sales

Open and Limited Edition prints of images from this book are available at *store.jlphoto.co.nz*

For any other enquiries please contact Jason Law directly at *jason@jlphoto.co.nz* or follow his journey on his social media platforms.

All images published in *New Zealand | The Southern Realm* were captured using Nikon DSLR cameras (D3, D800E & D810 models)

First Published in 2016 by Law Media

Photography, Text and Design by Jason Law

Printed in China by 1010 Printing International Ltd

ISBN: 978-0-473-35697-2

:: Jason Law ::
Photography

www.jlphoto.co.nz